FREEDOM & ITS DISCONTENTS

FREEDOM & ITS DISCONTENTS

REFLECTIONS ON FOUR DECADES
OF AMERICAN MORAL EXPERIENCE

PETER MARIN

STEERFORTH PRESS

SOUTH ROYALTON, VERMONT

Grateful acknowledgment is made to the editors of the following magazines in which many of these essays first appeared, some in different form and under different titles: "The Fiery Vehemence of Youth," *The Center Magazine,* 1969; "The New Narcissism," *Harper's Magazine,* 1975; "Spiritual Obedience," *Harper's Magazine,* 1979; "Coming to Terms With Vietnam," *Harper's Magazine,* 1980; "Living in Moral Pain," *Psychology Today,* 1981; "Helping and Hating the Homeless," *Harper's Magazine,* 1987; "The Prejudice Against Men," *The Nation,* 1991; "Virginia's Story," *AFP Reporter,* 1992.

Library of Congress Cataloging-in-Publication Data

Freedom and its discontents: reflections on four decades
of american moral experience / Peter Marin. — 1st ed.
p.   cm.

ISBN 1-883642-24-8
1. United States — Social conditions — 1980– 2. United States — Moral conditions. 3. Social values — United States. 4. Ethics — United States.
I. Title.
HN59.2.M36   1994
306 .097338—dc20   94-34344   CIP

Manufactured in the United States of America

First Edition

CONTENTS

PREFACE

THE ESSAYS COLLECTED in this book were written over a period of twenty-five years, but what strikes me now, as I re-read them, is the persistent appearance, from the first essay to the last, of certain ideas and themes, all of which refer in one way or another to *morality*. I can see, reviewing these essays, that for me all questions pertaining to politics, or to policy, or to the formal relations among us are actually disguised questions about morality, questions which require a reconsideration of moral values, of ethical norms.

How to explain that? Morality, after all, is not a popular subject these days, especially on the political left or in the secular intellectual circles where I feel most at home. But I am regularly drawn back to the subject, perhaps because of my on-going sense that we are "men in dark times"—a phrase used by Hannah Arendt and borrowed from Brecht. That is, we are men and women in dark *moral* times, a time in which moral thought and moral frames of reference have fallen into such disrepair that one cannot talk coherently about any political or social or cultural problem without first trying to delineate or construct, almost from scratch, a moral context in which it can be understood.

In one sense, of course, moral times are always dark. Our own age, obviously, has no monopoly on cruelty, violence, or indifference to suffering; we are, as men and women, no better or worse than men and women anywhere. But there is another sense in which our age may indeed be darker than others, if only because the very idea of morality, for so long misunderstood and in disrepute, now rests mainly in the hands of those who speak religiously or repressively, though not always morally.

Perhaps, then, these essays can best be understood as attempts to wrest morality from those who presently lay arrogant claim to it in God's name, or to reconstruct new moral frames of reference that make room for, and welcome, the many suffering others and the forgotten truths now excluded from our shaky moral thought.

It is no accident that the subjects of these essays are so often the marginalized or ignored members of our communities: Vietnam vets who speak about the horrors of war; homeless men and women; pauperized welfare recipients; adolescents with their unruly and disruptive energies. I am drawn to them not only out of sympathy and affection, but also by what they *know*, what they have to reveal to us about America and ourselves, the human truths they bear and without which our moral notions remain neither complete nor moral.

What I have tried to do in these essays is to keep faith with such men and women, and with their truths. Beyond all theory and speculation, I have tried to see with their eyes, to hear from their mouths what their eyes have seen, and to say what they themselves might have said, were anyone willing to listen.

And I have tried, too, to keep another kind of faith: a faith with the distant possibility of a just human future, one that lies, still, so far ahead of us that we often forget that it exists, if only as a possibility. Something within me whispers that our difficult days are not close to their end, that we've still further to go, that something in us, in our natures, must reveal itself, in all of its horror, before we can begin to understand ourselves and change. The moral ground beneath our feet will grow stonier, will fall away more precipitously, will become more of a wilderness, before we ever sense before us, and within reach, the kind of just world that presents itself to us now only in imagination.

In such circumstance, in *our* circumstances, keeping faith in a moral sense must therefore mean a faith kept with three things at once: forgotten others, forgotten truths, forgotten possibilities. It is precisely that kind of faith I have tried to keep in these essays, if only by pointing out, in dark times, where a bit of light might be found. But one must understand that what I mean by "light" is nothing mystical or religious; it is merely the generosity of spirit, or the senses of reciprocity and fraternity, or the concern for others and their freedom, that may someday make of us fully moral, and therefore fully human, beings.

Peter Marin
December, 1994

THE FIERY VEHEMENCE OF YOUTH

IT IS MIDNIGHT and I am sitting here with my notes, enough of them to make two books and a half and a volume of posthumous fragments, trying to make some smaller sense of them than the grand maniacal design I have in my mind. I don't know where to begin. Once, traveling in summer across the country with a friend from Hollywood and my young son in a battered green Porsche, I stopped for lunch somewhere in Kansas on a Sunday morning. As we walked into the restaurant, bearded, wearing dark glasses and strange hats, and followed by my long-haired boy, one Kansas matron bent toward another and whispered: "I bet those two men have kidnapped that little girl." I took a deep breath and started to speak, but I did not know where to begin or how to explain in just how many ways she was mistaken. Now, trying to write clearly about education and adolescence, I feel the same way.

For that reason I have chosen an eccentric method of composition, one that may seem fragmentary, jumpy, and broken. This essay will be more like a letter, and the letter itself is an accumulation of impressions and ideas, a sampling of thoughts at once disconnected but related. There is a method to it that may disappear in its mild madness, but I do not know at this juncture how else to proceed. Shuffling through my notes I feel like an archeologist with a mass of uncatalogued shards. There is a pattern to all this, a coherence of thought, but all I can do here is assemble the bits and pieces and lay them out for you and hope that you can sense how I get from one place to another.

An entire system is hiding behind this, just beginning to take form, and these notes are like a drawing, a preliminary sketch. I feel comfortable with that notion, more comfortable than with the idea of forcing them together, cutting and pasting, to make a more conventional essay. I can perceive in myself at this moment what I also see in the young: I am reluctant to deal in sequence with my ideas and experience, I am impatient with transition, the habitual ways of getting "from here to there." I think restlessly; my mind, like the minds of my students, works in flashes, in sudden perceptions and brief extended clusters of intuition and abstraction—and I have stuck stubbornly to that method of composition. There is still in me the ghost of an apocalyptic adolescent, and I am trying to move it a few steps toward the future.

One theme, as you will see, runs through what I have written: we must rethink our ideas of childhood and schooling. We must dismantle them and start again from scratch. Nothing else will do. Our visions of adolescence and education confine us to habit, rule perception out. We make do at the moment with a set of ideas inherited from the nineteenth century, from an industrial, relatively puritanical, repressive, and "localized" culture; we try to gum them like labels to new kinds of experience. But that won't do. Everything has changed. The notions with which I began my job as a high-school director have been discarded one by one. They make no sense. What emerges through these children as the psyche of this culture is post-industrial, relatively unrepressed, less literate and local: a new combination of elements, almost a new strain. Adolescents are, each one of them, an arena in which the culture transforms itself or is torn between contrary impulses; they are the victims of a culture raging within itself like man and wife, a schizoid culture—and these children are the unfinished and grotesque products of that schism.

They are grotesque because we give them no help. They are forced to make among themselves adjustments to a tension that must be unbearable. They do the best they can, trying, in increasingly eccentric fashions, to make sense of things. But we adults seem to have withdrawn in defeat from that same struggle, to have given up. We are enamored, fascinated, and deluded by adolescence precisely because it is the last life left to us; only the young seem to rebel with any real passion against media, machines, the press of history itself. Their elders seem to have no options, no sense of alternative or growth. Adult existence is bled of life and we turn in that vacuum toward children with the mixed repulsion and desire of wanton Puritans toward life itself.

Has there ever been a community of adults so conscious and envious of children—and so fearful of growth! The family, each adult life, which might at best be like a vessel, an adventure, is instead a fort established on a hostile plain, and the child is its natural enemy, for he brings to it all the energy (that wind of chaos) that threatens it with change. Say the same for schools. Say the same for each of us. Instead of preceding children, leading them, we shove them forward like shields, like bodyguards. They seem to me at times like a wave of shock troops sent against barbed wire in the war. They throw themselves against it so that the next wave can pass over it unhindered. Anyone who has known them intimately can sense in these children their combined strength and fragility, a recurrent brittleness that stems from what is paradoxically an excessive exposure to culture and a dearth of participation. Neither family, school, tribe, nor a usable past supports them. Instead, they define themselves and seem to pass among us like alien beasts: the reverse image of ourselves, strange weddings of the elements bread out of our lives and returned to haunt us with the precise irony of Greek tragedy.

As for me, an adult, I think of myself as I write as an observer at a tribal war—an anthropologist, a combination of Gulliver and a correspondent sending home news by mule and boat. By the time you hear of it, things will have changed. And that isn't enough, not enough at all. Somebody must step past the children, must move into his own psyche or two steps past his own limits into the absolute landscape of fear and potential these children inhabit. That is where I am headed. So these ideas, in effect, are something like a last message tacked to a tree in a thicket or tucked under a stone. I mean: we cannot *follow* the children any longer, we have to step ahead of them. Somebody has to mark a trail.

Adolescence: a few preliminary fragments . . .

(From my student, V): *yr whole body moves in a trained way & you know that youve moved this way before & it contains all youve been taught its all rusty & slow something is pushing under that rusted mesh but STILL YOU CANNOT MOVE you are caught between 2 doors & the old one is much closer & you can grab it all the time but the other door it disappears that door you cant even scratch & kick (like the early settlers were stung by the new land) but this new land doesnt even touch you & you wonder if youre doing the right thing to get in.*

(From Franz Kafka): *He feels imprisoned on this earth, he feels constricted; the melancholy, the impotence, the sicknesses, the feverish fancies of the captive afflict him; no comfort can comfort him, since it is merely comfort, gentle headsplitting comfort glazing the brutal fact of imprisonment.* But if he is asked what he wants he cannot reply. . . . He has no conception of freedom.

(From tapes recorded in Pacific Palisades, 1966, several boys and girls aged 12-14):

—*Things are getting younger and younger. Girls twelve will do it now. One guy said I fuck a girl every Friday night. What sexual pleasure do you get out of this (he's very immature you know) and he would say, I don't know I'm just going to fuck.*

—or—

How old are you? —*Twelve.* —Will you tell us your first experience with drugs, how you got into it? —*Well, the people I hung around with were big acidheads. So one day my friend asked me if I wanted to get stoned and I said yes. That was about five months ago and I've been getting on it every since. Started taking LSD about one month ago. Took it eleven times in one month. I consider it a good thing. For getting high, smoking grass is better, or hashish—it's about six times stronger than marijuana.*

(From Paul Radin: *Primitive Man As Philosopher*): *It is conceivably demanding too much of a man to whom the pleasures of life are largely bound up with the life of contemplation and to whom analysis and introspection are the self-understood prerequisites for a proper understanding of the world, that he appreciate . . . expressions which are largely non-intellectual—where life seems, predominatingly, a discharge of physical vitality, a simple and naive release of emotions or an enjoyment of sensations for their own sake. Yet. . . it is just such an absorption in a life of sensations that is the outward characteristic of primitive peoples.*

Can you see where my thought leads? It is precisely at this point, adolescence, when the rush of energies, the thrust of the ego up through layers of childhood, makes itself felt, that the person is once more like an infant, is swept once more by energies that are tidal, unfamiliar, and unyielding. Adolescents are in a sense born again, given a fresh identity and beset inside and out by the rush of new experience. It is at this point, too—when we seem compelled by a persistent lunacy to isolate adolescents—that what is growing within them demands expression, requires it, and must, in addition, be received by the world and given form, or it will wither or turn to rage. Adolescence is a second infancy. It is then that the young desire solitude and at the same time contact with the vivid world; must test within social reality the new power within themselves;

need above all to discover themselves for the first time as bridges between inner and outer life, makers of value, vehicles through which culture perceives and transforms itself. It is now, ideally, that the young begin to understand the complex and delicate nature of the ego itself as a thin skin between living worlds, a synaptic jump, the self-conscious point at which nature and culture combine.

In this condition, with these needs, adolescents are like a primitive men, apocalyptic primitives; they exist for the moment in that stage of single vision in which myth is still the raw stuff of being; they know at first hand through their own energies the possibilities of life—but they know these in muddled, sporadic, contradictory ways. The rush of their pubescent and raw energy seems at odds with public behavior, the *order* of things, the tenor of life around them, especially in a culture just emerging—as is ours—from a tradition of evasion, repression, and fear.

The contradictions within the culture itself intensify their confusion. We are at the moment torn as a culture between the future and the past, in the midst of a process of transformation we barely understand. The development of adolescent energy and ego—difficult at any time—is complicated in our own by the increase in early sexuality, the complicated messages of the media, and the effects of strong and unfamiliar drugs. These three elements are, in themselves, the salient features of a culture that is growing more permissive, less repressive. They are profound, complex, and strong: heavy doses of experience demanding changes in attitude, changes in behavior. The direction and depth of feeling responds accordingly; adolescents try—even as a form of self-defense against the pressure of their own energies—to move more freely, to change their styles of life, to "grow." But it is then that they find themselves locked into culture, trapped in a web of ideas, law, and rituals that keep them children, deprive them of a chance to test and assimilate their newer selves. It is now that the culture turns suddenly repressive. Their gestures are evaded or denied; at best they are "tolerated," but even then their gestures, lacking the social support of acknowledgment and reward, must seem to them lacking in authenticity—more like forms of neurosis or selfishness than the natural stages in growth.

They are thrust back upon themselves. The insistent natural press within them toward becoming whole is met perpetually by unbudging resistance. Schools, rooted as they are in a Victorian century and seemingly suspicious of life itself, are their natural enemies. They don't help, as they might, to make that bridge between their private and the social worlds; they insist, instead, upon their separation. Indeed, family, community, and school all combine— especially in the suburbs—to isolate and "protect" youth from the adventure, risk, and participation they need; the same energies that relate them at this crucial point to nature put them at odds with the social environment.

Thus the young, in that vivid confrontation with the thrust of nature unfolding in themselves, are denied adult assistance. I once wrote that education through its limits denied the gods, and that they would return in the young in one form or another to haunt us. That is happening now. You can sense it as the students gather, with their simplistic moral certainty, at the gates of the universities. It is almost as if the young were once more possessed by Bacchanalian gods, were once again inhabited by divinities whose honor we have neglected. Those marvelous and threatening energies! What disturbs me most about them is that we lack rituals for their use and balance, and the young—and perhaps we ourselves—now seem at their mercy. The young have moved, bag and baggage, into areas where adults cannot help them and it is a scary landscape that they face, crowded with strange forms and forces, and if they return from it raddled, without balance and pitched toward excess, who can pretend to be surprised—or blameless?

At times they seem almost shell-shocked, survivors of a holocaust in which the past has been destroyed and all the bridges to it bombed. I cannot describe with any certainty what occurs in their minds, but I do know that most adults must seem to the young like shrill critics speaking to them in an alien language about a Greek tragedy in which they may lose their lives. The words we use, our dress, our tones of voice, the styles of adult lives—all of these are so foreign to that dramatic crisis that as we approach them we seem to increase the distance we are trying to cross. Even our attention drives them further away, as if adolescents perceived that adults, coming closer, diminish in sense and size.

The inner events in adolescents create a demand on the world around them for life on a large scale, in a grand style. This is the impulse to apocalypse in the young, as if they were in exile from a nation that does not exist, and yet they can sense it, they know it is there, if only because their belief itself demands its presence. Their demand is absolute and unanswerable, but nonetheless it exists, and we seem unable at this point in time to suppress or evade it. For one reason or another, massive shifts in cultural balances, the lessening of repression for whatever reasons—economic, technological, evolutionary—new energies, like gods, have appeared among us again. But what can we make of them? The simple problem is that our institutions are geared to another century, another set of social necessities, and cannot change quickly enough to contain, receive, or direct these energies—and as we suppress or refuse them they turn to rage.

Primitive cultures dealt with this problem through their initiation rites, the rites of passage; they legitimized and accepted these energies and turned them toward collective aims; they were merged with the life of the tribe and in that way acknowledged, honored, and domesticated—but not destroyed. In most initiation rites participants are led through the mythical or sacred world (or a symbolic version of it) and are then returned, transformed, to the secular one as a new people, with new roles. They are introduced through these rites to a dramatic reality coexistent with the visible or social one and at its root; they are put in direct touch with the sources of energy, the divinities of the tribe. In many cultures the symbolic figures in the rites are unmasked at the end, as if to reveal to the initiate the interpenetration of the secular and sacred worlds. Occasionally the initiate is asked to don the ritual mask himself—joining one world with another and assuming the responsibility for their connection. This shift in status, in *relation,* is the heart of the rite; a liturgized merging of the individual with shared sources of power.

Do you see what I am driving at? These rites are in a sense a social contract, a binding up, occurring specifically, profoundly, and on a deep psychic level. Individuals are redefined in the culture by their new relation to its mysteries, its gods, or to nature and its powers. The experience of that hidden and omnipotent mythical world is the basis for a new relation to the culture and its members, each of whom has a similar bond—deep, personal, and unique, but also somehow shared, invisibly but deeply. These ritualized relationships of the individual to the shared gods bind the group together; they form the substance of culture: an invisible landscape that is real and felt, commonly held, a landscape which resides in each man and woman and in which, in turn, each man and woman resides.

I hope that makes sense. That is the structure of the kaleidoscopic turning of culture that Blake makes in "The Crystal Cabinet," and it makes sense, too, in America today, in relation to adolescents. What fascinates me is that our public schools, designed for adolescents—who seem, in their apocalyptic condition, to require this kind of drama, release, and support—educate and "socialize" their students by depriving them of everything the rites bestow. They manipulate the young through the repression of their energies; they isolate them and close off most parts of the community; they categorically refuse to make use of the individual's private experience. The direction of all these tendencies is toward a

cultural schizophrenia in which students are forced to choose between their own relation to reality or the one demanded by the
institution. The schools are organized to weaken the students so
that they are forced, in the absence of their own energies, to accept
the values and demands of the institution. To this end we deprive
students of mobility and experience; through law and custom we
make the only legal place for them the school, and then, to make
sure they remain dependent, malleable, we empty the school of all
vivid life.

We appear to have forgotten in our schools what every primitive tribe with its functional psychology knows: allegiance to the
tribe can be forged only at the deepest levels of the psyche and in
extreme circumstance demanding endurance, daring, and awe; that
the participant must be given *direct* access to the sources of cultural
continuity by and in themselves; and that only a place in a coherent community can be exchanged for allegiance.

I believe that it is precisely this world that drugs replace.
Adolescents provide for themselves what we deny them: a confrontation with some kind of power within an unfamiliar landscape involving sensation and risk. It is here, I suppose, that they
hope to find, by some hurried magic, a new way of seeing, a new
relation to things, a way to discard one identity and assume another. They mean to find through their adventures the *ground* of
reality, the resonance of life we deny them, as if they might come
upon their golden city and return still inside it: at home. You can
sometimes see the real veterans on the street in strange costumes
they have stolen from dreams, American versions of the Tupi of
Brazil, who traveled thousands of miles each year in search of the
land where death and evil do not exist. Theirs is a world totally
alien to the one we discuss in schools; it is dramatic, it enchants
them; its existence forms a strange brotherhood among them and
they cling to it—as though they alone had been to a fierce land
and back. It is that which draws them together and makes of them

a loose tribe. It is, after all, some sort of shared experience, some kind of foray into the risky dark; it is the best that they can do.

When you begin to think about adolescence in this way, what sense can you make of our schools? None of the proposed changes so fashionable for the moment makes sense to me: revision of curriculum, teaching machines, smaller classes, encounter groups, redistributions of power—all of these are stopgap measures, desperate attempts to keep the young in schools that are hopelessly outdated. The changes suggested and debated don't go deeply enough; they don't question or change enough. For what needs changing are not the methods of the school system but its aims, for what is troubling the young and forcing upon their teachers an intolerable burden is the *idea* of childhood itself, the ways we think about adolescents and their place in the culture itself. More and more one comes to see that changes in the schools won't be enough; the crisis of the young cuts across the culture in all its areas and includes the family and the community. The young are *displaced*; there is no other word for it. They are trapped in a prolonged childhood almost unique in human history. In few other cultures have persons of fifteen or eighteen been so uselessly isolated from participation in the community, or been deemed so unnecessary (in their elders' eyes), or so limited by law. Our ideas of responsibility, our parental feelings of anxiety, blame, and guilt, all of these follow from our curious vision of the young; in turn, they concretize our vision, legitimize it so that we are no longer even conscious of the ways we see childhood or the strain that our vision puts upon us. That is what needs changing: the definitions we make socially and legally of the role of the young. They are trapped in the ways we see them, and the school is simply one function, one aspect, of the whole problem. What makes real change so difficult in the schools is only in part their natural unwieldiness; it is more often the difficulty we have in escaping our preconceptions about things.

In general the school system we have inherited seems to me based upon three particular things:

- What Paul Goodman calls the idea of "natural depravity": our puritanical vision of human nature in which children are perceived as sinners or "savages" and in which human impulse or desire is not to be trusted and must therefore be constrained or "trained."
- The necessity during the mid-nineteenth century of "Americanizing" great masses of immigrant children from diverse backgrounds and thereby creating, through the schools, a common experience and character.
- The need in an industrialized state for energy and labor to run the machines: the state, needing workers, educates persons to be technically capable but relatively dependent and responsive to authority so that their energies will be available when needed.

These elements combine with others—the labor laws that make childhood a "legal" state, and a population explosion that makes it necessary now to keep adolescents off both the labor market and the idle street—to create a school system that resists change even as the culture itself changes radically. But teachers can't usually see that, for they themselves have been educated in the system and are committed to ideas that they have never clearly understood. Time and again, speaking to them, one hears the same questions and anguish:

"But what will happen to the students if they don't go to school?" "How will they learn?" "What will they do without adults?"

What never comes clear, of course, is that such questions are, at bottom, statements. Even while asking these questions teachers reveal their unconscious attitudes. They can no longer imagine what children will do "outside" schools. They regard them as young monsters who will, if released from adult authority or help, disrupt the order of things. They are no longer capable of imagining learning or child-adult relationships outside the schools.

But mass schooling is a recent innovation. Most learning—especially the process of socialization or acculturation—has gone on outside schools, and more naturally, in the fabric of the culture. In most cultures the passage from childhood to maturity occurs because of society's need for responsible adults, and it is marked by clear changes in role. Children in such cultures seem to have learned the ways of their culture or tribe through constant contact and interchange with adults, and it was taken for granted that the young would learn continually through their place close to the heart of the community.

We have lost all sense of that. The school is expected to do what the community cannot do and that is impossible. In the end, we will have to change far more than the schools if we expect to create a new coherence between the experiences of the child and the needs of the community. We will have to rethink the meaning of childhood; we will begin to grant greater freedom *and* responsibility to the young; we will drop the compulsory-schooling age; we will take for granted the "independence" of adolescents and provide them with the chance to live alone, away from parents and with peers; we will discover jobs they can or want to do in the community—anything from mail delivery to the teaching of smaller children and the counseling of other adolescents. At some point, perhaps, we will even find that the community itself—in return for a minimum of work or continued schooling—will provide a minimal income to young people that will allow them to assume the responsibility for their own lives at an earlier age and learn the ways of the community outside the school; finally, having lowered the level of compulsory schooling, we will find it necessary to provide different *kinds* of schools, a wider choice, so that students will be willing voluntarily to continue the schooling that suits their needs and aims.

All these changes, of course, are aimed at two things: the restoration of the child's "natural" place in the community and lowering the age at which a person is considered an independent member of the community. Some of the changes, to be sure, can be made in the schools, but my sense of things, after having talked to teachers and visited many schools, is that trying to make them in schools *alone* will be impossible.

One problem, put simply, is that in every school I have visited, public or private, traditional or "innovational," the students have only these two choices: to drop out (either physically or mentally) or to make themselves smaller and smaller until they can act in ways their elders expect. One of my students picked up a phrase I once used, "the larger and smaller worlds." The schools we visit together, he says, are always the smaller world: smaller at least than his imagination, smaller than the potential of the young. The students are asked to put aside the best things about themselves—their own desires, impulses, and ideas—in order to "adjust" to an environment constructed for children who existed one hundred years ago, if at all. I wonder sometimes if this condition is simply the result of poor schooling, but I am more inclined to believe that it is the inevitable result of mass compulsory schooling and the fabrication of artificial environments for children by adults.

Is it possible at all for adults to understand what children need and to change their institutions fast enough to keep up with changes in culture and experience? Is it possible for children to grow to their full size, to feel their full strength, if they are deprived of individual volition all along the line and forced to school? I don't know. I know only that during the Middle Ages they sometimes "created" jesters by putting young children in boxes and force-feeding them so that, as they grew, their bones would warp in unusual ways. That is often how the schools seem to me. Students are trapped in the boxes of pedagogic ideas, and I am tempted to say to teachers again and again: you must go further, create more space in the schools, must go deeper in thought, create more resonance, a different feeling, a different and more human, more daring style.

Even the best teachers, with the best intentions, seem to diminish their students as they work through the public school system. For that system is, at bottom, designed to produce what we sometimes call good citizens but what more often than not turn out to be good soldiers; it is through the schools of the state, after all, that we produce our armies. I remember how struck I was while teaching at a state college by the number of boys who wanted to oppose the draft but lacked the courage or strength to simply say no. They were trapped; they had always been taught, had always tried, to be "good." Now they wanted to refuse to go, but they could not, for they weren't sure they could bear the consequences they had been taught would follow such refusal: jail, social disgrace, parental despair. They could not believe in institutions, but they could not trust themselves and their impulses, and they were caught in their own impotence: depressed and resentful, filled with self-hatred and a sense of shame.

That is a condition bred in the schools. In one way or another our methods produce in the young a condition of pain that seems very close to a mass neurosis: a lack of faith in oneself, a vacuum of spirit into which authority or institutions can move, a dependency they feed on. Students are encouraged to relinquish their own wills, their freedom of volition; they are taught that value and culture reside outside oneself and must be acquired from the institution, and almost everything in their education is designed to discourage them from activity, from the wedding of idea and act. It is almost as if we hoped to discourage them from thought itself by making ideas so lifeless, so hopeless, that their despair would be enough to make them manipulable and obedient.

The system breeds obedience, frustration, dependence, and fear: a kind of gentle violence that is usually turned against oneself, one that is sorrowful and full of guilt, but a violence nonetheless, and one realizes that what is done in the schools to students is deeply connected to what we once did as a nation to the blacks or are doing now in Vietnam. That is: we don't teach hate in the schools, or murder, but we do isolate the individual; we empty him of life by ignoring or suppressing his impulse toward life; we breed in him a lack of respect for it, a loss of love—and thus we produce gently "good" but threatened men, men who will kill without passion, out of duty and obedience, men who have in themselves little sense of the vivid life being lost nor the moral strength to resist authority.

From first to twelfth grade we acclimatize students to a fundamental deadness and teach them to restrain themselves for the sake of "order." The net result is a kind of pervasive cultural inversion in which they are asked to separate at the most profound levels their own experience from institutional reality, self from society, objective from subjective, energy from order—though these various polarities are precisely those which must be joined together during adolescence.

I remember a talk I had with a college student.

"You know what I love to do," he said. "I love to go into the woods and run among the trees."

"Very nice," I said.

"But it worries me. We shouldn't do it."

"Why not?" I asked.

"Because we get excited. It isn't *orderly.*"

"Not orderly?"

"Not orderly."

"Do you run into the trees?" I asked.

"Of course not."

"Then it's orderly," I said.

In a small way this exchange indicates the kind of thinking we teach in the schools: the mistaking of rigidity and stillness for order, the equating of order as the absence of life. We create and preserve an order which depends upon the destruction of life both inside and out and which all life, when expressed, must necessarily threaten or weaken.

The natural process of learning seems to move naturally from experience through perception to abstraction in a fluid continuous process that cannot be clearly divided into stages. It is in that process that energy is somehow articulated in coherent and meaningful form as an act or thought or a made object. The end of learning is wisdom and wisdom to me, falling back as I do on a Jewish tradition, is, in its simplest sense, "intelligent activity" or, more completely, the suffusion of activity with knowledge, a wedding of the two. For the Hassidic Jews every gesture was potentially holy, a form of prayer, when it was made with a reverence for God. In the same way a gesture is always a form of wisdom—an act is wisdom—when it is suffused with knowledge, made with a reverence for the truth.

Does that sound rhetorical? I suppose it does. But I mean it. The end of education is intelligent activity, *wisdom,* and that demands a merging of opposites, a sense of coherent process. Instead we produce the opposite: immobility, insecurity, an inability to act without institutional blessing or direction, or, at the opposite pole, a headlong rush toward motion without balance or thought. We cut into the natural movement of learning and try to force upon the students the end product, abstraction, while eliminating experience and ignoring their perception. The beginning of all real thought is in the experience through one's self of a particular environment—school, community, culture. When this is ignored, as it is in schools, the natural relation of self and knowledge is broken, the parts of the process become polar opposites, antitheses, and the young are forced to choose between them: objectivity, order, and obedience as against subjectivity, chaos, and energy. It doesn't really matter which they choose; as long as the two sets seem irreconcilable their learning remains incomplete. Caught between the two, they suffer our intellectual schizophrenia until it occupies them, too. They wait. They sit. They listen. They learn to "behave" at the expense of themselves. Or else—and you can see it happening now—they turn against it with a vengeance and may shout, as they did at Columbia, "Kill all adults," for they have allied themselves with raw energy against reason and balance—our delicate, hard-won virtues—and we should not be surprised. We set up the choices ourselves, and it is simply that they have chosen what we hold to be the Devil's side.

If this is the case, what are the alternatives? I thought at one time that changes in schooling could be made, that the school itself could become at least a microcosm of the community, a kind of halfway house, a preparatory arena in which students, in semi-protective surroundings, would develop not only the skill but the character that would be needed in the world. But more and more, as I have said, it seems to me impossible to do that job in a setting as isolated and restrictive as our schools. Students don't need the artificiality of schools; they respond more fully and more intelligently when they make direct contact with the community and are allowed to choose roles that have some utility for the community and themselves. What is at stake here, I suppose, is freedom of volition in all its complexity, for this is the basic condition with which people must learn to deal, and the sooner they achieve within that condition both daring and responsibility, the stronger they will be. It seems absurd to postpone the assumption of that condition as long as we do. In most other cultures, and even in our own past, young people have taken upon themselves the responsibility of adults and have dealt with it as successfully as most adults do now. The students I have seen can do that, too, when given the chance. What a strain it must be to have that capacity, to sense in one's self a talent for adventure or growth or meaning, and have that sense continually stifled or undercut by the role one is supposed to play.

Thus, it seems inescapably clear that our first obligation to the young is to create a place in the community for them to act with volition and freedom. They are ready for it, certainly, even if we aren't. Adolescents seem to need at least some sense of risk and gain "out there" in the world: an existential sense of themselves that is vivid to the extent that the dangers faced are real. The students I have worked with seem strongest and most alive when they are in the mountains of Mexico or the Oakland ghetto or out in the desert or simply hitchhiking from place to place to see what's happening. They thrive on distance and motion—and the right to solitude when they want it. Many of them want jobs; they themselves arrange to be teachers in day care centers, political canvassers, tutors, poolroom attendants, actors, governesses, gardeners. They returned from these experiences immeasurably brightened and more sure of themselves, more willing, in that new assurance, to learn many of the abstract ideas we had been straining to teach them. It was not simply the experience in itself that brought this about. It was also the feeling of freedom they had, the sense that they could come and go at will and make any choice they wanted—no matter how absurd—if they were willing to suffer what real consequences followed. Many wanted to work and travel and others did not; they wanted to sit and think or read or live alone or swim or, as one student scrawled on my office wall, "ball and goof." What they finally came to understand, of course, was that the school made no pretense at either limiting or judging their activities; we considered them free agents and limited our own activities to advice, to what "teaching" they requested, and to support when they needed it in facing community, parents, or the law.

What we were after was a *feeling* to the place: a sense of intensity and space. We discarded the idea of the closed and protective school and replaced it with an increased openness and access to the larger community. The campus itself became a place to come back to for rest or discussion or thought; but we turned things inside out to the extent that we came to accept that learning took place more naturally elsewhere, in any of the activities that our students chose, and that the school was in actuality wherever they were, whatever they did. What students learned at the school was simply the feel of things: the sense of themselves as makers of value, the realization that the environment is at best an extension of men and women and that it can be transformed by them into what they vitally need. What we tried to create was a flexible environment, what a designer I know has called permissive space. It was meant to be in a sense a model for the condition in which all of us now find ourselves and in which the responsibility of the individual is to make connections, value, and sense. We eliminated from the school all preconceptions about what was proper, best, or useful; we gave up rules and penalties; we refused at all levels to resort to coercive force and students were free to come and go at will, to do anything. What we were after was a "guilt-free" environment, one in which the students might become or discover what they were without having to worry about preconceived ideas of what they had to be.

What we found was that our students seemed to need, most of all, relief from their own "childhood"—what was expected of them. Some of them needed merely to rest, to withdraw from the strange grid of adult expectation and demand for lengthy periods of introspection in which they appeared to grow mysteriously, almost like plants. But an even greater number seemed to need independent commerce with the world outside the school: new sorts of social existence. Nothing could replace that. The simple fact seemed to be that our students grew when they were allowed to move freely into and around the adult community; when they were not, they languished.

We came to see that learning is natural, yes, but that it results naturally from most things adolescents do. By associating learning with one particular form of experience and insisting upon that in school we make a grave error. When students shy away from that kind of experience it doesn't mean they are turning away forever from learning or abstractions; it means simply that they are seeking another kind of learning momentarily more natural to themselves. That may be anything from physical adventure or experimental community work to withdrawn introspection and an exploration of their fantasies and dreams.

Indeed, it is hard for them to do anything without some kind of learning, but that may be what we secretly fear—that those other forms of learning will make them less manageable or less like ourselves. That, after all, may be one reason we use all those books. Claude Levi-Strauss insists on the relation of increased literacy and the power of the state over the individual. It may well be that the early and premature dependence on print or abstraction is one of the devices we use to make students manageable, as if we meant to teach them that ideas exist in talk or on the page but rarely in activity. We tried to avoid that. When we permitted students freedom of choice and gave them easy access to the community, we found that ideas acquired weight and value to the extent that students were allowed to try them out in action. It was in practical and social situations that their own strength increased, and the merging of the two—strengthened self and tested knowledge—moved them more quickly toward manhood than anything else I have seen.

One might make a formula of it: to the extent that students had freedom of volition and access to experience, knowledge became important to them. But volition and access were of absolute value; they took precedence over books or parental anxiety. Without them, nothing worked. We had to trust the students to make their own choices, no matter what we thought of them. We learned to take their risks with them—and to survive. In that sense we became equals, and that equality may in the end be more educational for students than anything else. That, in fact, may be the most important thing we learned. New ways in seeing the young were more effective than changes in curriculum, and without them nothing made much difference. But we must understand too that the old way of seeing things—the traditional idea of childhood—is in some way baked into the whole public-school system at almost every level and also hidden in most pedagogy.

In some ways it is compulsory schooling itself which is the problem, for without real choice students will remain locked in childhood and schools, away from whatever is vivid in life. But real choice, as we know, includes dominion over one's own time and energies, and the right to come and go on the basis of what has actual importance. And I wonder if we will ever get round, given all our fears, to granting that privilege to students.

One thing alone of all I have read has made recent sense to me concerning adolescents. That is the implicit suggestion in Erik Erikson's *Young Man Luther* that all sensitive people experience in themselves the conflicts and contradictions of their age. Those who become great, he suggests, are those who articulate and resolve these conflicts in a way that has meaning for their time; that is, they themselves, as was Luther, are victims of their time and at the same time its vehicle and, finally, a means for its resolution. But all men and women, not only the great, have in some measure the capacity to experience in themselves what is happening in the culture around them. I am talking here about what is really shared among the members of a particular culture: a condition, a kind of internal "landscape," the psychic shape that a particular time and place assumes within each person as the extent and limit of their perceptions, dreams, pleasure, and pain.

If there is such a shared condition it seems to me a crucial point, for it means that there is never any real distance between men and women and their culture, no real isolation or alienation from society. It means that adolescents are not in their untutored state cut off from culture nor outside it. It means instead that each individual adolescent is an arena in which the contradictions and currents sweeping through the culture must somehow be resolved, must be resolved by the persons themselves, and that those individual resolutions are, ideally, the means by which the culture advances itself.

Do you see where this leads? I am straining here to get past the idea of the adolescent as an isolate and deviant creature who must be joined—as if glued and clamped—to the culture. For we ordinarily think of schools, though not quite consciously, as the "culture" itself, little models of society. We try to fit the students into the model, believing that if they will adjust to it they will in some way have been "civilized." That approach is connected to the needs of the early century, when the schools were the means by which the children of immigrant parents were acculturated and moved from the European values of their parents toward more prevalent American ones. But all of that has changed now. The children in our schools, all of them, are little fragments of *this* culture; they no longer need to be "socialized" in the same ways. The specific experiences of adolescents—their fears, their family crises, their dreams and hallucinations, their habits, their sexuality—all these are points at which the general culture reveals itself in some way. There is no longer any real question of getting adolescents to "adjust" to things.

The problem is a different one: What kind of setting will enable them to discover and accept what is already within them; to articulate it and perceive the extent to which it is shared with others; and, finally, to learn to change it within and outside themselves? For that is what I mean when I call adolescents the "makers of value." They are trustees—trustees of a world that already exists in some form within them—and we must all learn, adolescents and teachers alike, to respect it.

In a sense, then, I am calling for a reversal of most educational thought. The individual is central. The individual, in the deepest sense, *is* the culture, not the institution. Culture resides in the individual, in experience and memory, and what is needed is an education that has at its base the sanctity of the individual's experience and leaves it intact.

What keeps running through my mind is a line I read twelve years ago in a friend's first published story: *The idea in that idea is: there is no one over you.* I like that line: *There is no one over you.* Perhaps that signifies the gap between these children and their parents. For the children it is true, they sense it: there is no one over them; believable authority has disappeared. It has been replaced by experience. As Thomas Altizer says, God is dead; he is experienced now not as someone above or omnipotent or omniscient or "outside," but inwardly, as conscience or vision or even the unconscious or Tillich's "ground of being." This particular generation is a collective dividing point. The parents of these children, the mothers and fathers, still believe in "someone" over them, insist upon it; in fact, demand it for and from their children. The children themselves cannot believe it; the idea means nothing to them. It is almost as if they are the first real Americans—suddenly free of Europe and somehow fatherless, confused, forced back on their own experience, their own sense of things, even though, at the same time, they are forced to defy their families and schools in order to keep it.

This is, then, a kind of Reformation. Arnold was wrong when he said that art would replace religion; education replaced it. Church became School, the principal vehicle for value and "culture," and just as men once rebelled against the established Church as the mediator between God and man, students now rebel against the *public* school (and its version of things) as the intermediary between themselves and experience and the making of value. Students are expected to reach "reality" (whether of knowledge or society) through their teachers and school. No one, it is said, can participate in the culture effectively without having at one time passed through its hands, proven his allegiance to it, and been blessed. This is the authority exercised by priests or the Church. Just as men once moved to shorten the approach to God, they are moved now to do the same thing in relation to learning and to the community. For just as God was argued to appear within the individual—unique, private, and yet shared—so culture is, in some way, grounded in individuals; it inhabits them. The schools, like the Church, must be the expression of that habitation, not its exclusive medium. This is the same reformative shift that occurred in religion, a shift from the institutional (the external) to the individual (the internal), and it demands, when it occurs, an agony, an apocalyptic frenzy, a destruction of the past itself. I believe it is happening now. One sees and feels it everywhere: a violent fissure, a kind of quake.

I remember one moment in the streets of Oakland during the draft demonstrations. The students had sealed off the street with overturned cars and there were no police; the gutters were empty and the students moved into them from the sidewalks, first walking, then running, and finally almost dancing in the street. You could almost see the idea coalesce on their faces: The street is ours! It was as if a weight had been lifted from them, a fog; there was not at that moment any fury in them, any vengefulness or even politics; rather, a lightness, delight, an exhilaration at the sudden inexplicable sense of being free. George Orwell describes something similar in *Homage to Catalonia:* that brief period in Barcelona when the anarchists had apparently succeeded and men shared what power there was. I don't know how to describe it except to say that one's inexplicable sense of invisible authority had vanished: the oppressive father, who is not really there, was gone.

That sudden feeling is familiar to us all. We have all had it from time to time in our own lives, that sense of "being at home," that ease, that feeling of a Paradise which is neither behind us nor deferred but is around us, a natural household. It is the hint and beginning of freedom: a promise, a clue. One's attention turns to the immediate landscape and to one's fellows: toward what is there, toward what can be felt as a part of oneself. I have seen the same thing as I watched Stokely Carmichael speaking to a black audience and telling them that they must stop begging the white man, like children, for their rights. They were, he said, neither children nor slaves, no, they were—and here they chanted, almost cried, in unison—a beautiful people: *yes our noses are broad and our lips are thick and our hair is kinky . . . but we are beautiful, we are beautiful, we are black and beautiful.* Watching, you could sense in that released joy an emergence, a surfacing of pride, a refusal to accept shame or the white man's dominance—and a turning to one another, to their own inherent value.

But there is a kind of pain in being white and watching that, for there is no one to say the same things to white children; no elders, no brothers, no sisters to give them that sense of potency or pride. The adolescents I have seen—white, middle-class—are a long way from those words *we are beautiful, we are beautiful.* I cannot imagine how they will reach them, deprived as they are of all individual strength. For the schools exist to deprive one of strength. That is why one's own worth must be proven again and again by the satisfaction of external requirements with no inherent value or importance; it is why one must satisfy a set of inexplicable demands; it is why there is a continual separation of self and worth and the intrusion of a kind of institutionalized guilt: the demands and judgments not of God but of the system, the nameless "others," the authority that one can never quite see; and it explains the oppressive sense of some nameless transgression, almost a shame at Being itself.

It is this feeling that pervades both high schools and colleges, this Kafkaesque sense of faceless authority that drives one to rebellion or withdrawal, and we are all, for that reason, enchanted by the idea of the Trial, that ancient Socratic dream of confrontation and vindication or martyrdom. It is then, of course, that Authority shows its face. In the mid-fifties I once watched Jack Kerouac on a television show and when the interviewer asked him what he wanted he said: to see the face of God. How arrogant and childish and direct! And yet, I suppose, it is what we all want as children: to have the masks of authority, all its disguises, removed and to see it plain. That is what lies in large part behind the present riots in the schools. Their specific grievances are incidental; their real purpose is to make God show his face, to have whatever pervasive and oppressive force makes us perpetual children reveal itself, declare itself, commit itself at last. It is biblical; it is Freudian; it reminds me of the initiation rites: the need to unmask the gods and assume their power, to become an equal—and to find in that the manhood one has been denied.

The schools seem to enforce the idea that there is someone over you; and the methods by which they do it are ritualized, pervasive. The intrusion of guilt, shame, alienation from oneself, dependence, insecurity—all these feelings are not the accidental results of schools; they are intentional, and they are used in an attempt to make children "good citizens" and useful to the state. The schools are the means by which we deprive the young of life—that is what I mean to say—and we must not be surprised when they seek that life in ways that must of necessity be childish and violent.

But I must admit this troubles me, for there is little choice between mindless violence and mindless authority, and I am just enough of an academic, an intellectual, to want to preserve much of what will be lost in the kind of rebellion or apocalypse that is approaching. And yet, and yet . . . the rapidity of events leaves me with no clear idea, no solution, no sense of what will be an adequate change. It may be that all of this chaos is a way of breaking with the old world and that from it some kind of native American will emerge. There is no way of knowing, there no longer seems any way of estimating what is necessary or what will work. I know only that the problem now seems to be that our response to crisis is to move away or back rather than forward, and that we will surely, for the sake of some imagined order, increase in number and pressure the very approaches that have brought us to this confusion. I believe that the young must have values, of course, be responsible, care, but I know too that most of the violence I have seen done to the young has been done in the name of value, and that the well-meaning people who have been so dead set on making things right have had a hand in bringing us to where we are now. The paradox is a deep and troubling one for me. I no longer know if change can be accomplished—for the young, for any of us, without the apocalyptic fury that seems almost upon us. The crisis of youth and education is symptomatic of some larger, deeper fault in our cities and minds, and perhaps nothing can be done consciously in those areas until the air itself is violently cleared one way or another.

So I have no easy conclusions, no startling synthesis with which to close. I have only a change in mood, a softening, a kind of sadness. It may be, given that, that the best thing is simply to close with an unfinished fragment in which I catch for myself the hint of an alternative:

> . . . I am trying to surround you, I see that, I am trying to make with these words a kind of city so natural, so familiar, that the other world, the one that appears to be, will look by comparison absurd and flat, limited, unnecessary. What I am after is liberation, not my own, which comes often enough these days in solitude or sex, but yours, and that is arrogant, isn't it, that is presumptuous, and yet that is the function of art: to set you free. It is that too which is the end of education: a liberation from childhood and what holds us there, a kind of midwifery, as if the nation itself were in labor and one wanted to save both the future and the past—for we are both, we are, we are the thin bridge swaying between them, and to tear one from the other means a tearing of ourselves, a partial death.
>
> And yet it may be that death is inevitable, useful. It may be. Perhaps, as in the myth, Aphrodite can rise only where Cronos's testicles have fallen into the sea. It may be that way with us. The death of the Father who is in us, the death of the old authority which is part of us, the death of the past which is also our death; it may all be

necessary: a rending and purgation. And yet one still seeks another way, something less (or is it more) apocalyptic, a way in which the past becomes the future in ourselves, *in which* we *become the bridges between: makers of culture.*

Unless from us the future takes place, we are Death only, *said Lawrence, meaning what the Chassids do: that the world and time reside within, not outside, men; that there is no distance, no "alienation," only a perpetual wedding to the world. It is that—the presence in oneself of Time—that makes things interesting, is more gravid and interesting than guilt. I don't want to lose it, don't want to relinquish that sense in the body of another dimension, a distance, the depth of the body as it extends backward into the past and forward, as it contains and extends and transforms the world it inhabits.*

What I am after is an alternative to separation and rage, some kind of connection to things to replace the system of dependence and submission—the loss of the self—that now holds sway, slanted toward violence. I am trying to articulate a way of seeing, of feeling, that will restore to the young a sense of freedom and possibility and potency without at the same time destroying the past. That same theme runs through whatever I write: the necessity for each of them to experience themselves as an extension and maker of culture, and to feel the whole force of the world within themselves, not as an enemy, but *as* themselves:

> *. . . An act of learning is a meeting, and every meeting is simply the discovery in the world of a part of oneself that had previously been unacknowledged by the self. It is the recovery of the extent of one's being. It is the embrace of an eternal but elusive companion, the shadowy "other" in which one truly resides and which blazes, when embraced, like the sun.*

THE NEW NARCISSISM

WHERE TO BEGIN an essay like this? Its original subject was ostensibly an Esalen conference on "spiritual tyranny." But that was for me merely a way of getting at a more general subject: the present trend in therapy toward a deification of the isolated self. And that subject was in turn a part of an even more general concern: the ways in which selfishness and moral blindness now assert themselves in the larger culture as enlightenment and psychic health. A broad-based retrenchment is going on, a pervasive and perhaps unconscious shift in value—not only on a national level but in the moral definitions and judgments we make as individuals.

I think offhandedly as I write of several recent conversations I have had with friends or students, or what I have heard proclaimed from lecture platforms or seen on television and in popular journals. I am, for instance, dining with a close friend in a New York restaurant, and as we eat our steaks and drink our brandy and smoke our fat cigars he explains to me that the world is obviously overpopulated, and that somebody must starve, and that we, as a nation, must decide who it will be, and that it might as well be those who already suffer from protein deficiency, for they are already "useless." Or I finish a lecture to the members of the American Association for Humanistic Psychology, and a therapist rushes up to me afterward and asks me whether or not I believe in the "ethics of the lifeboat," and when I tell her that I don't know why we are in the lifeboat while the others are drowning, she

whispers knowingly to me: "We have a higher consciousness." Or
I am invited to meet with a well-meaning California legislator
who is beginning a political movement based on the therapeutic
values of "authenticity" and "warmth," and he draws for me on a
napkin the button he designed: the simple letter *I* on a blank white
background. Or I attend a dinner sponsored by the Population
Institute at the Century Plaza in Los Angeles, where Paul Ehrlich
addresses a thousand well-heeled people about the "coming end of
affluence," and when I leaf through a copy of his book given away
for free I see that he recommends filling the cellar with food and
buying a gun and relying on neither friends nor neighbors but
only on oneself. Or, finally, I listen for two hours in a graduate
seminar to two women therapists explaining to me how we are all
entirely responsible for our destinies, and how the Jews must have
wanted to be burned by the Germans, and those who starve in the
Sahel must want it to happen, and when I ask them whether there
is anything we owe to others, say, to a child starving in the desert,
one of them snaps at me angrily:"What can I do if a child is determined to starve?"

That, precisely, is what I am talking about here: the growing
solipsism and desperation of a beleaguered class, the world view
emerging among us centered solely on the self and with individual
survival as its sole good. It is a world view present not only in
everything we say and do, but as an ambiance, a feeling in the air, a
general cast of perception and attitude: a retreat from the worlds of
morality and history, an unembarrassed denial of human reciprocity and community.

A few months ago I went to dinner at the house of a woman who
had just been through a weekend of *est* (Erhard Seminar Training),
the latest and most popular new therapeutic enthusiasm. The training is designed to provide its participants with a new sense of
fulfillment and competence, and it seemed to have worked with

my hostess, for she assured me that her life had radically changed, that she felt different about herself, that she was happier and more efficient, and that she kept her house much cleaner than before.

Nothing in that is very startling or distressing, but in the course of the evening she also added that because of the training she now understood: (1) that the individual will is all-powerful and totally determines one's fate; (2) that she felt neither guilt nor shame about anyone's fate and that those who were poor and hungry must have wished it on themselves; (3) that the North Vietnamese must have wanted to be bombed or else it could not have happened to them; (4) that a friend of hers who had been raped and murdered in San Francisco was to be pitied for having willed it to occur; (5) that in her weekend at *est* she had attained full enlightenment; (6) that she was God; (7) that whatever one thought to be true was true beyond all argument; (8) that I was also God, and that my ideas were also true, but not as true as hers because I had not had the training; and (9) that my use of logic to criticize her beliefs was unfair, because reason was "irrational," though she could not tell me why.

There is no telling whether or not this is precisely what she learned at *est,* and no doubt other adherents would deny it, but I have talked by now to at least a dozen of its enthusiasts, and each one of them has blankly recited to me, word for word, the same ill-taught and ignorant catechism. No doubt they were happier for the teaching; invariably they expressed complete satisfaction with their newfound philosophy. Like my hostess, they had learned it all in a kind of manufactured daze at a weekend which cost them $250, in the company of hundreds of others. By now more than 50,000 people have "taken" the training, which was developed by Werner Erhard, who was once known simply as Jack Rosenberg, and who was a trainer for a short time with Mind Dynamics, a franchise operation that trained businessmen in humane managerial techniques. *Est* itself is a step past all that. It is a mixture of ideas and techniques borrowed from the behavioral sciences, Eastern philosophy, the traditional American classroom, Marine boot camp, and modern brainwashing methods. Participants at the weekend workshops are bombarded from the lectern with simplistic truths while being simultaneously bullied and soothed by an army of attendants. They are prevented from leaving their seats to stretch or eat or go to the bathroom, and if—as sometimes happens—they throw up in their places or urinate on themselves, well, that is all part of the training.

It is not hard to understand how it all works, and one need only read the first few pages of Freud's *Group Psychology and the Analysis of the Ego* to see what intelligent use Erhard makes of individual confusion. He has managed to compress into one activity half a dozen techniques for creating power over others: the underlying anxiety of the audience and its need for simple order; the strangeness and power of the extraordinary situation; the gradual befuddlement of the senses; the combined effects of repetition and fatigue; the credulity of others near you; the manufactured impotence of the audience; the masochistic relief that results from placing oneself in the hands of a man to whom one has granted omnipotence.

Clearly Erhard has a genius—not only for the efficiency with which his program is organized and sold, but also for the accuracy with which he tells his audience what it wants to hear. It is the latter which binds them to him. The world is perfect, each of us is all-powerful, shame and guilt are merely arbitrary notions, truth is identical to belief, suffering is merely the result of imperfect consciousness—how like manna all of this must seem to hungry souls. For if we are each totally responsible for our fate, then all the others in the world are responsible for *their* fates, and, if that is so, why should we worry about them?

It is all so simple and straightforward. It has the terrifying vacancy of the lobotomized mind: all complexity gone, and in its place the

warm wind of forced simplicity blowing away the tag ends of conscience and shame. It offers the kind of Orwellian enlightenment
an age like ours is bound to produce, but I do not spell it out in
detail or mock its enthusiasts for that reason alone, nor even because it marks the dead end of human desire or generosity. *Est* is,
after all, only a bit worse than our other popular enthusiasms, and it
is interesting in part because it makes clear so much of what is hidden in them. It is in many ways the logical extension of the whole
human potential movement of the past decade: an endless litany of
self-concern, self-satisfaction, self-improvement, self-assertion, self-
gratification, self-actualization, and self-esteem in which all else was
forgotten altogether, as if in the hope it would in that way disappear. Everything one finds in *est*—the refusal to consider moral
complexities, the denial of history and a larger community, the
disappearance of the Other, the exaggerations of the will, the reduction of all experience to a set of platitudes—all of that is to be
found in embryonic form in almost all modern therapy.

Yet compared to *est* the slightly older therapies (such as Gestalt
therapy or Abraham Maslow's self-actualization or Rogerian encounter groups) had a kind of innocence to them. They were, at
their worst, merely boring or silly. The people drawn to them were
obviously moved by a simple yearning for what was missing from
their lives, and if that yearning took sometimes puerile forms or
excluded moral concerns or genuine passion, that seemed excus-
able—like the play of children. But our newer therapies take upon
themselves a larger burden. Whereas the older therapies merely
ignored moral and historical concerns, the new ones destroy or
replace them. They become not only a way of protecting or changing the self, but of assessing the needs of others and one's responsibilities to them—a way of defining history and determining
morality.

Why that happens is not difficult to understand. It reveals the
impulse behind much of what we do these days: the desire to
defend ourselves against the demands of conscience and the world

through an ethic designed to defuse them both. Most of us realize at one level of consciousness or another that we inhabit an age of catastrophe—if not for ourselves then for countless others. Try as we do, we cannot ignore the routine inequities of distribution and consumption which benefit us and condemn others to misery. Many of us must feel a kind of generalized shame, an unanswerable sense of guilt. So we struggle mightily to convince ourselves that our privilege is earned or deserved, rather than (as we must often feel unconsciously) a form of murder or theft. Our therapies become a way of hiding from the world, a way of easing our pangs of conscience. What lies behind the form they now take is neither simple greed nor moral blindness; it is, instead, the unrealized shame of having failed the world and not knowing what to do about it. Like humiliated lovers who have betrayed what they love, we turn our faces from the world, if only (in Paul Goodman's phrase) "just to live on a while."

That is what makes our new therapies so distressing. They provide their adherents with a way to avoid the demands of the world, to smother the tug of conscience. They allow them to remain who and what they are, to accept the structured world as it is—but with a new sense of justice and justification, with the assurance that it all accords with cosmic law. We are in our proper place; others are in theirs; we may indeed bemoan their fate or even, if we are so moved, do something to change it, but in essence it has nothing to do with us.

What disappears in this view of things is the ground of community, the felt sense of collective responsibility for the fate of each separate other. What takes its place is a moral vacuum in which others are trapped forever in a "private" destiny, doomed to whatever befalls them. In that void the traditional measures of justice or good vanish completely. The self replaces community, relation, neighbor, chance, or God. Looming larger every moment, it obliterates everything around it that might have offered it a way out of its pain.

The end result of this retreat from the complexities of the world is a kind of soft fascism: the denial, in the name of higher truth, of the claims of others upon the self. Our deification of the self becomes equal in effect and human cost to what Nietzsche long ago called the "idolatry of the state." Just as persons once set aside the possibilities of their own humanity and turned instead to the state for a sense of power and identity no longer theirs, so we now turn to the self, giving to it the power and importance of god. In the worship of the state, life gives way to an abstraction, to the total submission of individual will. The result in both cases is the same. What is lost is the immense middle ground of human community. The web of reciprocity and relation is broken. The world diminishes. The felt presence of the other disappears, and with it a part of our own existence.

The real horror of our present condition is not merely the absence of community or the isolation of the self—those, after all, have been part of the American condition for a long time. It is the loss of the ability to remember what is missing, the diminishment of our vision of what is humanly possible or desirable. In our new myths we begin to deny once and for all the existence of what we once believed both possible and good. We proclaim our grief-stricken narcissism to be a form of liberation; we define as enlightenment our broken faith with the world. Already forgetful of what it means to be fully human, we sip still again from Lethe, the river of forgetfulness, hoping to erase even the memory of pain. Lethe, lethal, lethargy—all of those words suggest a kind of death, one that in religious usage is sometimes called *accidie*. It is a condition one can find in many places and in many ages, but only in America, and only recently, have we begun to confuse it with a state of grace.

It is in this context that the Esalen conference on Spiritual Tyranny becomes significant. It was called two years ago in San Francisco

by the Esalen staff as a response to the movement they had helped
to start. What apparently bothered them about the movement was
connected to what I have mentioned here: the proliferation of
sects and cults, and an attendant willingness on the part of many
persons to abandon individual responsibility in favor of submission
to narrow and shallow creeds or therapeutic "masters." The speakers invited were men whose names are familiar to those who read
Esalen's catalogues: Claudio Naranjo, Werner Erhard, George Leonard, Sam Keen, Jerry Rubin—all of them leaders of therapeutic
schools or theorists of what George Leonard has rosily called "the
coming transformation of humanity." As for the several hundred
members of the audience, some had come to cheer their favorite
gurus on and others merely to be present at what had taken on, in
therapeutic circles, the nature of a celebratory event—the equivalent of an all-star rock concert. But there were other reasons for
coming, too. Many people in the audience seemed to be looking
for direction to their lives, and they had come to the conference
for the same reason that they had attended workshops in the past:
to find help. The human potential movement had still not done
for them what it had promised; their lives had remained the same
or perhaps had worsened, and the new world, the promised transformation of self and community they had so long anticipated,
seemed very slow in coming.

So they came in a peculiar mood, one that combined equal
parts of celebration, yearning, and anger. But their mood was further complicated by the fact that the conference happened to be
taking place at the beginning of the Arab oil boycott. The audience
had thus recently been made aware of the possibility of a world
unlike the familiar one in which they felt privileged and safe. To
many of them the future must have seemed frightening, and, standing on the stage and looking out at them, one could feel in the air
and see in their faces the early signs of collective paranoia, as if they
were haunted by visions of the world's impending vengeance.
Packed into the huge hall, its walls lined with gigantic posters of

therapeutic heroes—Fritz Perls, William Reich, Abraham Maslow, and others—the crowd was restless, impatient, volatile; one could feel rising from it a palpable sense of hunger, as if those in it had somehow been failed by both the world and their therapies. It made one apprehensive—not for any specific reason, but simply because beneath the ruffled but still reasonable surface of the crowd lay a hysteria that would in other settings take on any one of several forms, none of them particularly pretty. They wanted someone to set matters right again, to tell them what to do, and it did not matter how that was done, or who did it, or what it required them to believe.

Most of the people in the audience were followers or clients of the various speakers, and as each one spoke his adherents responded with cheers and applause. Others, at odds with the speaker, answered with catcalls, whistles, or groans. I remember in particular the words "total obedience" and "submission to the perfect master" and "the adolescence of rebellion"—phrases which were used by several speakers and which drew from the crowd a surprising amount of acclaim. But even the speakers who took a stand against submission or obedience seemed somehow to diminish the world of experience and choice. In their words, too, there was a tyrannical refusal to acknowledge the existence of a world larger than the self, the total denial—by implication—of the necessity of human community or relation.

That missing element defined the conference and determined its nature: a massive repression all the more poignant because so much of the audience's feeling was engendered by the world denied. Their relation to that world—what it was, what it ought to be—lay at the heart of their discontent, but no one ever spoke of it. Even when those in the audience began to question the speakers, the questions they asked were invariably concerned with themselves, were about self-denial or self-esteem, all centered on the ego, all turned inward. Behind that, of course, they were asking something else, about problems for which they had no words,

about the proper human relation to an age of catastrophe. But neither they nor the speakers were capable of recognizing that fact,
and so those problems remained unarticulated, and they hung in
the room like shadows and ghosts, determining the tone of the
event but never permitted to enter it.

As I listened, I kept thinking about a conversation I had recently
had with a man much taken with mysticism and spirituality. He
was telling me about his sense of another reality.

"I know there is something outside of me," he said. "I can feel it.
I know it is there. But what is it?"

"It may not be a mystery," I said. "Perhaps it is the world."

That startled him. He had meant something more magical than
that, more exotic and grand, something "above" rather than all
around him. It had never occurred to him that what might be calling to him from beyond the self were the worlds of community
and value, the worlds of history and action—all of them waiting to
be entered not as a saint or a mystic, but in a way more difficult
still: as a moral man or woman among other persons, with a person's real and complex nature and needs. Those worlds had been
closed to him, had receded from consciousness as he had ceased to
inhabit them fully or responsibly or lovingly, and so he felt their
ghostly presence as something distant and mysterious, as a dream in
which he had no actual existence.

I saw that at work the first night of the conference and I saw it
again, in greater detail, the next day at the various workshops. I
remember one in particular: a seminar on astral travel held in one
of the local churches. In the huge reaches of the church the few
dozen participants seemed dwarfed and lost as they gathered
around the altar and the first few pews. Their voices echoed in the
empty space as they rose one by one to testify as to how they had
left their bodies while asleep, or how their friends had done so, or
how they had heard about someone who had. The tone was one of

strained yearning, a combined will to believe and to be believed, as if by sheer force of conviction they could bring into being a new world to replace the old one. They spoke about "space cadets" and "soul traps" and the ethics of psychic power, and after a while they shifted ground and spoke about the possibilities of using such power to get things changed in Washington.

"We'll get to the President while he's asleep," said someone. "We'll infiltrate his dreams."

"But that isn't right," said someone else. "That's tyranny, too. We can't intervene without his consent."

"It doesn't matter," said a third. "It won't work anyway. I've a friend who knows someone who tried it. He left his body and went to the White House. But he couldn't get in. The President has astral bodyguards. They know what's what in Washington."

So it went, a series of exchanges making the world of possibility a comic-strip cosmology. It was both absurd and sad; the exchanges and the pain implicit in them conveyed the participants' anguish at their own powerlessness. I thought automatically of the mysticism rampant in Germany in the thirties, or of the passion for shamans and mystics in prerevolutionary Petrograd, or of the Christian zealots in declining Rome. The seminar seemed to mix aspects of all three, and the church was a fitting place for it, for the participants were like lost pilgrims trying to create, in its shadows, a new faith to replace the one they had lost. The last remaining shreds of reason and hope mingled with emergent superstition and fantasy, and the end result was neither moral action nor a complex vision of the world, but a child's garden of absurdities, an impotent dream of power. Confronted by a world in which casual goodness was no longer sufficient as a response, the participants were groping for a way to restore to themselves a power and significance they could no longer feel. In this particular instance the salvationary course they took involved astral travel and psychic power, but it might just as easily have been *est* or scientology or submission to Guru Maharaj Ji or even a doctrinaire adherence to Reich's orgasm theory. As different as all those enthusiasms are, they have a common ground: behind the belief in each one is a sense of exhaustion, the bourgeois will to power mixed with impotence, and the ache of no longer feeling at home in the world.

Perhaps the best example of all this is the immense popularity of Castaneda's works about don Juan. What they offer the yearning reader is precisely what I am talking about here: the dream of an individual potency to be derived magically from another world. In essence it is an updated version of the Protestant dream of the salvation of the soul, and the important thing about the power celebrated by Castaneda and his readers is that it occurs neither in the actual polis nor in the company of significant others. It is found, instead, in a moral and human desert, a fictitious landscape emptied of comrade or lover or child, of every genuine human relation (save that of master and disciple) in which joy or courage might actually be found. Castaneda's myth of don Juan is not an alternative to our condition, but becomes a metaphor for it. It is simply the familiar myth of the solitary gunslinger translated into spiritual language, the comic-strip story of Superman or Captain Marvel made into a slightly more sophisticated legend for adults. It legitimizes our loneliness and solaces us with the myth that we can, in our isolation, find a power to make ourselves safe.

Contrast, for a moment, Castaneda's barren mysteries with the work of Lévi-Strauss, for whom the world of magic and myth is always a *human* world, a realm explored and inhabited by others like ourselves. For Lévi-Strauss the crucial human moment is not the moment of separate awareness; it is the moment of human meeting, in which the other's existence creates for us a sense of the depth and complexity of the world. That, precisely, is what is missing from Castaneda's world. We forget, reading it, that almost without exception the visionary experiences of Native American cultures are a collective work, prepared and defined and sustained by the community, by a world view which is, in effect, the product of cooperative labor. Visionary experience not only leads to the gods and into the self, but it also binds one to the world of myth and—through symbology and tradition—to the historical and social worlds. The individual seeker, though sometimes solitary, is never alone on the quest; the journey occurs within a landscape maintained inwardly by generations of men and women, and the experience is a wedding to them all. Returning from their vision quests, the American Indians recited their newly made poems and sang their songs to the tribe, feeding back to it the truths of a solitude that was *not* separate, but shared. Look, for instance, at the words of Black Elk, the visionary Indian leader, close to death and addressing the gods: "Hear me, not for myself but for my people. Hear me in my sorrow, for I may never live again. Oh, make my people live."

Make my people live! The tale in this instance is not of power but of love—not only for the gods or the self but for the world of others, those whose presence creates for the self a body as truly one's own as the flesh. That love, that sense of lived relation, is at the heart not only of tribal lore, but at the center of the legends of most cultures. One thinks of Odysseus surrounded by comrades seeking to return to his home, or of Gilgamesh driven to seek the secret of immortality by the death of Enkidu, his friend. Both of them are moved by what lies behind all myth and long-lived culture: the felt sense of relation and reciprocity. Indeed, that reciprocity is identical to culture: a collective creation and habitation of value sustained by what we carelessly call the "individual" self. But that, in our dream of power, is what we no longer remember. It disappears from our myths, it vanishes from our therapies, and we come to the worlds of mystery much as we came long ago to the new world: with greed and fear rather than awe and love. In the name of power we strip it of everything real, and it becomes nothing more than a reflection of our need.

What is lost in the whole process is a crucial part of our own human nature, our unacknowledged hunger for relation, for what might be termed "an appetence for Good": the needful reaching out for a life in a larger world. We are moved toward that world by the inner force Freud sometimes called Eros: the desire for relation is as much at work in our need for community and moral significance as it is in our need for coupled love.

Writing about the Athenian polis, Hannah Arendt said about the Greeks:

> The principal characteristic of the tyrant was that he deprived the citizens of access to the public realm, where he could show himself, see and be seen, hear and be heard, that he prohibited the *agoreuein* and *politeuein*, confined the citizens to the privacy of their households. . . . According to the Greeks, to be banished to the privacy of household life was tantamount to being deprived of the specifically human potentialities of life.

The same thing is true for us. To put it simply, it is as if each of us had at the same time a smaller and larger self, as if we inhabited at the same moment a smaller and larger world. The smaller world is the one familiar to us, the world of the individual ego and interpersonal relations, a reality acknowledged by our habits of thought and by our institutions and therapies. But we also inhabit a larger and unrealized world, one in which every gesture becomes significant precisely because it is understood to bind us to the lives of the invisible others.

The natural direction of human ripening is from the smaller to the larger world, is toward the realization and habitation of ever-widening realms of meaning and value. Just as the young are moved from the inside out through increasingly complex stages of perception and thought demanding corresponding changes in their environment, so, too, adults are moved from inside themselves through increasingly complex stages of relation: past the limits of ego and into a human community in which the self becomes other than it was. Seen in this way, human fulfillment hinges on much more than our usual notions of private pleasure or self-actualization, for both of those in their richest forms are impossible without communion and community, an acknowledgment of liability, and a significant role in both the polis and the moral world. To be deprived of those is to be deprived of a part of the self, and to turn away from them is to betray not only the world but also the self, for it is only in the realms in which others exist that one can come to understand the ways in which the nature of each individual existence is in many ways a collective act, the result of countless other lives.

The traditional image for what I am talking about has always been the harvest: the cooperative act in which comrades in a common field gather from it what they need. One finds the image repeated in the work of Camus, Giono, Kropotkin, Lawrence, Silone, and many others, but the most vivid example I know is the scene in *Anna Karenina* in which Levin labors in a field with his peasants, losing all sense of himself in the shared rhythms of the work, the deep blowing grain, and the heat of the sun on his body. It is an image of ecstatic relation which is as much an expression of Eros as is the emblem of two lovers tangled in embrace, and it can stand for almost every aspect of our lives. Every privilege, every object, every good comes to us as a result of a human harvest, the shared labor of others: the languages we use and the beliefs we hold and the ways we experience ourselves. Each of these involves a world of others into which we are entered every moment of our lives. Idly, for instance, we take coffee and sugar in the mornings, and even that simple act immerses us immediately in the larger world. Both the sugar and coffee have come from specific places, have been harvested by specific persons, most probably in a country where the land belongs by right to others than those who hold it, where the wages paid those who work it are exploitive and low. No doubt, too, the political system underlying the distribution of land is maintained in large part by the policies enacted and the armies acting in our name—and the reason we enjoy the coffee while others harvest it has nothing to do with individual will and everything to do with economics, history, and chance.

That, I believe, is what each of us already knows—no matter how much we pretend we do not. Our lives are crowded with the presence of unacknowledged others upon whom our well-being and privilege depend. The shadows of those neglected others—dying in Asia, hungry in Africa, impoverished in our own country—fall upon every one of our private acts, darken the household and marriage bed for each one of us. We try to turn away, but even the desperate nature of our turning is a function of the unacknowledged presence of others, and they are with us even in the vehemence with which we pretend they are not. Something in each of us—even among the enthusiasts of *est*—aches with their presence, aches for the world, for why else would we be in so much pain?

The question of the age, we like to think, is one of survival, and that is true, but not in the way we ordinarily mean it. The survival we ordinarily mean is a narrow and nervous one: simply the continuation, in their present forms, of the isolated lives we lead. But there is little doubt that most of us will survive more or less as we are, for we are clearly prepared to accept whatever is necessary to do so: the deaths of millions of others, wars waged in our name, a police state at home. Like the Germans who accepted the fascists, or the French who collaborated with the Germans, we too, will be able to carry on "business as usual," just as we do now. Our actual crisis of survival lies elsewhere, in the moral realm we so carefully ignore, for it is there that our lives are at stake.

Seen in that light, what might one expect from a therapy a grown man or woman might take seriously? First, a simple willingness to accept the existence of an objective reality equal in significance to the self, a reality which literally (as my friend John

Seeley likes to put it) *objects* as we try to act upon it. Second, a recognition that much of our present pain is the world's pain, the result of living in a catastrophic age in which we do violence to the best parts of our nature. Third, a consciousness of the natural force within us which demands a moral, political, and historical life in the larger world. Fourth, a humility in the presence of that larger world, a respect for the human meaning gathered there by others struggling both in the present and in the past. Finally, a recognition that the future depends directly upon the ways we act individually and in community; that it will never be more just, humane, generous, or sustaining than we ourselves are willing to be; and that the therapist and client, in the solitude of their encounter, create together—in how much of the world they admit to their discourse—a part of the social reality others will later inhabit.

Physicists sometimes use a lovely word, *elsewhere*, to describe the realms of being which we can postulate in thought but can never enter or demonstrate to exist. It is as if they existed side by side with the known world but were beyond all human habitation or touch. In a sense, *elsewhere* also exists in the moral realm, for whatever we fail to love or inhabit fully fades into it, is like a ghostly presence around us, a reality we vaguely remember or intuit but which is no longer ours. Thus, in a very real way the nature of the shared human world does depend on our actions and words, and we can destroy it not only with bombs, but through our failure to inhabit it as fully and humanly as we should. That, in part, is what Freud had in mind, decades ago, when at the very end of *Civilization and Its Discontents* he called for a resurgence of "eternal Eros" in its timeless battle with Death. Now, half a century later, Eros is not yet among us. Whether it ever will be is still an open question. But if the answer to that question is to be found anywhere, it will not be in our popular therapies or creeds like *est* or Castaneda's myths. There, where self is all, Eros can have no life.

SPIRITUAL OBEDIENCE

A LETTER CAME the other day from a good friend of mine, a poet who has always been torn between radical politics and mysticism, and who genuinely aches for the presence of God. A few years ago, astonishing us all, he became a follower of the Guru Maharaj Ji—the smiling, plump young man who heads the Divine Light Mission. Convinced that his guru was in fact God, or at least a manifestation of God, my friend gave his life to him, choosing to become one of his priests, and rapidly rising—because of his brilliance and devotion—to the top of the organization's hierarchy. But last week I received a phone call from my friend, who told me he intended to leave the organization, mainly because, as he said, he could neither "give up the idea of the individual" nor "altogether stop myself from thinking."

Then, a few days later, the letter came, scrawled unevenly on lined yellow paper, in a script more ragged than I remembered, and made poignant by the uneven tone:

> The decision in me to hang it up is the one bright light within me for the time being. Because what is actually the case is that I've lived very much the lifestyle of 1984. Or of Mao's China—or of Hitler's Germany. Imagine for a moment a situation where every single moment of your day is programmed. You begin with exercise, then mediation, then a communal meal. Then the service (the work each member

does). As the director of the House in which I lived and the director of the clinic, it was my job daily to give the requisite pep talks or Satsangs to the staff. You work six days a week, nine to six—then come home to dinner, and go to two hours of spiritual discourse, then meditate. There is no leisure. It is always a group consciousness. You discuss nothing that isn't directly related to 'the knowledge.' You are censured if you discuss any topics of the world. And, of course, there is always the constant focus on the spiritual leader.

Can you imagine not thinking, not writing, not reading, and no real discussion? Day after day, the rest of your life? That is the norm here.

What is the payoff? You are allowed access to a real experience of transcendence. There is a great emotional tie to your fellow devotees and to your Guru—your Guru, being the center stage of everything you do, becomes omnipresent. Everything is ascribed to him. He is positively supernatural after a while. Any normal form of causal thinking breaks down. The ordinary world with its laws and orders is proscribed. It is an 'illusion.' It is an absolutely foolproof system. Better than Mao, because it delivers a closer-knit cohesiveness than collective criticism and the red book.

Look at me. After a bad relationship, a disintegrated marriage, a long illness, a deep searching for an answer, I was ripe. I was always impulsive anyway. So, I bought in. That feeling of love, of community. The certainty that you are submitting to God incarnate. It creates a wonderfully deep and abiding euphoria which, for some, lasts indefinitely.

To trip away from such a euphoria, back to a world of doubt and criticism, of imperfection, why would anyone reject fascism or communism—in practice they are the same—once one had experienced the benefits of these systems?

Because there is more to human beings than the desire for love or the wish for problems to go away. There is also the spirit—the reasoning element in man and a sense of morality. My flight now is due out Dec. 5. I am hoping to last that long. I think that with a little luck I will. If not, I'll call.

Love to you, K

But nothing is simple. A few days later my friend called again, his voice a bit stronger, still anxious to leave, asking me to make his travel arrangements. But this time he began talking about William Buckley, how he liked his work, how he had written to him and gotten a moving letter in return. I could hear, as he talked, the beginning of a new kind of attachment, the hints, ever so faint, of a new enthusiasm, a new creed, something new to believe in, to join. Never having been to China, he had once extolled its virtues; now, still without having seen it, he denounced its faults. His moods are like the wild swings of a quivering compass needle, with no true pole.

I remember going a few years ago to a lecture in which the speaker, in the name of enlightenment, advocated total submission to a religious master. The audience, like many contemporary audiences, was receptive to the idea, or at least more receptive than they would have been a while back. Half of them were intrigued by the idea, drawn to it. Total submission, obedience to a "perfect master"—one could hear, inwardly in them, the gathering of breath for a collective sigh of relief. At last, to be set free, to lay down one's burden, to be a child again, not in renewed innocence, but in restored dependence, in admitted, undisguised dependence. To be told, again, what to do, and how to do it.

The yearning in the audience was so palpable, their need so thick and obvious, that it was impossible not to empathize with it in some way. Why not, after all? Clearly there are truths and kinds of wisdom to which most persons will not come alone; clearly there are in the world authorities in matters of the spirit, seasoned travelers, guides. Somewhere there must be truths other than the disappointing ones we have; somewhere there must be access to a world larger than this one. And if, to get there, we must put aside all arrogance of will and the stubborn ego, well, why not? Why not admit what we do not know and cannot do and submit to someone who clearly knows and does, who will teach us his truths if we merely put aside all judgment and obey with goodwill?

The audience in question was white and middle-class—in spiritual need perhaps, but not only spiritual need. They were in all probability politically and psychologically exhausted; though privileged, they had been deprived of full participation in a vital polis or in a vivid communal or social world; they had been raised in various institutional settings that had simultaneously taught them to be both responsible for their own behavior and to the expectations of others and had also demanded from them (if they were to succeed) an almost total submission to authority. As a result, the condition in which they found themselves, the frustrations at work at the heart of their lives, their desire for spiritual submission and thereby salvation, may have revealed less of a spiritual yearning than a capacity for submission in general, or a yearning for anything that might relieve them of their discomfort and locate them in the world. Submission in such a situation becomes a value and end in itself, and unless it exists side by side with an insistence upon political power and participation or on a just and moral world, it becomes a frightening and destructive thing, not only because it fails to provide what is really needed, but because it makes us forget precisely *what* we need.

There are many things to which a man or woman can submit: to one's own work, to the needs of others, to passionate love, to lust, to experience, to the rhythms of nature—the list is endless and includes almost anything men or women might do, for almost anything, done with wholeheartedness, takes us beyond ourselves and into a relation with other things, and that is *always* a submission, for it is always a joining, a kind of wedding to the world. There is, no doubt, a need for that, and without it we grow exhausted with ourselves, with our wisdom still unspoken and our needs unmet.

But that general appetite is twisted and used tyrannically when we are asked to submit ourselves unconditionally to "masters," or to unquestioned authorities—whether they wear the masks of the state or of the spirit. In both instances our primary relation is no longer to the world or to others; it is to the master, and the world or others diminish with that choice, because our primary relation to them is broken, and with it our sense of obligation, responsibility, and possibility. In our attempt to restore to ourselves what is missing we merely intensify the deprivation rather than diminish it.

During the summer of 1977, I taught for several weeks at Naropa Institute, a Buddhist school in Boulder, Colorado, begun by Chögyam Trungpa, Rinpoche, who is considered by his American followers to be a sort of spiritual king. While there, I made most of the entries and notes that appear on the following pages. But they are selected from a longer manuscript, and I suppose they will not make much sense without an explanation of Naropa and what I was doing there.

Trungpa is certainly no fraud. Prepared from childhood to be the abbot of several monasteries in Tibet, he fled the country when the Communists took it over in 1959, and in 1970 he came to the United States. He is believed by his followers to be the incarnation of Trungpa Tulku, an earlier Tibetan master, and to be heir to a tradition of "crazy wisdom" dating back 1,800 years to Milarepa and Padmasambhava, revered Tibetan saints. Trungpa's earliest American followers were drawn mainly from the counterculture, and I suspect that they may have been generally more intelligent, literate, and profligate than those drawn to other contemporary spiritual leaders. Forty years old, bright, witty, and a hard drinker, Trungpa also appealed to a number of artists and writers, many of whom—like Allen Ginsberg—became both his students and teachers at Naropa.

Trungpa's disciples are not nearly so well organized as members of most other modern spiritual groups. Though they sometimes live communally at the spiritual centers set up in different parts of the country, for the most part they live independently and separately and owe Trungpa allegiance or obedience only in terms of their spiritual lives. Nonetheless, Trungpa does wield immense power over some of them. His disciples apply to him for counsel as they might to a rabbi, and Trungpa has upon occasion strongly "suggested" to people whom they should marry or how and where they should live. Many of his followers believe him to have magical powers gathered in Tibet. In general, however, the power that Trungpa wields is as much a result of what his disciples project upon him as of what they are taught.

I came to Naropa because I was curious about it, and because some people there, familiar with my writing, had contacted me hoping that I would write something about the school. When I first explained my misgivings about teaching there, the staff said to come anyway, and I went, having certain mild but not decisive prejudices, feeling a bit guilty about a summer spent so far from things I really cared about, but also curious and self-indulgent enough to want a few easy weeks in the mountains.

I taught two courses, both of which I had suggested: one on autobiography, which was filled to overflowing, and one on social action and morality, which drew only a handful of students. Not knowing quite how to fit me into their scheme of things, the administrators thrust me upon the poets in Naropa's "Kerouac School of Disembodied Poetics." Perplexed by my presence, a bit resentful of those who stuck me there, and as competitive and hermetic as poets can often be, they left me pretty much to myself. For the most part I went about my private business, knowing enough about summer schools in general to construct a separate life for myself, and finding my real pleasures in the mountains or among friends with little interest in Buddhism.

Naropa, which is a year-round school, attracts most of its students during its two summer sessions. The guest faculty is impressive: artists, intellectuals, and academicians who are flattered by the invitation to teach and apparently hope to enhance their own work with Buddhist ideas and meditative teachings. The 600 students who were there for each summer session ought not be confused with Trungpa's regular disciples, who number perhaps 1,500 and are scattered across the country. The real disciples run, rather than attend, Naropa, and they are associated primarily with Vajradhatu, an essentially religious organization coordinating the various activities and meditative centers Trungpa has set up. Vajradhatu and Naropa are legally separate; though Trungpa often lectures at Naropa, his spiritual teaching is offered mainly in the activities of Vajradhatu, and Naropa is—or so its administrators claim—an attempt merely to leaven Western culture with Eastern wisdom. Whereas Vajradhatu is organized around a single truth and obedience to a single master, Naropa is supposedly more secular and various, with several points of view represented. Nonetheless, Tibetan Buddhism forms the heart of each summer's teaching. Most of the students there seem drawn by an interest in Buddhism, meditation, or enlightenment, and the most popular events of the summer are the weekly lectures conducted by spiritual teachers and the activities associated with them: studies in the Buddhist tradition and instruction in mediation, without which, it is carefully explained, one cannot fully understand Buddhist ideas.

The school has no campus of its own. Its central offices, along with a rehearsal hall, are on the second floor of a building on Boulder's mall close to the modish center of town and the hip bars and health food stores. Classes were held several blocks away in a large Catholic high school rented for the summer. Most of the summer faculty members were housed, along with some students, in a nearby apartment complex which took on, as the summer progressed, the untidy and noisy, but not unpleasant, vitality of unmanaged tenement life. Trungpa's disciples were scattered around town in their own houses, and they spent most of their time in another building altogether, where Vajradhatu's affairs were conducted. There things appeared to be more orderly; the building—efficiently busy, manned at the entrances—resembled a bank or a mini-Pentagon. Trungpa himself was not at Naropa while I was there. He was off "on retreat" for the summer. His place had been taken by an American named Ösel Tendzin, the "Vajra Regent," who had been Trungpa's prize student before being elevated to his new role.* Trungpa had in no way abdicated his place at the center of the school and its disciples, but the trappings of royalty, and the attitudes of the disciples toward them, had passed entire from Trungpa to Ösel. It is the position and not the man that commands obedience—not so very different from the Catholic attitude toward the Pope. Ösel was constantly attended in public, as is Trungpa, by a small legion of Vajra guards, rather muscular and doggedly loyal young men whose sole job is to do his bidding. Their presence, as with many things at Naropa, was partly symbolic. But that does not mean it was purely ornamental. Symbols at Naropa take on immense weight and significance, often superseding everything else. I remember a friend telling me he had been asked by one of the guards to prepare a performance for Ösel's birthday.

"What sort of performance?" he had asked.

"We don't care," answered the guard. "Just make sure you do it as if it were for a king."

As for Boulder itself, it is a complex and curious place, as is all of Colorado. Nature is so overpoweringly present one feels that one has escaped the ordinary world and arrived at a place more beautiful and innocent. But that is not the case. For a while, bored with

---

*Several years later, following Trungpa's death, Ösel Tendzin took his place. He, in turn, died of AIDS after reportedly sleeping indiscriminately and without protection with both male and female disciples and never informing them of his condition.

Naropa, I wandered the town, picking up stories and myths. The state is a paranoiac's dream, with drugs flowing into towns from the south, and drug money from the southwest, and guns being run to Latin America, and ex-Green Berets and soldiers of fortune and agents from nine different federal security agencies, and the same odd mix of interests, influences, and alliances that turns up in Miami and Panama or on the drug routes of Southeast Asia. Rocky Flats is nearby, were we reprocess fissionable material from all our nuclear weapons, and so is Cheyenne Mountain, America's underground headquarters in case of war. The Rockies are honeycombed from one end to the other with military installations of all sorts; a great war is brewing in the state over mineral and water rights; the state's powers include the Rockefeller and Coors families; branches of the Mafia contend with one another; many of the university's professors are said to have extensive ties with the CIA; this is where several years ago a mysterious busload of Tibetans turned up stranded in a ditch, preparing for a counterinsurgent invasion of Tibet; where Thomas Riha worked at the University of Colorado on a secret project before disappearing without a trace in Eastern Europe; where his confidante, Gayla Tannenbaum, is said to have committed suicide from a dose of cyanide in the same hospital where they once hid Dita Beard; where the young man who murdered his uncle, the King of Saudi Arabia, went to school and was, some insist, recruited by CIA agents working in the Drug Enforcement Agency. And it is here, too, that the wife of the Shah of Iran arrived with her full retinue on three private planes to lecture at the Aspen Institute about social justice.

In short, this is America, and the underside of town, invisible to tourists and Buddhist residents, is inhabited by bikers and hoodlums, outlaws and adventurers, rebels and loonies, all percolating under the surface and at the edges of town and perhaps a better measure of our age than the stained glass and ferns of the singles' bars or the herb displays at the health food stores. Though I love these details and tales, I have no room for them here, and I mention them only as a way of setting the scene, for they are not unrelated to what goes on at Naropa. This, too, is *the world*: the mix of power and violence and sophistication from which the students turn away as if hoping to leave it behind even as it presses close.

And finally, one note of caution. What goes on at Naropa and Vajradhatu is by no means as excessive or oppressive as what some other sects inflict upon their members. I do not intend here an exposé. In many ways it is the sect's relative innocuousness that interests me, because even in Naropa's comparative normality one can see the tendencies that lead elsewhere to far more troubling forms of tyranny and foolishness. Lastly, I should say that while passing through Boulder in 1978 I passed many of these pages on to someone at Naropa, explained that I intended to publish them, and asked if Trungpa would like to discuss them. The answer was no.

June 16

Of course, one must not forget this is Vajrayana Buddhism, a particular tradition—an aristocratic Tibetan line set free of moral constraint, in which all action is seen as play, and in which the traditional (if somewhat hazy) notions at work in Buddhism about our moral responsibilities to other living creatures are largely set aside. For the most part, moral and social questions disappear from all discourse and even from idle conversation, save when they are being raised by outsiders. Then they are dealt with a bit grudgingly, and always briefly.

Naropa embodies a feudal, priestly tradition transplanted to a modern capitalist setting. The attraction it has for its adherents is reminiscent of the attraction the aristocracy had for the rising middle class in the early days of capitalistic expansion. These middle-class children are drawn irresistibly not only to the submissive discipline involved, but also to the trappings of imperial hierarchy. Stepping out of their limousines, hours late for their talks, surrounded by satraps, the masters seem alternately like Arab chieftains or caliphs. Allegiance to the discipline means allegiance to the lineage, to the present Vajra, as clearly as if it were allegiance to royalty on the throne.

If there is a compassion at work here, as some insist, it is so limited, so diminished, so divorced from concrete changes in social structure or from direct contact with suffering others, that it makes no difference at all. Periodically someone will talk about how meditation will lead inevitably to compassion or generosity. But that, even according to other Buddhists, is nonsense. Certainly here it is nonsense. Behind the public surface lies the intrigue and attitude of a medieval court, and this shows up in the peculiar and supposedly playful way in which Buddhists enter the world of hip and modish capitalism, expanding their empire, running a variety of businesses all over town: restaurants, bars, clothing stores. It is no accident that they are in Boulder, where such businesses flourish. America is what it is, and business is play, and so the Buddhists happily take part in the moneymaking, unconstrained by any notion of a common good, and certainly unconcerned about what happens to individual conscience in a context dominated by the entrepreneurial self and the primacy of property.

For Vajrayana Buddhists, the "open space" of the world is an arena for play and not for justice. Nothing could be further from their sensibilities than the notion of a free community of equals or a just society or the common good. In their eyes justice is merely another delusion, and interest in it only another proof of personal confusion. Given this, one begins to see how well the institute fits into the life of Boulder and why it has such an attraction for certain modern intellectuals and therapists.

June 17

For the various sages here, every form of pain can be understood simply in terms of attachment or ego. Conscience does not exist, nor does what Blake long ago called a yearning for Jerusalem: a glory made part of daily life. Precisely those joyous powers and passions that reveal, in the self, the presence of life are taken to be fictions, and discounted or abused. In that, ironically, Naropa becomes, as its founders want, a normal part of American intellectual life. In its denial of the felt world of varied and suffering persons and the lessons to be learned there, it shares the limitations of intellectual America, and it caters to its weakness.

This particular brand of Buddhism is neither quite so morally aware as some Buddhist traditions nor so humble as others. Because it is elitist, aristocratic, and feudal, there lies at its heart, or at least close to the heart of Trungpa's aristocratic thought, a disdain for politics and for the yearnings behind it. His spiritual views lead inevitably and sometimes quite prettily to theories of radical aesthetics (see, for example, how another brand of Buddhism leavens the work of John Cage), and though one can even base upon them a fairly radical psychology, somehow they emerge, in his talks, in terms of politics, as reactionary, establishmentarian—something Trungpa has in common with most spiritual leaders who appeal to America's lost souls. The zeal one feels at work at the institute is simply a zeal to establish itself at the heart of American mainstream life, to conventionalize itself and make itself respectable. In that regard, Trungpa's early connections with the hippie or fringe community appear in retrospect to have been simply the easiest or only available way to build a foundation for his aristocratic program.

June 18

When Trungpa does touch upon politics, as he sometimes will in his lectures, it is always to devalue it, to set it aside. And when one raises with his disciples various questions about moral reciprocity and value, human responsibility, or political action, they dismiss such inquiries, muttering platitudes about "all sentient creatures" or "a confused and misdirected attachment to the world." But one must not make the mistake of thinking that they are otherworldly. Far from it. Trungpa and his students are very much of the world, and neither Trungpa nor his followers seem to have trouble with the structure of American capitalism, the idea of property, the underlying relations between castes and classes of persons. These, I believe, appear to him as divinely ordered—a kind of spiritual hierarchy hardened into human norms. The notion that individual well-being hinges on change does not occur to him any more than it seems to have occurred to his predecessors in feudal Tibet.

The fact that this notion is taught by a privileged class of priests to their followers ought to make it somewhat suspect, of course. But one can also understand its appeal to middle-class Americans, whose nervousness is such that they would like to believe that spiritual progress is possible without further upheavals in history or the loss of their own privileged condition.

Trungpa's implicit conservatism seems, then, both appealing to his followers and also destructive to the qualities of human decency still feebly struggling in them to stay alive. And that is to say nothing of its real consequences in the concrete world: those that will show up not in the destinies of these middle-class Americans, but in the fates of the poor and black and disenfranchised who invariably find themselves suffering the results of reactionary American politics. For those whose well-being rests upon either the transformation of society or changes in dominant American notions about justice, moral philosophies like Trungpa's can only spell further pain, for if they are widely taken seriously, what will happen to those who are marginal or dispossessed or without a place in the world as it is? I do not mean to suggest that Trungpa actually intends harm to anyone, or is an incipient fascist. Certainly the eclecticism at work in the summer institute, and the plethora of views expressed, and the relative freedom of their expression, leave intact at least a minimal sense of the free play of thought and a willingness to subject Buddhist views to challenge and criticism. But to claim for Vajrayana Buddhism (as is often done) a supremacy of vision, or to denounce in its name all other devotions, attachments, or senses of obligation as confusion (as is also done), is to do violence to all those present, and also to the millions of those who are not. It becomes, in that instance, not the healing that it might be, but a still further cause of pain.

June 19

Yesterday a friend and I sought among the places on our map a town still untouched by the development that has overwhelmed these mountains. Everywhere now there rise from the steep valleys row upon row of condominiums and chalets, and the signs of the culture that accompanies them: the stores and restaurants catering to the fancies of a white American self-celebration now coming into its own. To find something older and easier-going one must go to the outermost avenues, to the traditional gas stations and cafes that, though scars on the landscape, have at least a reality the make-believe cuteness of the towns—Dillon, Vail, Georgetown, Boulder, and Aspen—long ago lost or never had.

In all of these towns one feels oneself at the precious, airless dead end of culture among fashionable sleepwalkers. Each town seems to mimic and repeat what its builders remember of their college campuses. Complete with apartments, pools, tennis courts, groceries, jewelry stores, and bars made to look like old-time saloons, these towns close in on the soul at the same time that they supposedly sustain its life. They remind one of the "sundomes" Ray Bradbury once described in a story about rain swept Venus: self-enclosed pockets of weather creating a world totally separate from the planet's life.

A few nights ago, watching the faces of the rapt students as they listened to a Buddhist speaker, it occurred to me that the world into which they seemed compelled to move was the spiritual version of these towns. Though they sought surcease from the tribulations of the self, they seemed trapped in themselves by precisely the absence of what the speaker denounced: a passion for the world. Peculiarly, they seemed engaged in trying to escape an appetite that no longer seemed alive in them. Though the administrators of the institute are calm and have a kind of clarity, the atmosphere around them seems humanly empty, too hygienic, too claustrophobic by far. Lacking both irony and joy, the atmosphere is watery, insubstantial. Watching it, moving through it, one feels very little. There is not enough passion present in it to engender any kind of response. The larger world itself is so absent, so distant, that the dislocation between this reality and that other feels as if it has itself become unreal.

June 20
Sometimes the entire institute seems like a great joke played by Trungpa on the world: the attempt of an overgrown child to reconstruct for himself a kingdom according to whim. It is no accident that he should construct it here, in Boulder, through the agency of yearning Americans whose ache for a larger world is easily reduced to a passion for aristocratic form and myth. He makes easy use of the voracious elitism by which American members of the middle class increasingly justify their wealth or rationalize their sense of separation from others. What makes it painful to see is that there exists in many of these students a pain and shame and unused power that issues from the deepest and best parts of themselves and that cries out for attention and change. But there is no way for that to happen through this kind of Buddhism, no teacher to help them, no teaching to reveal to them what they feel. Instead, their human yearning, the ache of conscience, the inner need for justice, the felt sense of unused freedom, are all passed off as illusions, as Western childishness. These impulses, ironically, are suppressed or destroyed in the name of a spiritual wisdom that might, in other circumstances, help to complete them. But that destruction is not in any way inherent in Buddhist wisdom or even in the tradition of meditation. It is inherent in the priestly class. Aristocrats of any sort, after all, especially those given to pomp and hierarchy, are not the best sages to consult about political frustration and moral discomfort.

As is true of people in almost any contemporary institution, these students are better than what they are taught. Just as, in the sixties, the truths of their rebellion, garbled as they were, exceeded in their wisdom the institutional truths of their teachers, so, too, the yearning of these students and their unused powers are diminished by the institution that now defines reality and truth for them. Troubled not only by their loss of a felt connection to the world, these students also experience the pain of a vision of self or human nature that allows no room for what they feel about the world and offers no way to express it. Their pain is not fundamentally spiritual; it is moral. Their problem is to regain their moral lives in the same way that Americans have only recently begun to regain their sexual lives. But just as we looked mistakenly to sexuality for certain political and moral satisfactions, and thereby corrupting that realm, so now we mistakenly search in the spirit's world for the wrong satisfactions and do ourselves a similar damage. Just as Columbus, sailing among the American isles, thought himself to be in the Indies and called everything by the wrong names, we too drift in a landscape that we do not understand and where we have the wrong names for things.

June 21

We have come to Denver, to Lakeside, an amusement park built in the 1920s, to picnic on the lawn under the cottonwood trees. Just yesterday we were in the mountains, crossing a series of passes at 12,000 feet, above the timberline, where the tundra was covered everywhere with small blue and white flowers. The wind played about us as we wound our way among melting snow banks to come finally to what seemed like the top of the world. In the distance we could see nothing human, merely the high saddles of mountains, their tree-covered flanks, and the tall cloudy skies above them barely distinguishable from the white peaks. There was a beauty to that almost beyond belief, but there is something no less beautiful in all of this: the amusement park with its small lake and weathered, brightly painted buildings, the mechanical fat lady laughing above the ride through the fun house, lovers and children passing on the narrow paths or gathered at tables under the trees, and beside me, a good comrade. This, too, is a gift, perhaps more profound than that other, because its beauty is crowned by human presence. Sometimes, somehow, almost as if by accident, we get things right; the spaces we create for one another—like this small amusement park—reveal the presence of the human heart. The indifferent generosity of nature gives way to the human generosity of the accidentally just city.

Now at noon, we sit on the grass beneath this tall tree, having within reach the fruits of countless harvests: wine, bread, cheeses, fruit, chocolate. I look at the grass, the sky, the passersby, my companions, and my heart fills with a joy equal to any more obviously mystical or religious sentiment I have ever had. There is nothing beyond the absolute beauty of the transience of this day—this wind, this ease, this flesh. It arises from the heart in answer to a human presence, and one understands—if only for a moment—what it would mean to be free.

There are those, back at Naropa, who would escape all this. A few nights ago, in answer to some questions about the nature of joy, one of the sages in residence, a Buddhist monk, answered that joy was always followed or equaled by suffering, and that enlightenment meant leaving them both behind. Nobody in the audience bothered to argue. Yet there is, I think, a discipline graver and more demanding than the one offered to the audience. It is open to those whose joy in life seems to justify whatever suffering is entailed. It is a passion beyond all possessiveness, a fierce love of the world and a fierce joy in the transience of things made beautiful by their impermanence. I would not trade this day for heaven, no matter what name we call it by. Or rather, I think that if there is a heaven, it is something like this, a pleasure taken in life, this gift of momentary ease under the trees, and the taste of satisfaction, and the promise of grace, alive in one's hands and mouth.

The discipline of living with this grace, of seeking it out, is what calls to some of us as surely as the escape from pain calls to others. This is not the cessation of passion, but its completion, its *humanization*. The question posed by this discipline is a simple one, demanding a lifetime to answer. It is: *Can one live as man?* It is a question that echoes in the soul with the significance of Being itself. And when one can answer yes to that question, then the answer makes itself felt beneath all thought and fills the flesh with a power beyond all further questioning; it provides a certainty of belonging in a world that often seems, on its face, indifferent to our presence. Here, in the city, where we have made our homes, there lives a beauty that exceeds—when it is present—the beauty of the mountains, because it is a human beauty, and thereby lifts the heart even higher. It is not antithetical to the mountains, it calls to the same thing in the soul; it, too, is what one might call, with Giono, "the song of the world." Stone, sky, earth, and tree—these beckon to us as enigmas, facts, and gifts: a world *beyond* that suddenly opens in the soul to reveal itself, outside of us, as a home. That same thing is true of this city, this place, these human others. They, too, open in the soul, reveal themselves as our home. This beauty, not accidental, issues from the human hand, is a song of human joy. It is like the beauty of certain cities, of certain man-made landscapes, in which human habitation merges with sky and sea to form a world that would vanish if either were missing.

June 23

Today, when a student asked me what I thought of Naropa and its trappings, I filtered through my mind all the polite or witty things I might say, and then responded with what I really meant: "I think it is beneath contempt." And that is true. Beyond the reasonableness of my controlled responses, all of this seems worse than absurd, mainly because at the heart of its senselessness lies a smug self-congratulation beyond all belief. Things here are too closed, small, careful, secure. I remember, as a child, hating my obligatory visits to the synagogue, hating them with the passion of a secularized Jew, as if still stirring in my blood were the currents of the impulses that took a whole people out of their towns and shtetls and into the larger world—gasping for air, seeking a home. If there is a god, it is a god of the open world, of oceans and deserts, of great distances and beasts, and infinite variety and possibility. How such a god must shudder at these shuttered truths, these betrayals of the world.

June 24

Two summers ago, a well-known poet, William Merwin, came to Naropa to teach for the summer, accompanied by a lovely Asian woman, Dana.*

Trungpa befriended and apparently impressed them both. At the end of the summer Merwin, who had already had experience with Catholic modes of meditation, asked Trungpa if he and Dana could attend a fall retreat ordinarily open only to regular disciples. Admission to these retreats is always much sought after, in part because it is a sign of Trungpa's approval, but also because it is here that certain truths are supposedly revealed for which the other aspects of the discipline are simply a preparation. For several weeks Trungpa magically becomes the "Vajra Master": an absolute authority in all things, a spiritual master who is himself divine. The retreat involves alternating periods of meditation and formal teaching, but these are not nearly so serious as one might imagine; they are also marked by much celebration, drinking, and horseplay, and

---

*I tell this story with some hesitation because I have heard so many different versions of it from so many different people. Though I first learned most of the story in 1977, some of the details in my account are drawn from a full-length manuscript compiled at Naropa by the members of Ed Sanders's class in investigative poetry. In 1977, they interviewed all those involved and tried to reconstruct not only the events but the attitudes of the witnesses. Their manuscript includes several verbatim transcripts of interviews with participants. It is on file at Naropa's library—much to the institute's credit—and available to anybody who wants to see it. This fact, I should note, sets apart those who run Naropa from members of more secretive religious groups.

rumors abound about their sexual aspects—lovemaking, wife-swapping, and the accompaniment of devotion with communal debauchery.

The particular retreat in question, held at a rented ski lodge in Snowmass, Colorado, and involving about 125 people, apparently was no exception. During the first several weeks there were the usual incidents of roughhousing and hazing, most of which make the retreat sound more like an extended fraternity weekend than a religious event. There was a slow escalation of what began as playful violence: Trungpa took to using a peashooter on unwary students; there was a strenuous snowball fight between Trungpa's Vajra guards and his other disciples; at one point the disciples trapped Trungpa in his car and rocked it violently in the snow; there were playful student plans (in which some claim Merwin participated) for releasing laughing gas at one of Trungpa's lectures; and once, apparently, some of the students trashed Trungpa's chalet.

During all of this Merwin and Dana kept to themselves, just as they had done at Naropa during the summer. They spent their free time together in their room, coming down only for lectures, rituals, or meditation. Their aloofness, which the community members had resented all summer, took on, in the new context, a more disturbing quality. Many of the disciples later described it as antisocial, or an insult to Trungpa, or a form of rebellion or egotism—precisely the kind of personal attachment and self-protectiveness that this brand of Buddhism is meant to dissolve. In the claustrophobic atmosphere of the retreat, this communal resentment escalated in much the same way as had the initially playful roughhousing, and both of these elements found their final expression on Halloween night.

A party takes place—though nobody is quite clear whether Trungpa himself has arranged it. These parties have traditionally been more or less bacchanalian. Everyone is expected to come in costume; some disciples spend days planning and making their outfits. That night, at the party, Trungpa is slightly drunk and perhaps feeling bad-tempered. One of the participants later described the way Trungpa greeted her: "He was being so brutal, and, like, clawing my arm, and just biting my lip, so vicious." But she was, to be fair, dressed as a biker, and perhaps Trungpa's approach was satiric and mocking, as is sometimes his way. Earlier in the evening a woman had been stripped naked, apparently at Trungpa's joking command, and hoisted into the air by the Vajra guards and passed around—presumably in fun, though the woman herself did not think so. Merwin and Dana had apparently put their heads in earlier in the evening, stayed about an hour, dancing only with one another, keeping apart, perhaps made wary by the tales they had heard of sexual excess. Later, when Trungpa begins to lecture his students about the meaning of the ball and its relation to his teaching, he notices their absence and sends someone to get them. They come downstairs again, peer in, don't enter, and go back upstairs. Trungpa sends someone up after them, and he tells them politely, "The Vajra Master has extended an invitation to William Merwin to come." Merwin says through the closed door that he has gone to sleep, and that, anyway, he was at the party before. When Trungpa hears this he responds: "Well, he is sort of *required* to come." But when that message reaches Merwin he answers that nobody can tell him when to go to sleep.

Hearing this, Trungpa grows angrier. He addresses his listeners: "You know, a certain kind of resistance is going on . . . I want you to realize I'm going to insist he come down."

His students try to stop him, realizing perhaps that he is too drunk to know quite what he is doing. "Drop it," they say. "Let it go."

But he is adamant. "I want that door broken down," he says.

Now a whole gang goes upstairs. They crowd the hallway outside the room, explaining to Merwin what is going on, asking him again to come out, telling him to come out, warning him what will happen if he doesn't. A few of them, afraid of what is coming, and caught between common sense and their promised obedience to the master, *plead* with them to come out. Inside, Merwin and Dana (as they will later explain), are both angry and a bit frightened. It must seem to them as if everyone at the retreat is arrayed against them. Merwin, who ordinarily professes pacifism, is aware only of trying to protect Dana, and he has pushed furniture against the wall and broken a beer bottle in readiness, waiting to attack whoever comes through the door.

The crowd sends word again to Trungpa, telling him they are unable to break through the door. He tells them to go in from the balcony, breaking the window, and this is what they do, shattering the window and bursting through the door at the same time. As they do, Merwin lunges at the first few who enter, going for their faces, cutting several people around the eyes, on the chin, along the arms. There is a scuffle, shouts, and screams. Blood is everywhere. Merwin realizes what he has done, suddenly stops fighting, hands over the bottle. The wounded are taken off for doctoring. Merwin and Dana are brought by the crowd downstairs to stand in front of Trungpa while the assembled and costumed disciples watch.

Trungpa is apparently drunk and not particularly coherent. Merwin is angry but contained; Dana is more volatile, struggling with those who hold her, calling Trungpa names: Fascist, Hitler, Bastard, Nazi, Cop. Trungpa says a variety of things in no clear sequence. He wants them to reveal themselves, to give themselves up, or *over*, in some way. "I mean you no harm," he explains at one point. "What is your secret?" But he is also abusive. He mutters something about "my country ripped out from under me, the Chinese Communists did it." And he mentions Dana's race, implying an ethnic solidarity with her and some sort of betrayal on her part, asking her what she is doing with a white man.

Then he wants them to strip. He "asks" them to do it, but warns them that he will have it done by force if necessary. When they refuse, he orders his guards to proceed. Merwin, who is passive about it, is stripped first. But Dana looks around at the onlookers, staring each one in the face for a moment, asking for help. "Someone call the police," she says. Nobody intervenes. Nobody moves. All watch. Then Trungpa tells his guards to strip Dana. She struggles. One of the guards hesitates. Trungpa insists that he continue. The guard proceeds. Now a solitary male witness tries to intervene, but he is quickly overpowered by the guards, then moved out of the way. Finally both Merwin and Dana are naked. Trungpa seems satisfied. The lovers huddle together. Nobody speaks. Then Merwin looks around the room. "Why," he asks, "are we the only naked ones?" Then a few others begin to strip, then many others take off their clothes. Trungpa says: "Let's dance." The crowd begins to dance. Perhaps forgotten, or perhaps simply adequately chastised, Merwin and Dana go back upstairs.

The next day Trungpa posts an open letter to everyone at the retreat, saying, among other things, "You must offer your neurosis as a feast to celebrate your entrance into the Vajra teachings." There is no note of apology, only an explanatory justification. Merwin and Dana meet with Trungpa, who says that nothing like it will happen again. They consider leaving, but they finally, perhaps a bit oddly, decide to stay on. Merwin explains later: they were, after all, about to receive the Tantric teachings, and he did not want to miss them.

It would be possible, of course, to dismiss these events as unimportant: a kind of roughhousing that got out of hand or a momentary drunkenness with embarrassing consequences. It would also be possible to tell the story in a more dramatic way, stressing the almost literary symbolism of the details: the shattered glass, the cries of *Fascist* and *Hitler,* the naked lovers exposed and vulnerable, surrounded by guards, and the gradual transformation of the "innocent" onlookers into passive participants. Certainly there are almost mythic elements in the story, and even now it retains those elements, not only for those directly involved, but also for many of Trungpa's other followers, who cannot quite stomach the event and for whom it has had a shadowy and continual presence, like a bad dream they cannot quite forget.

What concerns me here is less the event itself, or Trungpa's behavior, than the reactions of his followers and the way they now try to explain away what happened. To someone who sees Trungpa—as I do—as simply an ordinary man dressed in the make-believe robes of a mystical king, his behavior is not particularly surprising. Power and alcohol go to most men's heads, and if you raise a man from childhood to believe in his own divinity, it is not surprising that he sometimes abuses his power. Nor am I surprised either by the behavior of his followers in the midst of the event. Most of them, looking on, were frozen into immobility. Though that is sad, it is not startling; people have an immense capacity for passivity and obedience, and it takes more ego and courage than most of them have to speak out forcefully in a situation where what they believe to be genuine mystical powers stand over and against them. Whether it is a tribesman with a shaman, a private with a general, or a student with a teacher, most people are too timid, too unsure of themselves, and (at times) too sensibly scared to oppose authority in a situation where it has been vested in a single man or a few individuals. No doubt many of the onlookers at Snowmass felt the stirring in themselves of a desire to intervene, but they were conscious after the fact of a paralysis of will, an impossibility of movement, which was not so much a failure of nerve but the immobilizing conflict between conscience and a learned obedience to authority, a submission to someone in whom they had vested immense power. No, the real problem lies elsewhere: in both what happened *before* the incident, in how the disciples had been taught to accept authority, and also in what followed after, in their inability even after the fact to see that Trungpa might have made a mistake, or that he was merely human.

"I was wrong," Trungpa might have said. Or, "he was wrong," his disciples might have said. But they *cannot* say such things. It would interfere too much with the myth they have chosen to believe. And that means they must then further skew the world, deny their own sensibilities, twist things out of focus, assigning virtue to Trungpa's action and seeing Merwin's and Dana's resistance as "mere" ego, or ignorance, or the denial of truth. It is there, then, that the whole event takes on its full significance, as the disciples struggle to rationalize the event, and to explain away the facts that might call their faith into question. They must shrink the world into something intolerably small and less than fully human, doing whatever violence to truth or conscience is required to maintain their beliefs. I have heard the same thing over and over from cultists of all sorts. In the face of the immense complexities of experience, they must deny whatever truths threaten their faith, projecting outward, onto the world, the paper-thin trompe l'oeil "realities" with which they have comforted themselves. One sees, called into the play, the immense human capacity for self-securing self-delusion, Plato's cave dwellers shutting their eyes as the cave explodes, pretending that they are still safely protected from truth.

June 25

Once while teaching a course to some high school teachers, I became embroiled in a bitter debate over the rights of students. I showed the teachers a film about Stanley Milgram's experiments, in which he measures the extent to which ordinary individuals will do what they are told. Subjects are chosen randomly, brought into an office, and told by a scientist behind a desk that they are going to participate in a learning experiment. They are introduced to a "plant," who they are told will be doing the "learning," and somewhere along the way the plant mentions that he has been ill, has just recovered from a heart attack. They go into another room where the plant is hooked up to a machine and seated out of sight behind a panel. The chosen subject is then told that he must ask a series of questions in rapid succession, and that each time the plant makes an error, he is to "correct" him with what he believes to be an increasingly severe but in fact imaginary electrical shock administered by pressing a button on the machine.

When the plant begins to make a few mistakes the chosen subject administers the first few shocks, making them slightly stronger each time. For a while everything goes smoothly, but then the plant begins to complain, claiming the shocks are too painful. As the shocks grow stronger, so do the exclamations and protests, and after a while the chosen subject usually begins to look questioningly at the scientist in charge, often saying he wants to stop. The expert always says go on, the experiment *must* continue. Sometimes the subjects argue, trying to reason with the expert, but they almost always go on. The shocks grow stronger, the cries grow louder, until finally the plant is screaming with pain and talking about his vulnerable heart, pleading for things to stop. Through it all the supposed expert remains adamant, and though some subjects somewhere along the line refuse to administer any more shocks, at least half of them obediently see the experiment through to the end, when the plant, after screams and pleas, has been reduced to ominous silence, and is apparently unconscious or dead.

The most significant aspect of the experiment is that not one participant refuses to continue when the planted subject *first* asks them to stop. It is only later, with a threat of death or grave illness, that people refuse to go on with the shocks. It is always and only the scream that is heeded, and never its antecedent, never the beginnings or first hints of pain—the simple, quiet human voice saying *no* or *stop*. Amplified, magnified, horror becomes visible; but its earlier stages are never acknowledged, never perceived; matched against authority, that small voice of choice is never accredited, does not seem to even register in the mind.

One sees the same thing at work in cults: a refusal to recognize in early excesses, early signs, the full implications of what is going on and will follow later. Relinquishing step by step the individualities of conscience, followers are slowly accustomed to one stage of abuse after another, becoming so respectful of the authority that they never quite manage to rebel, or else rebel when it is too late. How many in America, after all, would not respond in this way?

The teachers to whom I showed the movie were disturbed by it. Some were shaken. Obviously, they said, the subjects administering the shocks ought to have stopped, ought to have said no. But when I asked the teachers about their own students' rights to choose, or refuse to do what they are told, they insisted as a group that the students neither needed nor deserved those rights. "How," they would ask, over and over, "can we teach anything, or preserve order, if our students need not obey?"

June 26

I think back to a conversation I recently had with the director of Naropa's summer academic program. I liked him; he was quiet, literate, interested in many things besides Buddhism. But when, in the course of the conversation, I asked him whether Trungpa can make a mistake, he answered: "You know, a student *has* to believe his master can make no mistake. Sometimes Trungpa may do something I don't understand. But I must believe what he does is always for the best."

And when I asked him whether there are other truths in the world equal to his, he said, simply, "No, I think this is the way. I believe that without a meditative discipline others cannot come to truths akin to this."

As he talked, I looked out the window. I could see the afternoon sky, blue and infinite in its depths, and the mountains, green and complex, and, in another direction, an avenue full of people of all sorts, with different dreams and visions and partial truths hidden behind each gaze, with countless adventures folded into their flesh. For all of this, a single truth, a single discipline, a single master! The man talking to me was quiet, reasonable, curious, attentive; he meant me no harm at all, and he tried as we talked to hear what I was saying and to integrate it into what he already knew. But still, behind it all, there was another and harder edge, one that hides, always, behind the thought of those who believe the truth has already been given and has a single source. For how, then, can another man's truth, issuing from a different source, and contradicting one's own, be given a value equal to one's own? And if that is so, then how can one fully credit the other man's experience and thought?

I think too of two remarks made by a woman I know who was present at the retreat. She was close to Trungpa and not on bad terms with Merwin and Dana. After the events she went to see them, hoping to make them "understand" what had occurred and to explain Trungpa's actions. "I was trying to say," she said, "that Vajra teachings are ruthless, compassion takes many forms. But they had some rapid-fire answer to every statement which one way or another defended their sense of 'self'—their sense of propriety. It was impenetrable."

Impenetrable! As if it were a weakness, or something that stood between them and wisdom. No modesty permitted, no privacy, no integrity of choice. All of that seen as failure of nerve, a neurosis, or even—God help us—a form of aggression against the community.

It is here, finally, that living others begin to disappear, superseded by fantasy. And when those living others intrude themselves into the dream, threatening it with their actions or words, just as Merwin and Dana did, then their behavior must be classified as antisocial, or sick, or perverse, if only to protect the dreamers from the truths that might expose them to the ambiguities of the world. They make the other their victim, but only partially out of envy or animosity. The other is also victimized by their fear and their greed, their desire for safety, and their stubborn insistence on locating the truth in one man alone and creating for themselves an authority beyond all question.

And then there is what the same woman said much later, describing the event itself: "Merwin and Dana are standing together, facing Rinpoche, just completely huddled around each other. Very beautiful. Adam and Eve," she laughs. "Gorgeous bodies. . . . The whole thing, just visually, was elegant somehow. . . ."

It is that last phrase that echoes in the mind. *The whole thing, just visually, was elegant somehow.* It is this that offers the key to this particular discipline, in which aesthetic delight replaces all ethical notions, and in which the visual replaces the passions of sympathy or the heart. It is *all* visual—the little throne, the Vajra guards, the limousines—and distressingly common. I have seen other forms of it dozens of times around the world, in Mayan temples, Aztec shrines, Egyptian pyramids, the gold and kingly ornaments over which American tourists exclaim in Latin America, or the treasures of King Tut on exhibit in New York. These are all the emblematic, visual aspects of history removed from the truth of things, from flesh and blood, from the facts of life itself: the circumstances under which they were made, the systems of power they celebrate, the hierarchies of authority and injustice they reveal. The world flattens itself into spectacle; it becomes a film; a film envelops and coats what we see; behind it, the truth vanishes—and with it vanish the parts of the self that might have inhabited or changed, rather than merely *watched*, the world.

It is easy, I know, looking at what went on at Naropa, to recoil in instinctive horror, and mutter, "My God!" and wonder how some people get this way, and to bemoan what others do to themselves, and see it as somehow contrary to the American way. But, to tell the truth, it seems to me that what went on at Naropa, although more dramatic than what we usually see around us, was simply the lurid equivalent of what endlessly repeats itself in America in most systems of coercive authority, not only those at Naropa.

Trungpa's behavior toward Merwin and Dana was essentially no different—in essence or extent—from what we ordinarily accept without question between doctors and mental patients, or teachers and students, or military authorities and recruits. It is here, where we always think discipline is necessary, that we habituate people to doing what they're told, to acceding to authority, and to accepting without question the ways they are treated. If we think to ourselves that Trungpa's disciples ought to have rebelled, ought to have refused Trungpa's orders or interceded, then we would have to accept—as few of us are willing to do—the obligation, for example, of patients to rebel, and students, and recruits, and our own responsibility to resist whenever we witness (and who does not witness it daily?) the humiliation of others, or the denial of their full humanity.

I am familiar with all of the standard explanations about the growth of sects and cults—future shock, the nation's size, the collapse of the family, the failures of our churches, the absence of community, and so on. Certainly there is some truth in all such explanations. But what we tend to forget is the people drawn to such groups are behaving in precisely the ways we have *taught* them to behave.

The issue here is not merely the unquestioning acceptance of authority, though we tend to teach that everywhere in America. It is also the inability to hear the still, small, quiet human voice that says *no*, that speaks for nothing but itself, that makes no claim to any authority other than our common humanity, that asserts no power other than its own. It is to this voice, fragile but binding, that one owes allegiance, rather than to the thunderings of authority, or the whisperings of secret powers, or even the promise of salvation itself. It is the truly human, the "merely" human, that is, in the end, morally significant and the source of truth. Only those who believe that, only those whose home is made in the fragility of the flesh, among equal others, will be able to recognize the absurdities of power when they first present themselves, and to perceive what is wrong long before the final drama occurs, in the first requests for submission, in the first assault on independent thought. The only real alternative to hierarchy, submission, and unquestioning obedience is a passion for freedom and a belief in the true community of equals, one in which every member and each human voice is acknowledged as a source for truth or meaning, and in which truth and meaning are forever being formed, never fully given, never fully possessed by any master, any church.

And yet how many people in America—not just among the cults, but among us all—feel as if this is the real nature of experience, or that the truth that binds our moral lives is fully human, grounded in flesh, coexistent with the living members of their community? How many children are raised to the fierce independence or the generosity of spirit such a way of being requires, and how many adults can feel, as the heart of their existence, the immense responsibility of their moral life, and open continually their eyes and hearts to others like themselves?

June 27
Perhaps Naropa and its students make sense only when seen in the light of the sixties, for many of those who follow Trungpa are survivors of those years, and many of the younger students here are the unknowing heirs of that decade's experiences. Trungpa and his teachers never seem to tire of insisting upon both the futility of politics in general and the infantilism of Americans during the sixties. There is some truth, of course, in what they say. The forms of rebellion in the sixties were raw and often childish. But that childishness, we must remember, was often not generated from within, but was itself called forth by the behavior of adults, who forced the young—through their unresponsiveness and brutality— to fall back on forms of behavior we see today, in retrospect, as adolescent. Of course there was something undeniably adolescent in that behavior, but is was nonetheless something that might have ripened in other circumstances into a richer kind of rebellion, into more powerful forms of communal action and social change. For what moved beneath it was not merely adolescent; it was an inward yearning as old as the human heart and close to the bone of Western history. It was as if the culture itself had risen up in shame and self-disgust to demand that the moral values essential to its forward progress be more fully established in the corrupt social world. What spoke through the young in those days was simultaneously a fuzzy dream of the future and a dim remembrance

of certain overarching values to which the culture was ostensibly committed, values that had been lost along the way.

Though that rebellion was in part successful, helping to end the war in Vietnam, establishing minimal civil rights, opening out into partial triumphs for such things as gay rights and women's liberation, students at Naropa, as elsewhere, seem to feel as an aftermath from the sixties a peculiar kind of defeat: a combination of sorrow and fatigue. One hears continually in what the students say the echoes of a humiliation the students have self-protectively forgotten: the intrusion of murder into the political arena—the killings at Kent State, Attica, and Orangeburg, the assassination of the Kennedys and Martin Luther King, Jr. Those events combined—in ways we have failed to fully explore—to create at the heart of private and public life a terror that we have barely, if at all, allowed into consciousness. And that, coupled with the complex shame of being well-meaning moral children in a privileged and sometimes brutal nation, has produced in the young a sense of frustration and paralysis which they feel as a personal defeat.

There seems to lie at the heart of that frustration something that spoke for a brief time through the young in the sixties and then fell silent. It is possible to imagine that with the right elders, the right comrades, the right sustenance, the young might bring at least into partial being the lost Western values that lie coded in their minds and lives as history and tradition: the wonderful dream of remaking the human world in a shape that both the heart and reason tell us is just. But this is the dream forbidden at Naropa and now forgotten or unspoken among Trungpa's students.

Emerging from the 1960s wounded and in distress, they seem to have found a way to keep themselves intact and to create tenuous lives, but they do this at the expense of something else. That "something else" might not have survived in any case, but it does seem still barely alive in the temporary summer students to whom Naropa opens its doors, and the uneasiness one feels at the institute is a response to the absolute denial of what moves in the young but has never been named in our modern psychologies: the yearning for cooperation and the common good, the prompting of reason and conscience, the hope of transcending a consciousness defined solely by class. But these are no more explored here than they are at our traditional universities.

The incompleteness of the moral rebellion of the sixties was caused by several things: the absence of a familiar tradition of political thought or binding moral frames of reference; a diminished view of human nature handed to the young by their teachers and leaders; an absurd view of politics; a lack of organizational ability; a wide-eyed innocence that led to retreat at the first signs of punitive violence or state terror. In some sense those who now follow Trungpa were the victims of those things and now find in the community he provides a partial answer to what was missing then. But it is only a *partial* answer and makes no real place for the yearning from which their rebellion arose. It was a yearning for what the French called *fraternity, equality, and liberty*, the three necessary parts of a social order in which the self comes simultaneously into its own and the world of others. It was a hunger, an appetence—by which one means an appetite extended into gesture or action. In the rhetorics of the East, in their modes of salvation, there is little room for an aching of the soul that demands a restructuring of the world. The fixed caste system, taken as fate, as something as final as the stars, drove the notion of salvation further inward than it has even been forced to go in the West. What we consider in the West the freedom of the polis, the public space belonging to equals, is internalized in the East, and is replaced by the abstract "open space" one discovers in meditation.

June 29

It is fashionable these days in intellectual or countercultural circles to decry the loss of mysticism, irrationality, and intuition, and to believe that their return would somehow restore the generosity and stability men have lost. But all this is nonsense. The great rationalist dream of the Enlightenment—that reason might lead men toward justice and lives of conscience—has never been proved unworthy or false; *it has hardly been tried.*

One can look back, if one wants, to the American Constitution, the attempt of fallible men to establish as the foundations of their society what reason had taught them about the just relations among men. But the history of America has in fact had little to do with reason, consisting instead of wave upon wave of zealotry and ideology, and religious excess, generations of superstition and foolish beliefs, and a yearning for salvation and the ceaseless abdication of the stoic virtues necessary to democratic life: independent thought; the acceptance of human weakness; humility in the face of complex truths; the refusal to abjure either choice or responsibility; and the willingness to choose conscience and uncertainty rather than submission and safety. These, I believe, are the marks of reasonable and passionate men, but they are virtues presently as rare in the university and the political arena as they are in the cults that abound among us, and if reason has "failed" as a way of conducting human affairs, it is not because reason is an insufficient guide, but because it has rarely been put to use.

And yet, and yet. . . . There is more to all this than I can adequately describe, or than a reasonable man can comprehend. One of the women I know here, one of Trungpa's most dedicated and insular disciples, described to me once, in moving detail, how she had been enabled by meditation and Trungpa's teaching to return home to her alcoholic mother and father, to see them through a crisis that brought them close to death, and then to nurse them back to sober health. Had she not learned patience and affection from Trungpa, she said, she would have been unable to do it, and her parents would no doubt have died. I believe her; I believe that in complex ways even this odd mixture of falsehood, authority, submission, and partial truth sometimes releases in those exposed to it sources of strength and love previously untapped by all that surrounded them. I have known the woman in question for years, and she usually appears to me to be both silly and self-concerned, but when she spoke about her parents she became suddenly human, her eyes filled with intelligence and affection, and her face took on a different cast altogether; she wore a face that had become hers through this teaching.

I say that to be fair, and to avoid the easy condemnation with which we smugly react to such things as these. The problem is more complex than we imagine, for these absurd sects often call forth or develop in some people powers that the larger and institutional culture has failed to liberate and has for the most part destroyed. What ties these disciples to their master is often the best part of human nature, the deepest aspect of human yearning—not merely fear or greed, but a love for the world that has found no outlet in the past, and has gone rejected or unused by conventional society. That is why, looking at all this, one is filled not only with anger but with sorrow, with an almost overwhelming sense of human waste and loss, and a pervasive sadness at the price people are forced to pay merely to come close to being human, or the way in which the mind must be sacrificed so that the heart can come into play.

July 1

Without a doubt, what the world demands from us is a kind of attentiveness, a *wakefulness*, and an open receptivity through which the world and others can be taken in and made a part of our own inner lives. Out of that arises a feeling of connectedness, out of which, in turn, the beginnings of conscience make themselves felt. It may well be that this is what some Buddhists mean by *compassion*—a word that has a softer and more generous sound, and strikes the ear less tyrannically, than what I have here called *conscience*. But call it what you will—compassion or conscience—neither is sufficient in itself. Each needs to be acted outward and into the world: not spontaneously but with the rigorous thought and care and even cunning demanded of us by the complexities of the realities around us, the complex realms we call *history* and *politics*.

"To make a home in history for flesh"—that is the phrase that sings itself in and out of my mind these days, meaning the struggle we all must make not only to feel at home in the world but to re-make the world so that it becomes a proper home for us. The great Western dreams of justice and fraternity, of a community of equals, of a freedom that brings in its wake a generosity of spirit towards all other creatures—these, though they may be unobtainable in any permanent way, must somehow be kept alive, if only in the private ways each of us determines right and wrong and what we find we should do in the world. It is here, finally, that the promptings of the heart, guided by thought, open out into the ambiguous realms for which we have learned such an unfortunate disdain: history, politics, morality—those realms in which we mix fact with value hoping to come as close as we can to what in our human fallibility we judge to be best or just.

July 4

I sit here near midnight wondering how to put together all these concerns—not into a piece that makes sense, but into a life that makes sense. Cars pass outside. The Colorado sky is heavy with rain, and the clouds are lit from the underside by the lights of distant towns. I want to think that these high mountains are answer, or the wind, or the sound the trees make as the wind blows among them. But that is not so. The only answer will come from what it is we *do*, in how we learn to act as moral creatures, while making a future that does justice to the heart. Seen in that light, this foolish brand of Buddhism is not a sufficient answer. But if there is one, it is one we have not yet spelled out in word or action. It waits, still, like a landscape to be entered: one simultaneously as beautiful and as treacherous as the mountains can sometimes be. I, like almost everyone else, am reluctant to enter it, but where else does it make sense to go? Of what use is any future or enlightenment that does not restore a just and fully human world? Now, as I work, I can hear its insistent calling, not unlike the wind in the trees.

COMING TO TERMS WITH VIETNAM

THE FEVERS OF WAR are once again upon us. They do not yet rage openly, but beneath the surface of recent American events can be felt the gathering strength of attitudes and emotions that permit us to think about the war in ways that were impossible even a year ago. We hear almost daily the militant pronouncements of our political candidates and news of escalating appropriations for arms. We seem to be witnessing the remilitarization of America, a process that has not yet brought us to the brink of war, but has already established in many minds the groundwork for war: a revitalized sense of our moral superiority, a heightened fear of the malevolent forces surrounding us, and a belief in our capacity to temper our use of violence.

Whether it be the Nicaraguan revolution, the hostage crisis, the rise in OPEC prices, the Russian invasion of Afghanistan, or the fighting in Iraq and Iran, our inability to control events and our habitually inept responses to them ought to have demanded from us a rethinking of our political and moral relation to the world. But we neglect this crucial task. Instead, we have lapsed comfortably back into the familiar attitudes that marked the Cold War in the 1950s and the Asian debacle of the sixties: we clench our fists and mutter comforting platitudes to ourselves, cheerfully lost among the same illusions that proved so disastrous a decade ago.

It is fashionable now, in some circles, to see this renewed military hubris as both inevitable and necessary. We are told that we are

merely leaving behind, as we must, the guilt that paralyzed us after
the war in Vietnam. But that, I think, misstates the case. What paralyzed us was not simply the guilt felt about Vietnam, but our inability to confront and comprehend that guilt: our refusal to face
squarely what had happened and why, and our unwillingness to
determine, in the light of the past, our future moral obligations. In
short, we spent a decade denying and evading guilt rather than
using it to our advantage.

Yet the moral quandaries remain. Vietnam is with us still, laden
with meaning, constraining some of us, eating at others, pushed
out of sight but present in the various shames we feel as we look at
the flag, in our naive dreams of easy peace, or in our violent fantasies of virtue and power. Sometimes, for a moment, one gets
glimpses of the barely hidden anger and guilt that lie at the heart of
the culture. When, for instance, California's Gov. Jerry Brown ap-
pointed Jane Fonda to the state's art council and the state senate
refused to ratify the appointment, the air was filled suddenly with
violent responses. To the senators, Ms. Fonda was "a traitor"; to her,
such critics were "fascists." One could feel once again the brutal
and still unresolved memory of the war.

The same volatility appears in private conversations. Mention
Vietnam, the veterans, guilt, or responsibility, and the air becomes
rife with accusations, defenses, justifications, and confusions. A split
is revealed not only among us but also within each one of us: many
of us live with the sense of having left undone a series of tasks we
can neither name nor understand, but which we know with a terrible intensity constitute the war's legacy.

None of us has faced the specter of his own culpability—not
Nixon's duplicity, not Kissinger's errors—but the particular ways in
which each one of us, actively or passively, may have contributed to
the killing in the terms of the taxes we paid, the officials we elected,
the lessons of obedience we taught in the classroom, the endless
round of incipient and complicit ways in which we participated in
the institutions and rituals that made countless young men willing

to kill for the worst of causes in the worst of ways. We have stubbornly avoided the kind of passionate and open self-investigation that members of a democratic society must conduct in order to protect others in the future from the errors and brutalities of the past. In setting the war aside we have failed to push ourselves far enough, have failed to raise the crucial questions about the war and ourselves we should have confronted. We have failed to indicate that we will ever be much different from what we have been in the past.

We have had our texts, that is true. Book after book about the war has come off the presses, placing blame, analyzing causes, condemning Nixon, Kissinger, and Westmoreland and their abuses of power. But most of these books seem to have missed the point, ascribing the war merely to political errors or to the excesses of a few powerful men, as if the rest of us in America had somehow been fooled into fighting.

That was not the case at all, of course. Though some Americans resisted from the start, the war was a popular one; we reelected Nixon in the middle of it; and we were led further into it not so much by lies as by our nationalistic sense of unsullied virtue and by the difficulty we have in seeing the reality of events, the justice of rival causes, or the suffering we inflict upon others. Few of the books on Vietnam confront the issues we should have faced: the full extent of the atrocities committed in the war and the participation in those atrocities of ordinary soldiers, ordinary citizens, our ordinary young.

The Vietnam novels produced so far have been encapsulated in American myths, even when the war has been seen in all its absurdity. No novelist has yet been willing to confront, directly, the realities of the war, or to consider it, at least in part, from the Vietnamese point of view—that is, in terms of their suffering rather than ours. The cultural bias that has traditionally marked our attitudes toward other races seems in these books to be firmly in place. The novels, for the most part, are jumpy, surrealistic. It is difficult, for example, to distinguish the tone or setting of Tim O'Brien's *Going After Cacciato* from Joseph Heller's *Catch-22* or Richard Hooker's *MASH*. The books reveal something about our soldiers' states of mind and about the corruption of our institutions, but they are universally lacking in both tragic dimension and the capacity to perceive the Vietnamese as anything more than stick-figures in an American dream. It is hard, reading these books, to find in them much hope for a change in America's self-perception, save for the skepticism and irony about authority that has become a national characteristic and sometimes our saving grace.

There are exceptions to all this, of course: Gloria Emerson's *Winners and Losers*, Frances FitzGerald's *Fire in the Lake*, or Ron Kovic's *Born on the Fourth of July*. Yet none of these books, for all their obvious passion and truth, suggests a way out of our present moral predicament or confronts its readers with their own responsibilities. Only Gloria Emerson, inconsolable in her rage and grief, manages to communicate that we, as a people, have no right to move beyond the war without examining our past and, in its context, determining our future.

There are, too, the veterans among us, enigmatic and for the most part silent, harboring the truths the rest of us do not want to hear. We have statistics on their suicide rate and the extent of their drug addiction, but nobody bothers much with the reality behind those figures, with what the vets saw and did or were *asked* to do, or with how the permutations of guilt (the guilt they feel, the guilt we deny) are at work within them. Here, too, silence reigns, perhaps in large part because we discourage the vets from speaking by refusing to listen to them. Even when the vets protest or speak out, they have little to say about the war itself. They almost always voice their own grievances: how they were treated, the paucity of their benefits, the refusal of their countrymen to pay attention to them. Their protests against Agent Orange are solely personal; they never remind us (nor do we care to remember) what the poison must also have done, and be doing even now, to generations of Vietnamese. What they avoid, as do we all, is the immense task of coming to terms with what went on in Vietnam—the killing and the attendant guilt—and the fact that neither they nor we know how to respond to those realities.

It is with all of that in mind that I began, a year or two ago, to go to each of the Vietnam films produced by Hollywood. I did not expect to find much there. But some of the films were being made by serious men and women with aesthetic skills and some political insight; more important, American audiences were apparently taking them seriously. Even intellectual critics and commentators were treating the films as if they might not only reveal to us something about ourselves, but might also define for us, at a popular level, our memories, myths, and attitudes about the war. The films seemed, on the surface, to have been prepared with as much gravity and perception as the best books about the war. With film, we might at last break our shared silence, forcing ourselves—en masse—to look at what we had previously avoided. They might become in a way our shared stations of the cross, stages on our ambiguous journey toward the truths of Vietnam.

I saw perhaps a dozen films, among them *Apocalypse Now*, *Dog Soldiers*, *Go Tell the Spartans*, *Heroes*, *The Boys in Company C*, *Coming Home*, *The Deerhunter*, *Who'll Stop the Rain*, and *Taxi Driver* (which, though not classed as a Vietnam film, more successfully communicates the war's continuation at home than any of the other films). There were perceptive moments in almost all of them. *Heroes*, for instance, had a few marvelous scenes of vets back home together; *The Boys in Company C* was dominated by a black street hero— something relatively rare and generous; and a few prebattle conversations in *Go Tell the Spartans* convincingly echoed the early days of the war. But for the most part these films owe more to other films than they do to the war. It is, in fact, difficult to remember while watching these films that there actually *was* a war, or that its causes and consequences might have something to do with one's own life.

The most significant Vietnam films were *Apocalypse Now, The Deerhunter,* and—to a lesser degree—*Coming Home.* These were not necessarily the best or most intelligent films. But they were more than films; they were *events.* Despite the fact that they failed to confront the moral issues of the war, they were treated with the same seriousness and granted the same attentiveness that we ordinarily reserve for important books. Many Americans regarded them as summary statements about the war, a fact which may tell us something about ourselves, if not about Vietnam.

The Deerhunter's faults were immediately visible and have been well-documented. Most notable among them were director Michael Cimino's intentional misrepresentations of the war, his implicit absolution of Americans for any illegitimate violence or brutality, and a xenophobia and racism as extravagant as anything to be found on the screen since our World War II films about the Japanese. And yet, for all of that, certain parts of *The Deerhunter* are more moving and memorable than any of the other films about the war. Cimino shows more humanity, more respect and generosity, toward his American characters than one can find, for instance, in either *Coming Home* or *Apocalypse Now.* His vision, despite the reactionary politics behind it, has a tenderness missing from those other films that are more strongly against the war.

The best parts of the film are those set in America, in and around the Pennsylvania steel town that is home to three friends (Robert DeNiro, Christopher Walken, John Savage) preparing to leave for Vietnam. Something powerful and moving comes through in these scenes of men drinking, hunting, and celebrating together: it is Cimino's respect and love for his characters, and a clarity of perception that brings persons and landscape sharply alive. Cimino has a fine eye and is faithful to what he sees; he captures with loving accuracy the slant of light on a deserted avenue, or a tavern's interior, or the startling purity of the hills outside of town. One feels, suddenly, the poignant and bittersweet pleasures of American lives led far from the centers of power: their loneliness, their fundamental innocence.

Cimino's central subject, after all, is innocence—his characters' and our own. His film confers upon its viewers a sort of absolution for Vietnam, returning to them precisely the illusion of superior virtue that ought to have been wiped away by the war. He has organized his film cunningly around the traditional literary themes of innocence versus decadence, small-town and wilderness virtues opposed to urban corruption. It is a familiar theme, one to which we respond almost without thought, and Cimino's use of it is both intelligent and perverse. His comforting moral equations mask the truths of the war by reversing them completely; innocent Americans become the war's only victims, and the Vietnamese—in reality an agrarian, village people—become big-city villains, smiling devils, corrupt gamblers, streetwise pimps, and whores. The irony is that the very same virtues Cimino ascribes to Americans— those in whose name America tried to destroy Vietnam—lie at the heart of the culture we brutalized. It is not clear whether Cimino is oblivious to this, or is lying about it intentionally.

What is at work here is probably a simple form of aesthetic ignorance or greed: the notion that if something "works" it must be right, for there is no other standard of judgment. Cimino has the talent to almost bring it off. He makes us forget, as we watch his film, that things were other than the way they are portrayed here. It is only when one *does* remember, and when one considers the actual causes of the war and the film's brute blindness to all but white American Christianity, that the extent of the film's cruelty—not only to the Vietnamese, but to the Americans Cimino supposedly loves—becomes clear. A decade from now, in foreign nations whose names we barely know, where death is not make-believe but real, young men like those in Cimino's film will die again, in part because of the myths he has helped to manufacture.

If those on the political Right can be simpleminded and reductive in their pursuit of virtue, so can those on the Left. The smugness and self-satisfaction at work in *Coming Home*, for which both director Hal Ashby and actress Jane Fonda are responsible, are almost as destructive to genuine thought and feeling as elements in *The Deerhunter*. Nancy Dowd, who wrote the film's screenplay, was reportedly outraged by what was done to her script, and one can see why. What may well have begun as a straightforward and somber attempt to deal honestly with the problems of returning veterans is reduced to a ritualized love story and a vehicle for Ms. Fonda's moral posturing.

Ms. Fonda plays a young housewife married to a patriotic army officer (Bruce Dern) anxious to be shipped to Vietnam. When he goes overseas, she volunteers to work in a veterans' hospital and meets a paraplegic vet (Jon Voigt) who is vehemently opposed to the war. They argue at first, then grow closer, and finally become lovers. A sexual metamorphosis begins: Ms. Fonda's hair comes down; her pantsuits give way to jeans; she has marvelous orgasms and turns against the war. Then Dern returns, slightly wounded and disillusioned by the war, and learns he has been cuckolded. Inconsolable, he kills himself by swimming out to sea. At the film's end we find Voigt, who will now live happily ever after with Ms. Fonda, lecturing a high school class about the evils of war.

There are a few shots in the film that ring eerily true: a sequence near the beginning in a hospital in which a few wounded vets argue about the war; a scene or two on an army base where officers and wives carry on in the foolish innocence that prepares the way for American brutality; and, when Dern returns home, a scene at an airfield with bodies stacked high in bags and a forklift ready to handle them. But such moments are washed away by what surrounds them; everything else in the film seems thin and contrived, unrelentingly trite, a cross between Hollywood tripe and Chinese opera—villains punished, virtue rewarded, and lovers riding—or rather one riding, the other pushing—into the sunset.

One finds every event and issue oversimplified, distorted by a peculiar greed for virtue and the need to be wholly right—as if good were never partial, or motive and consequence never ambiguous. This is not only bad art; it is also bad politics. In the name of goodness it feeds precisely the wrong hungers in the audience, makes no real demand upon it, renders fantastical the genuinely tragic complexity of moral life, and shrinks the moral realm to a set of commonplace attitudes and banalities.

And what can one make of *Apocalypse Now*, supposedly the ultimate Vietnam film? It is hard to get at the film itself, so surrounded has it been by Coppola's self-congratulating pronouncements about its significance. I know people who think the film is marvelous and that as time passes it will become a classic. But it seems to me to be morally inert at its center, morally *stupid*—not a "failed masterpiece," as critics have classed it, but an essentially unintelligent investigation of themes too complex for Coppola to handle: not the emperor without clothes, but the clothes with no emperor inside.

Loosely patterned after Joseph Conrad's novel *Heart of Darkness*, the film is an attempt to use the novel's themes, structure, and narrative devices to create what Coppola has called "a moral fable," not only about the war, but about every confrontation between "civilized" and "primitive" cultures. Lieutenant Willard (played by Martin Sheen, and Coppola's equivalent to Conrad's narrator, Marlowe) is ordered by his superiors in Saigon to travel upriver into what is apparently Cambodia and assassinate a Colonel Kurtz (Marlon Brando), a brilliant officer who has turned renegade and surrounded himself with an army of local tribesmen. Traveling first by helicopter and then by boat, Willard passes through a series of disconnected adventures, each of which reveals a different aspect of the war. With the sole surviving member of the boat's crew, he reaches Kurtz's compound and finds him alternately lucid and mad, reciting T. S. Eloit, reading *The Golden Bough*, and talking a sophomoric line of philosophy hard for the viewer—but not for Willard—to take seriously. Supposedly caught between admiration and revulsion for Kurtz, Willard eventually kills him—not for his superiors' reasons, but for his own. At the film's end we see him starting on his long journey home, presumably to deliver to Kurtz's young son the message Kurtz has sent him.

The film has its virtues, of course: occasionally vivid and powerful images, a few sequences in which Coppola captures the hallucinatory and dreamlike quality of the war, a conceptual sweep that sometimes breaks into a brilliant and savage clarity, and a technical proficiency in camera work and sound effects that have awed many people in the film industry. There are moments when Coppola, obviously in his element, is like an obsessed painter at work, using the screen and his technical mastery to create memorable effects that convince one, for a moment, that one is watching a great film.

But Coppola's technical skills and his eye for detail are not matched by his moral imagination. Something is missing here: the depth, coherence, and generosity of vision that mark the great moral texts of the sort that Coppola hoped to make. The best moments in the film are depreciated by sudden shifts of tone or attitude and lapses of intelligence; one can feel, *behind* the film, Coppola struggling with his footage and his ideas, trying to piece together from four years of work something that will pass as a whole and yet accommodate every confused aspect of his attitude toward the war. We are given, essentially, a kind of sampler, a variety show of Coppola's talents: bits and pieces of successive scripts, fragments of John Milius's originally hawkish screenplay, Michael

Herr's antiwar narrative added late in the day, set pieces of surreal exaggeration derivative of *Catch-22* or *MASH*, mawkish images of the Vietnamese, and, finally, the entire last convulsive third of the film, a pastiche of borrowed meanings and second-hand myths in which Coppola, striving to locate the significance of his work, loses his way completely.

The film is crippled by a morally incoherent attitude toward the war and its attendant issues. What supposedly holds the film together is the narrative explanation delivered by Willard and accompanying the action. But this device, borrowed from Conrad, is as ineffective as it is desperate; if one listens carefully to it, it proves ineffective and distracting, pasted onto the action like a label onto a bottle, a way of trying to create a significance that inheres neither in Coppola's thought nor in the film's implications.

What obsessed Conrad was not only the visible nature of men's acts but the struggle men wage inside themselves to remain decent or find something substantial and worthy of respect: a virtue or truth to hold against the darkness. Coppola recognizes the pertinence of this theme to the American experience in Vietnam, but he fails to understand how Conrad made it work, and nowhere is this more evident than in the film's last third. Here, for the film to succeed at all, its moral meanings must deepen and extend themselves, enveloping the audience, locating themselves finally not only in war, nor even in something as abstract or general as the human heart, but in each of us as individuals, in our actual lives, in the daily battle living men and women wage against their own savagery. Coppola never manages this shift. One wonders whether he knows it is supposed to occur. In the last part of the film he borrows wildly: from Conrad, from Eliot, and from the original myth of the Fisher King, which he apparently discovered while making the film. Even the most powerful images in this section seem derivative, reminiscent of those in Werner Herzog's *Aguirre, the Wrath of God*, a film with similar themes handled more imaginatively. But all of these sources, which have in their original versions a force of their own, seem emptied here of significance. They fail to touch or move us, or to have much to do with the real world or our actual lives.

Is it too much, I wonder, to expect from cinema what one expects from books: seriousness and depth of vision equal to both their subjects and the possibilities of human nature? The truly great films about war do far more than the directors attempt or accomplish in the films in question here. Jean Renoir's *Grand Illusion* or the film version of Erich Maria Remarque's *All Quiet on the Western Front* not only educate us to the horrors of war but also offer us something believable and real to hold against them: an enlightened way of seeing others, a generosity of spirit, and a vision of possible human allegiances more worthy of a man's devotion than the passions of war or the powers of the state.

The vision and the humanity one finds at the heart of such films are far more restorative and profound than anything at work in our Hollywood films. One thinks of the scene in *All Quiet on the Western Front* in which the narrator-soldier, having bayoneted a Frenchman, sits all night beside him in a trench as he slowly dies, gradually becoming obsessed with the idea of somehow taking the Frenchman's place after the war, as if in atonement for the human solidarity he has violated by killing. Or one thinks of the friendships conveying the main themes of *Grand Illusion*: between French and German officers, between French aristocrat and working-class Jew. In both cases one is offered as an alternative to war a human reciprocity that reaches across the distances created by war and replaces the arrogance of moral certitude and abstraction with a humbler sense of partial truths, of a human reality shared with living others.

The key to great moral art, as well as to a nation's moral life, is the capacity to understand two elusive truths: first, that our actions occur in a real world and have immeasurable consequences for countless others; and second, that those suffering others are also real—not emblems, not symbols, not abstractions, not merely "Vietnamese" or "Iranians" or "Communists" or "militants," but concrete persons in specific situations, men and women with lives and needs as real as our own.

Yet that, precisely, is what seems missing from these films: the capacity to stretch the aesthetic imagination far enough to include within the moral realm actual others in a real world. They are, instead, examples of what I would call an "imperial" art, one designed to appeal to the citizens of a powerful but declining empire by allowing us the luxury of "facing" reality while at the same time denying our role within it. Supposedly challenged, we are secretly soothed. It is all somehow like the television documentary *Roots*: how happy we are to see on the screen the progress black Americans have supposedly made, how self-satisfied now that we have had a program about them, and how oblivious, still, to the ghetto horrors in our midst.

The real problem with these films, I suspect, has something to do with the inadequacy of the visual image in dealing with political, historical, and, especially, moral matters. The interiority of events—both their inner, subjective significance and their concrete political meanings—is ordinarily preserved or created through language; but it is often lost when, as in these films, events are reduced to the merely visual. As Susan Sontag has argued in her work on photography, the reduction of experience to image tends somehow to bleed it of value and reflective power. Photography's flattening of moral content and its confusion of made objects with "reality" is intensified in cinema by the size of the screen, the verisimilitude of the action, and the increased possibilities for manipulation. Cinema tends toward the hypnotic; unless a director cuts consciously against the grain of the medium, film almost always neutralizes the audience's capacity for skepticism and moral reflection, and this is particularly true in films attempting to deal directly with history.

Without language history becomes meaningless. The proper vehicle for moral meaning and concern is *speech*; it is not only the words themselves but our sense of the human speaker that remind us in the midst of events of their human significance. In the great moral texts, whether book or film, it is only the believability and power of the human voice that engage us completely in the work. One thinks of the great war novels: *War and Peace, Parade's End, The Charterhouse of Parma, All Quiet on the Western Front.* The moral power of these books inheres not only in action and plot; it is also rooted in the quality and tone of language, in the narrative voice or the voices of particular characters that create in us, as readers, a kind of empathy and identification, a sense of being drawn towards and close to a human sensibility superior to the horrors it suffers or describes.

The same thing is true of great films. In *Grand Illusion* or *Hiroshima, Mon Amour* or *All Quiet on the Western Front* it is the human voice that somehow breaks the fictional and imagistic frame of reference. It seems to issue simultaneously from a world outside the film and from inside ourselves, reminding us of a moral and human reality larger than the film, one we ourselves inhabit—not as viewers, but as moral participants.

Unfortunately, the verbal absurdities of the Vietnam films amount to a kind of moral muteness in which the reality of events and the humanity of those involved vanish completely. If one listens to as well as watches these films, one discovers that nothing spoken or thought within them is intelligent enough to be taken seriously. People "say" things, of course. But what they say is so infantile, so manipulative, or so obviously present merely to move the plot along that we are demeaned as we watch.

There is something both tragic and ironic in this, for rarely has an American experience been marked by as much reflection, clarity, and consciousness of difficult issues as was the war in Vietnam. Side by side with America's acceptance of the war, and behind the mass demonstrations of protest, lay something altogether different and equally important: the willingness of many Americans—most of them very young—to determine for themselves the answers to the most serious questions human beings can face, those pertaining to obedience and rebellion, others' lives and deaths, the pull of conflicting allegiances, and the nature and cost of moral choice. It was a decade of genuine moral heroism and profound moral speech, not only in the endless conversations among comrades and peers or the spoken and printed criticism of the war and the state but also in the inward debates men held with themselves about what was just or best to do.

That was true not only of those who resisted the war but also of those who fought in it. Though many young men participated mindlessly, countless others, even in the middle of battle, made anguishing moral choices, the nature of which—given our present silence—we may never understand. Many went AWOL, not out of fear but in disgust; others refused orders; a few went over to the other side; a few sabotaged our side: vets have told me of firing continuously and intentionally over the enemy's heads.

Everywhere in the war, even among many of those who determined for themselves that it was right to fight, one found genuine moral seriousness and anguish and a depth and clarity of reflection that put to shame the theatrical, vacuous moral imagination one finds in the Vietnam films.

And the same moral seriousness prevails among the vets. In the past several months, trying to find ways to assess these films, I talked at length to many of them about the war. Not all of them wanted to say much about it, and most omitted the details. But time and again a few reluctant or cautious words about grief, anger, or fear revealed more about the specific nature of the war and its particular horrors than could the accumulated sound and fury of all of these films.

I remember, for instance, one veteran's story about his return to the States. He had been a part of what he called an "assassination squad," spending long periods of time on his own, out of touch with both his superiors and comrades, apparently working independently on his assigned tasks. He described coming home in a series of almost surrealistic vignettes: being harangued in the airport by an officer for playing cards with his buddies and "giving the service a bad name"; being asked by the first civilian he had met in months about "them niggers in the army, the ones too chickenshit to fight"; falling asleep in his seat on the airplane and then waking from a nightmare of war, shaking and sweating, to find that everyone close to him had moved several seats away; and, finally, meeting his parents at the airport and finding it impossible to speak. They drove home in silence and then sat together in the kitchen, and his mother, in passing, apologized for there being "nothing in the house to eat." That did it; he broke. Raging, he went from cupboard to cupboard, shelf to shelf, flinging doors open, pulling down cans and boxes and bags, piling them higher and higher on the table until they spilled over onto the floor and everything edible in the house was spread out in front of them.

"I couldn't believe it," he said, shaking his head as he told me. "I'd been over there for years, killing those poor bastards who were living in their tunnels like rats and had nothing to eat but mud and a few goddamn moldy grains of rice, and who watched their kids starve to death or go up in smoke, and she said *nothing to eat*, and I ended up in the kitchen crying and screaming: *Nothing to eat, nothing to eat!*"

This story is not particularly special; I might have recounted a dozen others like it, some about the war itself, and more dramatic.

But the point would be the same. No image, no technical effect, no posed theatrical scene, comes even close to the power and meaning of one man speaking quietly, telling the truth of his experience.

It is inevitable, then, that we come to the veterans themselves. If two of the keys to the comprehension of the past and the creation of the future are memory and speech, it is in the memories of the vets and in the possibilities of their speech that the antidotes to our silence and self-deception lie. It is their voices—real voices, grounded in real experience—that may have the power to call us back from our illusions to the discomforting concreteness of our acts. The questions of silence and speech, which remain for the rest of us abstract and theoretical questions, are for our veterans personal quandaries, sources of personal pain; at least some of them are forced by the circumstances of their lives to struggle inwardly, and apparently endlessly, with the problems all of us should, but do not, confront.

The real issue, to put it bluntly, is guilt: how, as a nation and as individuals, we perceive our culpability and determine what it requires of us. We must concern ourselves with the discovery of fact, the location of responsibility, the discussion of causes, the acknowledgment of moral debt and how it might be repaid—not in terms of who supposedly led us astray, but in terms of how each one of us may have contributed to the war or to its underlying causes. The "horror" of war is really very easy to confront; it demands nothing of us save the capacity not to flinch. But guilt and responsibility, if one takes them seriously, are something else altogether. For they imply a debt, something to be done, changed lives—and that is much harder on both individuals and a nation, for it implies a moral labor as strenuous and demanding as the war that preceded it.

Decades ago Karl Jaspers, the German philosopher who had fled his country during the Second World War, returned to Germany when the war was over and gave several lectures under the title "The Question of German Guilt." His purpose was neither to castigate his fellow citizens nor to find particular people to blame, but simply to establish the realms of discourse and thought in which, collectively and individually, they were responsible for reviewing their past acts and determining their future behavior. There are obvious differences between the Germans' situation and our own, but Jaspers's work is relevant to us, especially because we have spent so little time thinking productively about guilt.

We, like the Germans, fought a war marked by racism, atrocities, and what many saw as genocide; we too, as a people, actively supported or tolerated the annihilation of a civilian population; we too watched our neighbors, brothers, and children devastate a nation in our name; we too elected our leaders knowingly, welcomed their small reassuring lies, applauded the suppression of dissent at home, and were more concerned with our power than the suffering it caused; and, finally, we too, in the war's aftermath, have denied responsibility for what occurred, have pleaded ignorance, have blamed everyone but ourselves.

But all of us, according to Jaspers, are responsible for the acts of war, accountable for the personal and social acts that begin to contribute to war long before it has actually begun: the distractions, evasions, failures of nerve and resistance, mindless enthusiasms and neutralities with which we replace our responsibilities as citizens, as moral agents. We are all, then, at least partially guilty, or guilty enough to share the burden of guilt that we happily assign, after the war, only to those leaders and soldiers we ourselves produced.

Jaspers distinguished among four kinds of guilt: criminal, political, moral, and metaphysical. The first two types are essentially simple. Criminal guilt involves an individual breach of civil law; judgment is made by a judge and jury. Political guilt involves the collective crimes of a state, its leaders or its citizens; these are judged—as at Nuremberg—by the war's victors in accordance with international conventions. But the second two kinds of guilt—moral and metaphysical—are far more complicated, for they involve the judgments men make about themselves according to conscience, and it is these judgments, made privately and communally, that determine a nation's moral nature. It is quite possible and sometimes necessary, in Jaspers's eyes, for men who might be innocent in criminal and political terms to find themselves morally and metaphysically guilty, and to struggle to restore to themselves and to their community what they find missing from their moral lives.

Moral guilt, for Jaspers, involves the responsibility of all persons for all of their acts and the consequences of their acts—even under orders, even in the midst of war. "It is never true," he writes, "that 'orders are orders.' Every deed remains subject to moral judgment." He means *every* deed: not only the acts of those who gave or took orders but even the apparently innocuous acts of those who in civilian life contributed in any way to the institutions and social attitudes that made such violence possible. Even those not directly responsible for the war, and, yes, even those who stood against it, have in its aftermath an obligation to help create a moral climate in which all members of society can thoughtfully and cooperatively examine the complexities of guilt and the nature of moral obligation. "Moral guilt," Jaspers writes, "can only truthfully be discussed in a loving struggle between men who maintain solidarity among themselves."

Metaphysical guilt, for Jaspers, has to do with our relation to God and the way in which we have somehow betrayed our given covenant with God. It refers to our fundamental failure, at work not only in war but ubiquitously, to extend our own sense of human reciprocity or responsibility past the ordinary limits of family or nation to include those distant from and unlike ourselves.

With metaphysical guilt, as with moral guilt, the power of judgment belongs to each of us in relation to ourselves; we are answerable to both our own conscience and to God, and we remain responsible—at the heart of our own privacies—for setting right what we ourselves perceive as wrong.

One might argue with these categories, of course. For many of us the line between moral and metaphysical guilt is not as easily drawn as it is for Jaspers. But such arguments are not important. What is important is the fact that Jaspers takes guilt seriously and understands it as a natural and inevitable consequence of all human activity. Guilt has, for him, little to do with breast-beating and weeping, sackcloth and ashes. He does not see it, as we do in America, as a condition to be escaped or denied; it has nothing to do with punishment or retribution. It is, rather, a kind of awareness, a form of acknowledgment, a way of so clearly seeing one's relation to the past, and one's past actions, that one is moved by reason and conscience to rethink and remake the nature of one's moral life. It is a practical matter, a kind of perceived debt requiring and impelling further action. It is, in a sense, a question men pose to themselves and which they can only answer with what they are willing to become.

The purpose of such an answer has little to do with absolution or atonement. The dead, after all, remain dead. The maimed remain maimed. It is no more possible to "absolve" oneself of guilt than it is to bring the dead back to life or erase the suffering one has caused. But it may be possible to live in the future in a way that makes sense of the past, and to restore to one's life the moral legitimacy that has been lost. No one can determine for others precisely what it is that they, in their own privacies, may find they must do; but one can say that the legitimacy of all moral life depends on the willingness of each of us to struggle with such questions before we decide what we will do. All of us, like all nations, are tested twice in the moral realm: first by what we do, then by what we make of what we do. A condition of guilt, a sense of one's own guilt, denotes a kind of second chance; we are, as if by a kind of grace, given a chance to repay to the living what it is we find ourselves owing to the dead.

It is obvious that these notions—taken seriously—would require from us much more, as individuals, than we have so far been willing to accept as part of the debt conferred upon us by the war. We would have to consider, above all else, the institutions, collective attitudes, and systems of authority that made possible both our actions in Vietnam and the willingness of our young men to partake in them. We would have to ask ourselves about the extent to which we were responsible not only for the war but for the schooling we give our young and the ways we encourage obedience and the suspension of moral judgment: the violent and incipient racism at work in our streets and minds; the myths and distractions of media that wrap us endlessly in dreams and fantasies; the caste and class blindness that teach us, continuously, an indifference to all those unlike ourselves; the tendency at work everywhere among us, on both the Left and Right, to presume virtue and moral superiority for oneself while casting one's opponents as knaves; the failure of both our artists and thinkers to place at the heart of their concerns a passion for conscience or justice. Finally, in terms of "metaphysical" guilt, we would have to consider precisely what we believe one person owes another, or what we owe to *which* others, and how responsible each of us must be in relation to collective moral choices, especially in the face of what our country asks us to do.

But these questions, which hung in the air for the war's duration and ought now to inform the heart of every private existence, have ceased for most of us to have any power. The notion of conscience itself has become almost exotic; genuinely moral concerns, genuinely moral lives, have become so rare among us that they seem eccentric.

I remember once talking to a psychologist who worked for the Veterans' Administration. I asked him how he and his colleagues dealt with the problem of guilt.

"We *don't* deal with it," he said. "It does not exist for us. For us, everything is a problem in *adjustment*."

How different would it be anywhere else in our culture? What has changed radically in the last several decades is not so much our behavior, but how we think about it: the ways we measure action and its consequences, and how we hold ourselves or one another responsible for things. One can search in vain these days—not only in therapeutic theories, but in those dealing with morality or politics—for the word conscience. Our philosophers long ago reduced ethical questions to problems in epistemology, and even our religions have ceased to offer us much in this realm, concerned as they are with problems of salvation rather than the complexities of concrete moral life in the world.

This, in part, is what makes our veterans so important. The vets know conscience exists; they are immersed in it. They face daily, as a part of their private and personal lives, the questions that at best remain abstract for the rest of us. In a sense, they are still walking point for us, confronting a landscape as alien as anything they faced in Vietnam, still doing for the rest of us the dangerous tasks that we pretend do not exist.

Guilt, I know, is not the only possible explanation for the pain and rage they feel. Obviously, they suffer not only the alienation experienced by the participants of any war but also problems unique to the war in Vietnam: their disappointment at their treatment at home; their anger at the absence of gratitude, attention, respect, or aid; their resentment at having risked their lives and seen men die in a war now regretted or forgotten. But behind all of that, and mixed inextricably with it, is often something more, something not always privately admitted: the anger of the veterans at themselves, their grief at having fought and killed in the wrong war, for the wrong reasons, the wrong way. One cannot know how many veterans are thus troubled. Despite everything written about it, the war remains, still, a mystery for most of us. We will never know precisely what went on, how frequently atrocities occurred, how many men and women were wantonly slaughtered or raped, how many villages were carelessly destroyed—or how many of our soldiers were directly involved. But certainly all of that plays a part in what many of our veterans now suffer. I am thinking not only of the outspoken and angry veterans such as the Vietnam Veterans Against the War, but also about all those others in whom shame and guilt may take a disguised and unrecognizable form: the suicides reported and unreported; the cases of addiction, criminality, depression, schizophrenia, and all the other conditions that may be in part maladies of conscience; the devastated drifters and drinkers and compulsive talkers and weepers one can find in the cheap hotels and taverns of any American city; the armed and angry vets one finds in southern and mountain states awaiting Armageddon and hating both their government and those who criticize it; and even (or perhaps especially) the "well-adjusted" who go about their daily business without apparent doubt or dread or drama, who never speak about the war but nightly wake alone in the dark dreaming of war, caught in its terrors still.

No doubt complex forces are at work in all of these instances, but who can doubt that in many of them conscious or unconscious guilt plays a part? Even in the cases in which vets deny feeling guilty, how can one tell how much of that is true, or how much they may be hiding from themselves? The past, after all, has not held still; it has pursued us these last several years even as we have tried to leave it behind. Almost every bit of information we have had about the war since its end has called its legitimacy into question and revealed the cupidity of those who oversaw it. Devastating as this information ought to have been to all

Americans, it has disturbed many of our vets even more; and those among them who have consciously tried—as many have—to discover retrospectively the truths of the war find themselves in the predicament of Oedipus: every step they take toward the truth may also bring them closer to their own guilt.

I think, as I write, of several conversations I have had with vets in recent months. There is no way, really, in a few words, to describe the range of feelings and reactions that come into play in their voices and faces as they speak. Often what passes across their faces is at odds with their words; one feels as if one is listening to two voices at once, or as if they desperately want to tell you what they are busy keeping you from finding out. I recall, in particular, the way vets describe their reception in America after the war. They were shocked, they explain, to find themselves treated by their countrymen as if they were at fault. This was especially true, they say, on college campuses, where they were spat upon, ostracized, and called baby-killers and murderers. Something more than injury or confusion creeps into their voices: something plaintive, yearning. The words baby-killer and murderer become in their mouths a kind of self-accusation, as if the events they are reporting reveal more about their own self-doubt, their own anguish, than they do about how they were received.

At such times one finds oneself wanting to reach out to soothe away their pain. But how is one to do that? Many vets, in fact, find themselves more guilty than they appear to other members of the society; they judge themselves more harshly than they are judged by others. Yet their feelings about themselves, as painful as they are, may well be morally accurate. The guilt they feel is—dare one say it?—often appropriate. True, many killed out of ignorance; but though others may forgive them, certain men, as they grow older and learn more about the past, cannot forgive themselves.

Here one hesitates, of course. These are areas in which no man can adequately judge another; even though some sort of general guilt exists, who can say of any particular man, *this* is how much he must feel or suffer? Every vet had his own situation, his own war. Some, of course, killed gladly, arbitrarily. But others killed reluctantly, or in a hallucinatory fog, distanced from their actions by the music they listened to and the drugs they used. Still others killed against their will, lacking the courage or foolishness to resist; and others killed because they had been trained to do it, or for the reasons at work in almost any of us: because they were there, or were told to kill, or because others were trying to kill them. There are so many different stories, so many different motives, that one wants, perpetually, to shade every statement with explanations, excuses, and disclaimers. Three such forms of extenuation come to mind, which ought to enter into every judgment—about ourselves or others—that we make about guilt.

First, there is the complexity of guilt, the difficulty in separating out individual responsibility in the midst of war from the more general responsibility of a people or a nation. "Shee-it," a vet said to me once, "I come from Dallas, man. What in hell did I know back then? Even in '68, everyone I knew was for the war: teachers, parents, clergymen even. Dissenters? They were just dirty northern hippies to us. I was just *doin' right.*"

Behind the shared guilt for the war lies a deeper and more general guilt, one that includes all the other forms of obvious or incipient violence at home or abroad that prepare the way for war. Daily, even in supposed "peace," we are complicitous in distant places with brutality and murder, in political partnership with thugs and knaves. And the same thing goes on here at home in those quarters of our cities we carefully avoid. If our children in Vietnam were not trained to kill throughout their lives, they were at least readied for it through the mix of national pride, obedience, superiority, and racism we teach in our schools and encourage in our communities. In a way, few of the men who fought in Vietnam were ever really there, ever really saw the place and their enemies. They were locked, still, in our classrooms, in our national dreams, in our old Hollywood films, living out, almost like robots, the pervasive national myths of virtue, prowess, and power.

Second, there is the nature of the war itself. It was, after all, a civil war, a guerrilla war. Despite our immense technological advantage, down on the ground, in hand-to-hand combat, our young soldiers were often out of their league, confronted not only by sophisticated and dedicated soldiers, but also by an entire civilian population that saw them as intruders, invaders—a situation for which nothing had prepared them. For many of our troops the war was like a perpetual Halloween Night grown brutally real. A sense of trespass and illegitimacy shrouded every moment; they were like grown children in the wrong place, always in someone else's garden, ready to fire or flee in an instant. Even innocuous objects took on a malevolent life of their own. Viet Cong tripwires made each twig and stone a threat. Our soldiers carried bits of wire to fit over the mouths of soft-drink bottles to protect themselves from the glass shards planted by the Viet Cong; they held the bottles up to the light to make sure they were not half-filled with gasoline. Vets have repeated to me stories about whores in Saigon who lined their vaginas with razor blades to mutilate GIs. And I remember a vet who said to me (not without awe):

"It was the Viet Cong women scared me the most. If you were wounded in battle, the men would use the chance to escape. But the women! They'd come out to where you were and cut off your head and your balls."

Are such stories true? It almost does not matter. What does matter is that Americans believed them and that they reveal to us a bit of the nightmare landscape Vietnam became for our vets.

"It was like the goddamn West," another vet once said to me. "I was more frightened of other Americans than of the Viet Cong.

Guns everywhere, everyone armed. I got so used to it I carried a piece for months back in America, and I was ready to use it—not on the enemy but on Americans."

At times supplies were so short that vets traded the scavenged parts of enemy bodies in the Saigon markets for the very same supplies intended for them in the first place: weapons, boots, or rain gear. Others became so disgusted with the perpetual theft of their food that they wrote to American corporations, asking in vain for their food to be sent directly to them.

"I was from the city streets," a young man said to me, "and so I was used to it all—the graft, the theft, the crooked authority. I know all about American corruption. But the farm kids! Christ, when they saw all that, it damn near blew them away. It was worse than combat, to see their own country's shabbiness."

No doubt this was intensified by the effects upon our troops of what they saw in the midst of their own army: the stupidity and dishonesty of their leaders and the cupidity and corruption pandemic behind the lines. Every vet I know has stories to tell about vanishing supplies, open theft, drug trafficking, black-marketeering, and gangster-like confrontations that repeated in Vietnam the normal life of certain American neighborhoods.

And there is, thirdly, human nature itself, the apparent need and even the right of men to forget after a war what they have done or seen in it. The forgetfulness that no society can afford is undeniably a blessing for individual men, a kind of soothing boon that allows them to recover from the past. There are certain acts so terrible that only their victims can afford to remember them; those who committed them must forget, if only to stay sane.

I remember reading about a German ex-officer discovered years after the end of the Second World War hundreds of miles deep in the African bush in a house on stilts at a river's edge, where he lived with his native wife and five children. When his captors asked him whether he was the man they were seeking, he said: "I am another."

And perhaps he was. Nature has its own forms of absolution, and they have little to do with justice. Memory's power is countered by another power, perhaps as strong: the capacity to sunder the present from the past. One thinks of Lt. William Calley under house arrest, so typically American: baby-faced, soft-toned, with his southern-belle sweetie beside him, his evenings of television and TV dinners and ice cream for desert. His banality was equal in its small way to Eichmann's: no sorrow, no shame, no visible signs of memory or any apparent sense of what it might be that was so disturbing to those condemning him.

Horrible, one thinks at first. But is it? If it is horrible, it is also fully human, almost universal—and understandable. We have already seen the effects of the past on those of our veterans who can neither forget nor stand its memory. For every man who succeeds in making something of the past, several—who knows how many?—come to grief. Without the community of loving others about whom Jaspers spoke, those others whose burdens ease one's own, forgetfulness may be nature's kindest gift, and something that all men must be allowed, for perhaps that alone can heal their wounds.

And yet despite the universality of guilt and the extenuation of war, it seems only just that the war belongs to our vets, that they have become its keepers. I do not mean the keepers of its statistics or of the analysis of its causes or the particulars of blame; these will be pursued by others, the scholars who come later, dissecting the war, laying out its details at a safe distance. But the *nature* of the war, and the *fact and feel of it,* and the conflicts and private struggles of conscience, the horrors that existed simultaneously outside and inside a man—all of these belong to the vets, for who else has it in their power to keep us straight, and who else has the knowledge required to do it?

I remember a few years ago in Michigan, accompanying a woman to a graduate seminar in psychology given by a friend of hers. The students were supposed to be discussing conscience and ethics, but they were not up to it. They were young, inexperienced, over-schooled. All value, they kept insisting, was relative, arbitrary; truth was what anyone believed it was; who were we, asked one or two, to say the Germans ought not to have killed the Jews? It may have seemed right at the time.

Only one man among them was different. Black, older than the rest, he had been in Vietnam. Reluctantly, only because I asked, he described his experience there: how he had awakened one morning, after months of combat, weeping and shivering, unable to continue, frightened and ashamed of the killing he had done, full of self-hatred. Those in the room fell suddenly silent; reality had intruded upon them. But they were not up to it; they had to evade it. "Just shell shock," the army doctors had told the vet, and now the students had a similar explanation. "Conditioning," they said—that was all; first taught not to kill, then asked to kill, he had been caught between two arbitrary orders.

I still remember the look on the vet's face. He smiled at me and shook his head, as if to say: *You see it, man, who needs this shit?* And what could I respond? That what he had said needed saying, whether they heard it or not? That it was precisely because the others did not understand that it needed saying? That he must keep faith with the dead even if the living kept no faith with him?

The point is: the vets must speak—both for our good and for their own. They know firsthand, as most of us should but do not, that guilt is real and that men cannot be fully human or whole without coming to terms with their relation to suffering others.

Will the vets speak? Some of them, I suppose, have no choice. They are unable either to forget the past or come to terms with it without speaking. Every war, whatever its nature, is followed by a sort of lag time, a period of assimilation and silence during which, as most people forget the past, a few mine from the past what they later speak into the world. Two of the films I have mentioned earlier—*Grand Illusion* and *All Quiet on the Western Front*—appeared a decade and a half after the end of the First World War. And it has taken European filmmakers nearly forty years to confront the complex moral issues of the Holocaust. Perhaps something similar will happen with Vietnam. Our great texts, and a period of rich understanding, may yet be ahead of us: new books and new films—still working at the moment in the minds of silent men— may, a decade from now, confront us with the truths of the past in new ways.

The problem with that, of course, is that it may come too late to do much good. Even our young seem, at the moment, affected by our appetite for war. A few days ago a veteran I know who teaches a high school class told me about an experiment he conducted:

"I like to set up mock elections in historical contexts," he said. "Last week I chose the later stages of the Vietnam war, just about the time we mined Haiphong harbor. One of the student-candidates was a dove who promised to end the war. The other was a hawk who wanted not only to mine the harbor but also to use nuclear weapons."

"And who won?" I asked.

"The hawk," he said, "in a landslide."

I have little doubt we will come fully round, as nations usually do, to where we were before, perhaps a bit wiser, but not much, and subject continuously, each one of us and all of our children, to the pressures, influences, and conditioning that lead men everywhere to war. We are not much worse in America than people anywhere, but we are not much better either, and our shared national moral life—and therefore the destinies of countless others affected by our choices—hangs perpetually in a kind of uneasy balance, slanted toward violence but checked by decency. All that protects us from the worst aspects of our nature is simply the faint possibility of a humility grounded in the consciousness of our past errors and the memory of what we have done to others.

I am not arguing here for a pure pacifism—though given the human capacity for error there is an argument to be made on that count. What I am arguing for here is only the minimal moral ground required in any just society: the willingness of all men and women to accept full responsibility for the nature of their acts and their consequences—especially in those matters involving others and life and death. It is individual judgment, choice, and responsibility that leaven and define the nature of all shared moral life. Nations and their leaders must be forever constrained and circumscribed by the ethical stances maintained by each private citizen: the capacity to see others clearly, to understand the relationship of one's life to theirs, and to judge the demands of the state or resist its power in accordance with one's best and private sense of justice.

It has fallen to the vets to remind us of this, and what we owe them in return is everything we can do to make their task easier. This includes not only a willingness to consider the war itself and our own culpability, but also a willingness to begin the reexamination and re-creation of the debauched moral landscape in which their private struggles occur.

As it now stands, those veterans who take guilt seriously feel set apart from others, isolated by their seriousness. But it is, ironically, their guilt that joins them to others, thrusts them violently into the human world. They must understand not only that they may be guilty but that they are merely guilty *too*—that is, guilty in the same way that other men are guilty, and in a fashion that joins them to the human community rather than separating them from it. Their guilt derived from the war is not so different, really, from the guilt of the person who has two coats while another has none, or the guilt of the overfed in a hungry world, or the guilt of those who remain oblivious and protected by privilege in a world of impermissible pain. Only when all of us take seriously the possibility of our own culpability will the vets understand that their guilt, as terrible and demanding as it may seem, makes them human rather than monstrous.

Yet, having said all that, I must add that it is not likely to occur. For the most part the vets will be left to confront their guilt on their own. The only other Americans to confront their own guilt may well be those who stumble accidentally—and almost unwillingly—into its acknowledgment.

I am thinking, as I write, of something that happened that night in Michigan, after the seminar I've described. My friend and I sat in the kitchen with the professor's wife who told us what he had neglected to explain himself—that he had become a member of a charismatic Catholic sect, now spoke in tongues, and was convinced that all human evil could be traced to possession by the Devil. Later, my friend and I went down the street to a neighborhood bar. It was the night of the first Ford-Carter election debate, the one in which the equipment failed and the debate was frozen in time, like a tableau in wax, until it was fixed. As we sat at our tables, silently watching the bar's patrons watching in silence the two figures voiceless at their lecterns, a young man came over and talked to us. He was a veteran—hair in a ponytail, wearing an army jacket, carrying a guitar case. He set it down and introduced himself and launched into a soliloquy, the kind one sometimes hears from disturbed veterans: brilliant, heartbreaking, crazed, shifting in rapid, disjointed succession from his childhood to the war to America to God to Carter to Ford to his parents to the army doctors to the powers who run the country to the CIA's plot to cheat him of sleep and drive him insane. He would proceed with lucidity for a while, and then suddenly his language would come apart. Flashes of madness appeared; one could almost hear, behind his words, bomb blasts and rifle fire and the dead falling around him. And when he had finished he put one hand on my friend's arm and one on mine and said quietly, wistfully: "I don't know you, but you're all right. I'd like to have had parents like you, or maybe even kids."

Outside in the street at midnight, my friend, thinking about the seminar and the professor's wife and the vet, put her head on my shoulder and wept. "I did not think," she said, "it had come to this."

But it *has* come to "this," though my friend, like the rest of us, has trouble grasping what "this" means, or the extent of the pain and horror at work within us, or the full cost to others and ourselves of our careless posturing, arrogance, and violence.

Weeping, I know, solves nothing. Morality is an activity, not a sentiment. And yet there was something in my friend's weeping, as there was in the black veteran's tears in the midst of war, that seems to me to hold the key to the re-creation of ethical life if ever one is to occur.

For it was as if, in weeping, my friend had set free at last the stirrings of memory, the raw beginnings of speech, the angers and sympathies and griefs and regrets that lie unexpressed at the human center of the lost moral world. That, perhaps, was what her weeping signified: the beginning of moral awareness. And if it did, then may God or fortune grant her, as well as to the rest of us, the courage to see through to its end the ethical journey such weeping begins.

LIVING IN MORAL PAIN

TWO YEARS AGO I was asked by a magazine editor to write an essay on the Vietnam films that were then beginning to appear. Searching for a way to measure the quality and accuracy of the films, I began to talk to Vietnam veterans. What I found both astonished and moved me: a world of moral pain and seriousness that put to shame not only the films in question but also the way most Americans deal with their moral relation to the world. The films ceased to concern me; what became important, and what I eventually wrote about, were the vets themselves. They absorbed me not only in terms of what they themselves had become but also because of the questions their difficulties raised about the capacity of our society to deal with the psychological and ethical problems that beset them.

Those questions are not easily exhausted, and I have found them again on my mind these days as America's attention has turned back, grudgingly, to the vets. The veterans, still angered by the way they are treated, have grown increasingly vocal, increasingly visible, refusing to vanish into the past with the war. Their public complaints are varied and familiar: the paucity of their benefits; the ingratitude and indifference of their fellow citizens; the red tape and bureaucratic foul-ups in VA assistance; the unwillingness of the government to recognize its responsibility for many of their problems, including the effects of Agent Orange and what psychologists now label the "delayed-stress syndrome."

All of those complaints have validity. But something about them, and about the response being made to them, seems to me inadequate. *Time* magazine's cover story on the vets this past summer is a typical example of what I mean. It portrayed the vets as victims of the society that sent them to war, and argued that the solution to their problems lay in increased acceptance and gratitude for them here at home. Left unsaid in such analyses are two crucial aspects of the vets' suffering that no one seems to want to confront. The first is the unacknowledged source of much of the vets' pain and anger: a profound moral distress arising from what they saw and sometimes did in the war. And the second is the failure of our prevailing cultural wisdom, our models of human nature, and our modes of therapy to explain moral pain or provide ways of dealing with it.

Of course, many vets have problems directly traceable to sources other than the ones I've named, and no doubt there are vets who are not disturbed in any way by their participation in the war. Yet the fact remains that in private conversations with many vets, one begins to sense beneath the surface of their resentment the deep and unacknowledged roots of their anger. That is not only my experience. In the past several months a number of men and women who work with vets in clinics and rap groups have told me that both the stories related by the vets and their explicit concerns have clearly begun to change, and that the vets now reveal more and more of their moral distress.

Shad Meshad, western coordinator for the Veterans' Outreach Program, put it this way: "We aren't just counselors; we're almost priests. They come to us for absolution as well as help."

A psychologist said it more explicitly: "Day in and day out, now, we hear stories about atrocities and slaughter, things we didn't hear before. Why men were silent before and now speak remains a mystery to me. But something has changed, and sometimes you hear almost more than you can stand. It is, I swear, like being in Germany after World War II."

It is no accident that the war in Vietnam, by far the most morally suspect war America has fought in modern times, has raised the most problems for those who served in it. Some of the problems can be ascribed to the vets' youthfulness, to the unfamiliar horrors of a guerrilla war, and to the fact that the ambiguity of American attitudes toward the war has indeed denied the vets the gratitude and help they feel they deserve.

But none of these considerations should obscure the fact that what the vets now suffer is essentially a result of the same bitter reality that caused the schisms here at home: the nature of the war itself; its excessive brutality and cruelty; and the arbitrary violence—especially in relation to civilians—with which we fought it. True, stories similar to those emerging from Vietnam occasionally surfaced after World War II and the Korean War. But one would probably have to go back to the American Indian wars to find something similar to the way civilian populations were treated in Vietnam.

There were two fundamental kinds of violence. The first was programmatic, large-scale, widespread and intentional—the result of official policies established at various levels of command. It included the conscious and wholesale slaughter of civilians, something that other nations (and war critics here at home) called genocide. The modern precedent for this kind of violence was set decades ago, during the World War II firebombing of Dresden, when civilian, not military, sites became targets. In Vietnam, the policy was extended still further: in the name of ending the war and protecting "innocent" soldiers, the administration punished "guilty" civilians, choosing as a conscious strategy the murder of noncombatants. Of course, that did not happen everywhere. Many U.S. commanders and troops tried conscientiously to distinguish between civilians and combatants and to observe the ordinary rules of war. But far more often than Americans like to realize, those rules were broken, and the war literature indicates they were broken more often by the Americans than by the Vietnamese; as a nation, we were guilty of acts that would have appeared to most Americans, had they been committed by others, as barbaric.

The second kind of violence was more sporadic, arbitrary, and individualized, ranging from large-scale but apparently spontaneous massacres, such as those at My Lai, to the kinds of "recreational" violence in which a GI, just for the fun of it, might gun down a woman crossing a field or at the side of the road. How much of that went on is not clear and we will probably never have an accurate picture of it, but stories abound. One cannot read through books like Gloria Emerson's *Winners and Losers* or the interviews in Mark Baker's *Nam* without coming upon examples every few pages. Many veterans have tales of this sort. Few of them talk directly about their own actions, but there is always something they have seen, something a buddy described. Taken together, what the stories reveal is that many of our soldiers acted as if they had been granted an implicit permission to act out at will, upon an entire population, spontaneous and unnecessary acts of violence.

One cannot tell how many soldiers were involved, nor how many now suffer psychological and emotional disturbances from their involvement. We have few accurate figures for this sort of thing. Even the number of Americans who served during the Vietnam era remains in doubt. Whereas the figure was once estimated as 2.5 million, it has now been revised upward to 4 million. Studies suggest that one out of five veterans has been severely affected by stress, which would put the figure at 800,000, and researchers and therapists seem to agree that perhaps 50,000 need immediate help. But whatever the figures, no one who speaks to distressed vets can doubt that their involvement in the excessive violence of Vietnam is a fundamental source of their inner turmoil, or that their distress reveals not only psychological stress but also moral pain.

It is here that our collective wisdom fails the vets, here that our dominant approaches to human nature and our prevailing modes of therapy prove inadequate. We have as a society useful ways to approach moral pain or guilt; it remains for us a form of neurosis or a pathological symptom, something to escape rather than something to learn from, a disease rather than—as it may well be for the vets—an appropriate if painful response to the past. A VA psychologist once told me that he and his colleagues never dealt with problems of guilt. Nor did they raise the question of what, specifically, the vets did in the war: "We treat the vets' difficulties as problems in adjustment." That is true, I suspect, of most of the help the vets receive, save for what they, and the therapists closest to them, have begun to develop in their own rap groups and clinics, where they have now been struggling for a decade to discover and describe the true nature of their problems.

But even within that struggle there are difficulties. By now, a rather extensive body of written work pertaining to the vets exists: at least fifteen new papers were presented just at the American Psychological Association convention last August. Most of the literature concerns "the delayed-stress syndrome," a term whose widespread use arose in connection with Vietnam veterans: the psychological and emotional disturbances that surface well after the war's end in men who had previously seemed unscathed. The concept is an important and useful one and no doubt there is a syndrome of symptoms and behaviors that appears months or years after the war and that can be attributed, retrospectively, to its stresses. Such symptoms, all observers agree, include flashbacks, nightmares, uncontrollable anger, paranoia, anxiety, and depression.

But many researches also extend the range of symptoms to include a variety of other emotional states: feelings of guilt, perception of oneself as a scapegoat, alienation from one's feelings, an inability to trust or love. It is there that the trouble begins, for symptoms such as these are less persuasively attributable to the war as simple combat, especially when they appear individually and not as a set of interrelated symptoms. One suspects that in many cases their classification as delayed stress obfuscates the real nature of the veterans' experience.

Let me give an example. Imagine (as is often the case) a particular vet who has seen close up not only the horrors of war but forms of human suffering and despair that are altogether different from what he had seen before. He comes home sensing a complex relation between the lives of most Americans and the things he has witnessed, a connection between our privilege here at home and the suffering and deprivation elsewhere in the world. Is it surprising that such a man, having seen his own comrades senselessly killed, and reflecting upon the moral or immorality of the killing he himself has done, would find it increasingly difficult to come to terms with the "normal" life he returns to? How would the moral smugness and obliviousness of American life strike him? How would expensive restaurants filled with happy diners strike him, or our incessant talk about interest rates, or our cheerful and relentlessly mindless TV commercials?

No doubt such a man would be "irritable," would be angry, would find himself at odds with things, unable to resume his previous job, pursuits, or relationships. But to call all such problems delayed stress or to see them as explicable only in terms of battle fatigue would be to misstate the condition entirely; it would in effect avoid the real significance of the vet's condition, would *void* it in some way, would ignore entirely the moral heart of the problem or the complexity of his situation. Similarly, seemingly precise analytic terms for repressed guilt—"impacted grief," for one—and facile theories about psychological denial become in their turn cultural systems of denial: a massive, unconscious cover-up in which both those who fought and those who did not hide from themselves the true nature of the vets' experience.

Reading through the literature on the vets, one notices again and again the ways in which various phrases and terms are used to empty the vets' experience of moral content, to defuse and bowd-lerize it. Particularly in the early literature, one feels a kind of madness at work. Repugnance toward killing or the refusal to kill are routinely called "acute combat reaction," and the effects on men of slaughter and atrocity are euphemistically called "stress," as if the clinicians describing the vets were talking about an execu-tive's hypertension or an unhappy housewife's blood pressure. Nowhere in the literature is one allowed to glimpse what is actu-ally at work: the horror of the war and its effect on those who fought it. Much of this masking has its roots in the war itself, when army psychiatrists charged with keeping the troops ready to fight treated as pathology any rebellion against orders or a refusal to kill.

Such attitudes have persisted in peacetime. Some VA therapists are now talking about the need to "deresponsibilize" their pa-tients—that is, to get the Vietnam vets to attribute their actions to external causes rather than their own moral choices. Those who do mention guilt usually describe it as "survivor's guilt": shame not for what was done, but for having outlived one's comrades. Even a sympathetic observer like John A. Wilson, a psychologist whose work on stress was put into my hands by vets who found it useful, manages to render the moral aspect of the war less important than it is. Wilson ascribes most of the vets' pain to the truncation of the "normal" development of the ego. Drawing on the work of Erik Erikson, he uses a table that connects stressful experiences to "qualities of ego-development and personality integration" and lists eleven stress-producing events. The eighth reads, in its entirety, "Death of Buddies and Atrocities," as if the death of one's friends and the inflicting or witnessing of atrocities were all more or less the same thing and had the same moral or psychological impact.

There are, of course, other authors who go beyond such think-ing. Robert Jay Lifton's work comes first to mind, if only because his book *Home From the War* (1974), published relatively early, has had a more powerful impact on therapists working with vets than any other work. Lifton has been largely responsible for the idea of the vets as victims, and there is no doubt that he has radically affected the way his colleagues see the veterans' experiences. Others, too, come to mind: Chaim Shatan, B. W. Gault, Arthur Egendorf, Arthur Blank, Bill Mahedy, Robert Laufer, and Jack Smith. All of these men have either written about the war or worked extensively with vets; often, they have done both. And one can see in their work a slow-dawning recognition of what's troubling many vets, a recognition of a moral experience that will require from us a new thinking, a new language and new categories of moral or psychological experience, if we are ever to be of help to the vets in dealing with their pain.

Why has most psychological thinking about Vietnam avoided the categories of moral experience or moral pain? There are several reasons, I think. Much of the research on Vietnam veterans has been funded by government agencies or by veterans' organizations. Several psychiatrists who work with the vets tell me that in this area, as in any other, researchers tend to look for results that will keep their funding sources happy. Then, too, many of those writing about the vets are devoted to them; they want to see them get whatever they need from the government and they feel that the best way to do that is to portray the vets solely as victims by locating the source of their troubles in the war itself. And one also suspects that many shy away from the question of moral pain simply because it is likely to open up old wounds for which there is really nothing like a "cure." As one therapist told me regarding the atrocities and the shame that were sometimes discussed in his rap group: "That, my friend, is the hardest thing to deal with. When somebody brings it up, we all fall silent. Nobody knows how in hell to handle it."

Beyond those reasons lies perhaps the most significant one of all: the limits of the discipline itself, the present inadequacy of psychological categories and language to describe the nature and anguish of human conscience. The truth is, much of our confusion in regard to therapy and moral pain stems from the very nature of the therapeutic tradition itself. A strain of moral sensibility and respect for conscience was always at least implicit in the work of Freud. But two elements combined there to separate considerations of psychological health from moral concerns. The first was the need to isolate the self in the therapeutic process from its familiar or social connections in order to see it clearly and deal effectively with it. What began as a useful fiction gradually hardened into a central psychological motif or approach: the self in therapy is characteristically seen as separate from what surrounds it—an isolated unit complete in itself, relatively unaffected by anything but inner or local experience. Secondly, morality was often treated in Freud's work as a form of social tyranny or imposition from the outside, something fundamentally alien to the individual ego. There were good reasons for his view, of course, most notably the heavy and oppressive German morality of the time and the obviously destructive dissonance between individual inner life and the regulated social order around it. Nonetheless, in its accent on human need as opposed to social obligation, traditional psychoanalysis established habits of thought that have gradually been honed in America into a morally vacuous view of human nature.

Our great therapeutic dream in America is that the past is escapable, that suffering can be avoided, that happiness is always possible, and that insight inevitably leads to joy. But life's lessons teach us something else again, something that is both true of, and applicable to, the experience of the vets. Try as they do to escape it, the past pursues them; the closer they come to the truth of their acts, the more troubled they are, the more apart they find themselves, and the more tragic becomes their view of life.

The veterans' situation is Oedipus's situation, and not for the reasons Freud chose—the story as the touchstone of infantile life—but because Oedipus's fate reveals to us the irreversibility of certain kinds of knowledge, the power of certain actions and perceptions to change an individual's life beyond any effort to change it back. Oedipus saw and was blinded, came close to the truth and lost the world of men, and once in exile he suffered not so much because of what he had done, but because of what he *learned* he had done: a terrible and tragic knowledge that deprived him of the company both of men and of gods.

Such knowledge has come to many vets too. What they've learned is this: the world is real; the suffering of others is real; one's actions can sometimes irrevocably determine the destiny of others; the mistakes one makes are often transmuted directly into others' pain; there is sometimes no way to undo that pain; the dead remain dead, the maimed are forever maimed, and there is no way to deny one's responsibility or culpability, for those mistakes are written, forever, and as if in fire, in others' flesh.

Though this is perhaps a terrible and demanding wisdom, it is no more and no less than what all men should know; it is the ethical lesson life teaches those who attend to the consequences of their actions. But because our age is what it is and because most Americans flee from such knowledge, this wisdom is especially hard for the vets to bear. It ought to bring them deeper into the human community, ought to bring them close to the heart of all mature moral experience, but instead it merely isolates them, sets them irrevocably apart, locks them simultaneously into a seriousness and a silence that are as much a cause of pain as are their past actions. They become suffering pariahs not only because of what they have done, but because of the questions this raises for them— questions that their countrymen do not want to confront, questions for which, as a society, we have no answers.

A few months ago, after I had talked about guilt and the war to a group of vets, professors, and students, a vet came up to me.

"I left in the middle of your talk," he said angrily. "What you were saying didn't make sense. I feel no guilt. There was no right or wrong over there. All of that is nonsense. It was a dream. That's how

I leave it behind. I don't let it bother me. I couldn't understand what you were saying."

Yet he had returned to register his complaint, and as he spoke to me, his eyes filled with tears. There was a grief revealed by his gaze that he could not admit to me and perhaps not even to himself, probably because he had little hope of finding a way to deal with it. Its release, or at least its acknowledgment, might radically have changed him, radically changed his relation to the world, but it might also have been too much for him, and so his anguish made itself felt as denial, as refusal to consider the past in any moral way at all.

In responding, I tried to broaden the question of responsibility, tried to suggest that, yes, the vets were guilty, but that the rest of us were also guilty, and that we were guilty not only for the war but for countless other public and private acts that had directly or indirectly caused pain or suffering for others. All of us, I tried to say, ought to struggle to come to terms with human fallibility and culpability. The vets were not alone in that, or ought not to be alone. It was a struggle all men should properly share. When I said that, he relaxed. The tears were still there, but more obvious now, less masked. His voice was softer, no longer truculent.

"I see what you mean," he said. "But you didn't say that before. I can understand what you're saying now."

I *had* said it before, but I had said it in a way that made it impossible for him to hear. In making the guilt his alone, or in making it sound as if it were his alone, I had deprived him of precisely the kind of community and generous company that make it possible for people to see themselves clearly. What he needed, as do all of the vets, was not only a way of thinking and speaking about his life, but the willingness of other men and women to consider their lives *in the same way*.

This is the point at which the failure of therapy becomes tragic, and it is at this point that the future task of therapy becomes clear:

to see life once again in a context that includes the reality of moral experience and assigns a moral significance to human action. It may be that certain acts and certain kinds of guilt set individuals irrevocably apart from others; Oedipus, after all, entered a realm in which common wisdom was of no use to him. But one cannot help feeling that this is not entirely the case with the vets, and that their isolation has as much to do with our corrupt view of human nature as it does with their past actions. The moral anguish they suffer, as intense as it gets, might be more familiar to the rest of us if we paid as much attention to moral life in our therapies as we do to other forms of behavior.

What the problems of the vets ought to point toward are several categories of moral experience ignored in therapy but applicable to all men and women. Those categories, if we could bring them to bear on the problems of the vets, would be of immense use not only in alleviating their particular torment, but also in illuminating certain aspects of experience we all must confront.

The first category of moral pain is the common notion of "bad conscience": a person's reaction to past actions he or she finds inexcusable or inexplicable. Bad conscience causes the individual remorse, shame, and guilt, and demands setting right of what has been done. But it goes beyond this reaction, approximating what Sartre, in *Being and Nothingness*, called "bad faith": the underlying and general sense of having betrayed what you feel you ought to have been.

We are familiar with the feeling in the emotional realm; we know how those who settle for emotional or sexual lives that do not satisfy them, or who sacrifice desire to fear, can feel humiliated and depleted or experience an almost organic sense of shame. In some way, at some level, they know their lives to be a lie. The same thing can exist in the moral realm. We can experience in the present a pain engendered by past actions we find reprehensible, and to the extent that we merely try to outlive such events, forgetting or ignoring them, we may indeed feel ourselves to be guilty of a kind of bad faith, of breaking a covenant not only with others or with God, but with our own natures.

This, I think, may be the experience of Americans who cannot help measuring in their minds their privileged condition and the way they choose to spend their lives against the varieties of need, deprivation, and pain they see around them. Many of us suffer a vague, inchoate sense of betrayal, of having taken a wrong turning, of having said yes or no at the wrong time and to the wrong things, or perhaps of having taken upon ourselves a peculiar and general kind of guilt of having too much while others have too little, and yet proceeding, nonetheless, with our lives as they are.

How much more painful, then, must be such feelings for the vets, for whom the consequences of their own moral choices or errors were immediately and terrifyingly visible in Vietnam: the irrevocable suffering and death of often innocent others. Is it surprising that, back at home, many vets would suffer senses of bad faith or conscience, and of having betrayed both others and themselves?

The second category of moral pain has to do with what might be called "the world's pain"—the way we internalize and experience, as our own, the disorder, suffering, and brutality around us. Some people take on the pain of others as a personal burden; external suffering mixes with their own immediate emotional experience in a way that makes it difficult to sort out what has been produced by one and what by the other. We can call it empathy if we want, but it goes well beyond a specific response to someone else's particular misfortune. It can take the form of a pervasive sense of universal suffering, injustice, and evil: a response to the world's condition that produces a feeling of despair, disgust, or even a sort of radical species-shame, in which one is simultaneously ashamed of oneself and one's kind.

Who can forget, for example, the images of John F. Kennedy falling in the open car or of the young female student at Kent State kneeling above her fallen comrade, her mouth open in a scream? And who cannot remember the televised images from Saigon of South Vietnamese soldiers crowding into the last planes to leave, the women and children clinging to them and falling through the air as they took off? The horror one feels in relation to such sights can be traumatic and perhaps permanent; it works in ways we do not understand, depriving us of something essential to the ego's health: a sense of a habitable world and of trustworthy human connections.

Often this response to suffering is hidden away, repressed, or ignored. It eats at people from the inside out, but because they feel helpless in the face of what causes it, they try as best they can to ignore it or solve it in ways that have nothing to do with its causes. Much of the apparent "selfishness" at work in America, the tendency to turn inward toward self, is not a function of greed; it is instead an attempt to alleviate pain and guilt by turning away from the world, by trying to deny its significance, at least in terms of conscience. Time and again one hears vets say about the war and its issues: "It don't mean nothin'." They struggle to empty the past of meaning—not because they are hardened to what happened or because it means nothing, but because this is the only way they can keep themselves sane.

The veterans of Vietnam have discovered in their own behavior and the behavior of others truths about human nature and human suffering that will (and should) remain with them for the rest of their lives, calling into question the thin surface of ordinariness they see in the world around them. They suffer now, in a bitter way for which we have no words, the brute truth of the human condition, which is for them neither an abstraction nor an idea; it is, rather, what they know, how they feel, who they are. Their grief, akin to Oedipus's, or to Buddha's at the sight of suffering, or to

Christ's in the presence of human evil, is far more than a therapeutic problem; it raises instead, for each of them, the fundamental questions of how to live, who to be.

Here we come to the third category of moral pain: the way most of us suffer when we cannot act out in the world our response to the suffering we have seen in it. In the past several decades, therapy has concentrated on analyzing individual pain or frustration in terms of loss and deprivation: how our needs for warmth or love may have gone unanswered. The therapeutic answer to that condition has been to teach us how to get what we want. But in concentrating on that aspect of our inward pain we have underestimated the ways in which we also suffer when we cannot find ways to express our love or give back to the world in some generous way what we feel we owe to it. Morality, argued Kropotkin, is simply "an overflow of vitality." He meant that it is a natural and unconscious response to the world, a sort of spontaneous gratitude engendered by the interplay of private energies and the surrounding reality. In such a view, there is no such thing as a feeling separate from action; each response we have to the world naturally becomes and demands a gesture. But when the process cannot be completed, when it is truncated, when what we experience cannot find its way into language or action, then, as do the vets, we experience a sense of loss and humiliation, a sense of depletion akin to what we feel when rejected in love or frustrated in desire.

A few months ago, I attended a meeting of vets, academics, and therapists in which we were supposedly discussing "the healing process." The discussion had been rather dry and constrained until one vet began to speak. He had been in the war, he said, though not in combat. Coming back from it had been hard, and his feelings about it had grown steadily stronger since its end; nothing seemed right, he was unable to settle down or come to terms with life, but he wasn't sure why that was.

"I'm an artist," he said. "A sculptor. At least that's what I've been doing lately. Coming home from the war, I saw huge piles of shell-casings. And a couple of years ago I realized that I wanted to use them to make a gigantic sculpture, something to commemorate the dead, to let people know what the war had been like. For years I tried to get those casings. But they wouldn't let me have them. They were being recycled, they said, to make new shells. . . ."

And suddenly he was shaking and weeping, unable to go on, frustrated, as are many vets, by the impossibility of explaining to others what pains them. Later he came over to talk to me. "I don't know how to explain it," he said. "I keep thinking that if I could do this one thing, if I could just get it right, if I could make this one statement, then somehow everything would be all right, other people would see it, they'd know, and then it wouldn't happen again."

This impulse is, in essence, what one finds unacknowledged in many vets, and the inability to act upon it gradually drives them far deeper into distress than they were when they first came back from the war. We know how imprisonment affects animals, how they are affected by the loss of space and freedom. Often they sicken and die. The same things happen to men and women. But we are far more complicated creatures, and we inhabit history as well as nature. When we cannot act in history, when our response to the world around us cannot be spoken or turned into gesture, then we suffer inside—as do the vets—a set of experiences for which we as yet have no psychological name.

Most good therapy, Paul Goodman once said, cutting pragmatically to the heart of the matter, is a combination of a whorehouse and an employment agency. He meant that if it did not teach people how to make lives for themselves involving both useful work and deep loving, it would do no one much good. The same thing can be said in relation to the vets. Somewhere along the line, therapy must once again enter those areas in which the therapist and patient become comrades, and where what each has discovered in their own experience provides questions and answers not only about "happiness" or "health" but also about moral responsibility; about how we find, in relation to the suffering world around us, a response that assuages our pain and puts to use some of our powers. Without that, the vets will be left high and dry, alone in their anguish, and the rest of us will have lost one of our last remaining chances to take ourselves, as well as others, seriously.

There is one last point that must be made not only about the encounter between therapists and patients but also about any contemporary "helping" relationship (teacher and student, for example) that involves the shared redefinition of reality. For decades now, we have considered Buber's "I-thou" relationship the ideal model: a respectful intimacy in which the integrity of the other is fully perceived, understood, and embraced. No doubt all of that is necessary and good. But it is also morally insufficient. It is incomplete. For it does not fully take into account the inevitable presence of the invisible others, those distant witnesses who have suffered our past acts and who may suffer them in the future.

The proper consideration for therapists and vets, for all therapists and all Americans, is "I-thou-they": the recognition that whatever we do or do not do in our encounters, whatever we forget or remember, whatever human truths we keep alive or permit to die, will help form a world for others. Our actions will play a significant part in defining not only the social and moral life of our own people, but the future of countless and distant others as well, whose names we will not know and whose faces we will not see until, perhaps a decade from now, Americans view them through the sights of guns. The responsibility of the therapist neither begins nor ends with the individual client; the client's responsibility neither begins nor ends with the self. Both extend far outward, into the past and into the future and toward countless other lives.

Whether a consideration of all these elements will make a difference to the vets is not clear. It may well be that most of them will be forced to live alone with certain kinds of pain and regret for the rest of their lives, though one can hope that at least some of them will be lucky enough to turn the truths of the past to some use, to become keepers and bearers of these truths rather than their victims. What is clear is that their psychological well-being will inevitably depend in large part upon their own capacity to resolve the issues of conscience that they alone fully understand. Whatever skills or comfort they manage to salvage from traditional therapy, they will have to see through to the end—with or without our help—the moral journey they began in Vietnam.

One can only hope that the rest of us will accompany them on that journey when we can, and that we will follow them when we should; and that out on the edges of unacknowledged experience, in those regions of the self into which the vets have been led and for which the rest of us have few words and little wisdom, therapy will find at last a part of the gravity that has so far eluded it, and move a bit closer to a coming of age.

HELPING AND HATING
THE HOMELESS

WHEN I WAS a child I had a recurring vision of how I would
end as an old man: alone, in a sparsely furnished second-story
room I could picture quite precisely, in a walk-up on Fourth
Avenue in New York, where the secondhand bookstores then
were. It was not a picture which frightened me. I liked it. The idea
of solitude and marginality must have seemed to me, back then, for
reasons I do not care to remember, both inviting and inevitable.
Later, out of college, I took to the road, hitchhiking and traveling
on freights, doing odd jobs here and there, crisscrossing the country. I liked that too: the anonymity and the absence of constraint
and the rough community I sometimes found. I felt at home on
the road, perhaps because I felt at home nowhere else, and periodically, for years, I would return to that world, always with a sense of
relief and release.

I have been thinking a lot about that these days, now that transience and homelessness have made their way into the national
consciousness, and especially since the town I live in, Santa Barbara,
has become well known because of the recent successful campaign
to do away with the meanest aspects of its "sleeping ordinances"—
a set of foolish laws making it illegal for the homeless to sleep at
night in public places. During that campaign I got to know many
of the homeless men and women in Santa Barbara, who tend to
gather, night and day, in a small park at the lower end of town, not

far from the tracks and the harbor, under the roof-like, overarching branches of a gigantic fig tree, said to be the oldest on the continent. There one enters much the same world I thought, as a child, I would die in, and the one in which I traveled as a young man: a "marginal" world inhabited by all those unable to find a place in our ordinary world. Sometimes, standing on the tracks close to the park, you can sense in the wind, or in the smell of tar and ties, the presence and age of that marginal world: the way it stretches back and forward in time, parallel to our own world, always present, always close, and yet separated from us—at least in the mind—by a gulf few of us are interested in crossing.

Late last summer, at a city council meeting here in Santa Barbara, I saw, close up, the consequences of that strange combination of proximity and distance. The council was meeting to vote on the repeal of the sleeping ordinances, though not out of any sudden sense of compassion or justice. They had been pressured into it by the threat of massive demonstrations and national publicity— "The Selma of the Eighties" was the slogan one heard among the homeless. But the threat that had only frightened the council enraged the town's citizens. Hundreds of them turned out for the meeting. One by one they filed to the microphone to curse the council and castigate the homeless. Drinking, doping, loitering, panhandling, defecating, urinating, molesting, stealing—the litany went on and on, was repeated over and over, accompanied by fantasies of disaster: the barbarian horde at the gates, civilization ended.

What astonished me about the meeting was not what was said; one could have predicted that. It was the power and depth of the emotion revealed: the mindlessness of the fear, the vengefulness of the fury. Almost none of what was said had anything to do with the homeless people I know—not the ones I once traveled with, not the ones in town. They, the actual homeless men and women, might not have existed at all.

If I write about Santa Barbara, it is not because I think the attitudes at work here are unique. They are not. You find them everywhere. In the last few months I have visited several American cities, and in each of them I have found the same thing: more and more people in the streets, more and more suffering, and in the public mind, almost always, the same thing: confusion and ignorance, or rage, or simple indifference.

What follows is an attempt to explain that rage, undo some of the confusion, to chip away at the indifference. I want to illuminate some of the darker corners of homelessness, the ones we ordinarily ignore, and where much of what is useful is hidden.

The trouble begins with the word "homeless." It has become such an abstraction, and is applied to so many different kinds of people with so many different histories and problems, that it is almost meaningless.

Homelessness, in itself, is nothing more than a condition visited upon men and women (and, increasingly, children) as the final stage of a variety of problems about which the word "homelessness" tells us almost nothing. To put it another way, homelessness is a catch basin into which pour all of the people disenfranchised or marginalized by processes which are beyond their control and which lie close to the heart of American life. Here are the major groups packed into the single category of "the homeless":

- Veterans, mainly from the war in Vietnam. In many American cities, vets make up close to 50 percent of all homeless males.
- The mentally ill. In some parts of the country, roughly a quarter of the homeless would, a couple of decades ago, have been institutionalized.
- The elderly on fixed incomes whose funds are no longer sufficient for their needs.

- Men, women, and whole families pauperized by the loss of a job.
- Single parents, usually women, without the resources or skills to establish new lives.
- Runaway children, many of whom have been abused.
- Alcoholics and those in trouble with drugs (whose troubles often begin with one of the other conditions listed here).
- Immigrants, both legal and illegal, who often are not counted among the homeless because they constitute a "problem" in their own right.
- Traditional tramps, hobos, and transients who have taken to the road or the streets for a variety of reasons and who prefer to be there.

You can quickly learn two things about the homeless from this list: that many of the homeless, before they were homeless, were people more or less like ourselves, members of the working or middle class; and that the world of the homeless has its roots in various policies, events, and aspects of social and economic life for which many of us are responsible and from which some of us actually prosper.

We decide, as a people, to go to war, and we ask our children to kill and to die, and the result, years later, is grown men homeless in the street.

We change, with the best intentions, the laws pertaining to the mentally ill, and then, without intention, neglect to provide them with services, and the visible results, in our streets, drive some of us crazy with rage.

We cut taxes and prune budgets, we modernize industry and shift the balance of payments and trade and eliminate jobs and workers, or we sexualize our children too soon and inform them about birth control too late, or we let our schools fall into disarray and marginalize large numbers of adolescents, and the result of all these actions and errors, disparate as they are, can be read, sleeping form by sleeping form, on our city streets.

The liberals cannot blame the conservatives. The conservatives cannot blame the liberals. Homelessness is the sum total of our dreams, policies, intentions, errors, omissions, cruelties, kindnesses—all of it, when something goes wrong, recorded, in flesh, in the life of the streets.

You can also learn from this list one of the most important things there is to know about the homeless—that they can be roughly divided into two groups: those who have had homelessness forced upon them and want nothing more than to escape it; and those who have at least in part *chosen* it for themselves, and now accept, or in some cases, embrace it.

I understand how dangerous it is to introduce the idea of choice into a discussion of homelessness. It can all too easily be used to justify indifference or brutality toward the homeless, or to argue that they are only getting what they "deserve." And yet it seems to me that it is only by taking choice into account, in all of the intricacies of its various forms and expressions, that one can truly understand certain kinds of homelessness.

The fact is, many of the homeless are not only hapless victims but also half-voluntary exiles, "domestic refugees," people who have turned not against human society in general, but against our society, American society. Look for a moment at the vets. The price of returning to America was to forget what they had seen or learned in Vietnam, to "put it behind them." But some could not do that, and the stress of trying showed up as alcoholism, broken marriages, drug addiction, crime. And it showed up too as life on the streets, which was for some vets a desperate choice made in the name of life—the best they could manage. It was a way of avoiding what might have occurred had they stayed where they were: suicide, or violence done to others.

We must learn to accept that there may indeed be people, and not only vets, who have seen so much of our world, or seen it so clearly, that to live in it becomes impossible. Here, for example, is the story of Alice, a homeless middle-aged woman in Los Angeles, where there are, perhaps, 50,000 homeless people. It was set down a few months ago by one of my students at the University of California, Santa Barbara, where I taught for a semester. I had encouraged them to go find the homeless and listen to their stories. And so, one day, when this student saw Alice foraging in a dumpster outside a MacDonald's, he stopped and talked to her:

> She told me she had led a pretty normal life as she grew up and eventually went to college. From there she went on to Chicago to teach school. She was single and lived in a small apartment.
>
> One night, after she got off the train after school, a man began to follow her to her apartment building. When she got to her door she saw a knife and the man hovering behind her. She had no choice but to let him in. The man raped her.
>
> After that, things got steadily worse. She had a nervous breakdown. She went to a mental institution for three months, and when she went back to her apartment she found her belongings gone. The landlord had sold them to cover the rent she hadn't paid.
>
> She had no place to go and no job because the school had terminated her employment. She slipped into depression. She lived with friends until she could muster enough money for a ticket to Los Angeles. She said she no longer wanted to burden her friends, and that if she had to live outside, at least Los Angeles was warmer than Chicago.
>
> It is as if she began back then to take on the mentality of a street person. She resolved herself to homelessness. She's been out West since 1980, without a home or job. She seems happy, with her best friend being her cat. But the scars of

memories still haunt her, and she is running from them, or should I say him.

This is, in essence, the same story one hears over and over again on the street. You begin with an ordinary life; then an event occurs—traumatic, catastrophic; smaller events follow, each one deepening the original wound; finally, homelessness becomes inevitable, or begins to seem inevitable to the person involved, the only way out of an intolerable situation. You are struck continually, hearing these stories, by something seemingly unique in American life: the absolute isolation involved. In what other culture do you find such a total absence of support from familial, social, or institutional sources? Even more disturbing is the fact that it is often our supposed sources of support—family, friends, government organizations—that have caused the problem in the first place.

Everything that happened to Alice—the rape, the loss of job and apartment, the breakdown—was part and parcel of a world gone radically wrong, a world, for Alice, no longer to be counted on, no longer worth living in. Her homelessness can be seen as flight, or as failure of will or nerve, or even, perhaps, as disease. But it can also be seen as a mute, furious refusal, a self-imposed exile far less appealing to the rest of us than ordinary life, but *better*, in Alice's terms.

We like to think, in America, that everything is redeemable, that everything broken can be magically made whole again, and that what has been "dirtied" can be cleansed. Just the other day, on television, I saw that one of the soaps had introduced into the plot a homeless woman. One of the female characters in her thirties discovers that her long lost mother has appeared in town and is living on the streets. After much searching the mother is located, identified, embraced and then cleansed, scrubbed and polished, dressed in style, and restored in a matter of days to her former upperclass habits and role.

A triumph—but one more likely to occur on television than in real life. Yes, many of those on the streets could be transformed, rehabilitated. But there are others whose lives have been irrevocably changed, damaged beyond repair, and who no longer want help, who no longer recognize the need for help, and whose experience in our world has made them want only to be left alone. How, for instance, would one restore Alice's life, or reshape it in a way that would satisfy *our* notion of what a life should be? What would it take to return her to the fold? How to erase the four years of homelessness, which have become as familiar to her, and as much a home, as her "normal" life once was? Whatever we think of the way in which she has resolved her difficulties, it constitutes a sad peace made with the world. Intruding ourselves upon it in the name of redemption is by no means as simple a task—or as justifiable a task—as one might think.

It is important to understand too that however disorderly and dirty and unmanageable the world of homeless men and women like Alice appears to us, it is not without its systems of caution, prudence and order, and its rules and rituals. The homeless in our cities mark out for themselves particular neighborhoods, blocks, buildings, doorways. They impose on themselves, often obsessively, strict routines. They reduce their world to a small area, and thereby protect themselves from a world that might otherwise be too much to bear.

As I write this, I keep thinking of the old woman who sleeps every night, summer and winter, in the vestibule of my cousin's apartment house in Brooklyn, huddled among her sacks and bags between the unlocked outer door and the locked inner door, muttering to herself, even in sleep, in a slurred, barely audible voice.

She frightens my cousin, and so whenever he comes in at night, no matter how late or cold it is, he drives her out into the street as if she were a dog, just so he can feel safe while unlocking the inner door. Sometimes, late at night for no good reason, he makes special trips down to the lobby to drive her away, but as soon as he leaves, she comes back.

One of his neighbors, a kindly woman disturbed about the old lady for different and more decent reasons, takes another approach. She calls around town to various agencies and shelters, then takes the old lady to those who say they will help her. But in a couple of days the old woman is back again, huddled once more among her possessions, muttering to herself.

"For my own peace of mind," is what my cousin will say. "For her own good," is how the neighbor might put it. But different as these responses are, neither one has much to do with what the old lady herself wants. To my cousin and the neighbor she is "homeless." But in fact she has a home. The doorway is her home, or at least the vestige of a home: a cave, say, in which she has taken shelter in a storm the way a lost traveler might. Those trying to dislodge her out of fear, like my cousin, or out of charity, like his neighbor, are both making her homeless. At least in her eyes they are depriving her, against her rather powerful will, of the last bit of space left her in the world, and beyond which, in her mind, all is danger and void.

Pavlov, the Russian psychologist, once theorized that the most fundamental reflexes in all animals, including humans, are those involving freedom and orientation. Grab any animal, he said, and it will immediately struggle to accomplish two things: to break free and to orient itself. And this is what one sees in so many of the homeless. Having been stripped of all other forms of connection, and of most kinds of social identity, they are left only with this raw stuff of nature, something encoded in the cells—the desire to be free, the need for familiar space. Perhaps this is why so many of them struggle so vehemently against us when we offer them aid. They are clinging to their freedom and their space, and they do not believe that this is what we, with our programs and our shelters, mean to allow them.

Years ago, when I first came to California, bumming my way west, the marginal world, and the lives of those in it, were very different from what they are now. In those days I spent much of my time in hobo jungles or on the skid rows of various cities, and just as it was easier back then to "get by" in the easygoing beach towns on the California coast, or in the bohemian and artistic worlds in San Francisco or Los Angeles or New York, it was also far easier than it is now to survive in the marginal world.

It is important to remember this, important to recognize the immensity of the changes that have occurred in the marginal world in the past twenty years. Whole sections of many cities—the Bowery in New York, the Tenderloin in San Francisco—were once ceded to the transient. In every skid row area in America you could find what you needed to survive: hash houses, free-lunch saloons, pawnshops, surplus clothing stores, and, most important of all, cheap hotels and flophouses and two-bit employment agencies specializing in the kinds of labor transients have always done. Jobs were comparatively plentiful: seasonal agricultural labor, shape-up work on the docks or in construction, and a wide range of odd jobs and temporary work implicitly reserved for transient, part-time workers.

It was by no means a wonderful world. But it *was* a world. Its rituals were spelled out in ways most of the participants understood. It had its own codes, its own forms of civility, never written down but observed nonetheless. In hobo jungles up and down the tracks, whatever there was to eat went into the common pot and was divided equally. Late at night, in the jungles or in the freight-train empties crisscrossing the country, men would speak with a certain anonymous openness, for all the world like Chaucer's travelers in their coach. The shared condition of transience created among them a sense of temporary community. You met many men from whom you did not part without a sense of loss.

What most people in that world wanted was simply to be left alone. Some of them had been on the road for years, itinerant workers. Others were recuperating from wounds they could never quite explain. There were young men, and a few women, with nothing better to do, and older men who had no families or had lost their jobs or wives, or for whom the rigor and pressure of life had proved too demanding. The marginal world offered them a respite from the other world, a world grown too much for them.

But things have changed. There began to pour into the marginal world—slowly in the sixties, a bit faster in the seventies, and then faster still in the eighties—more and more people who neither belonged nor knew how to survive there. The sixties brought the counterculture and drugs; the streets filled with young dropouts. Changes in the law loosed upon the streets mentally ill men and women. Inflation took its toll, then recession. Working-class and even middle-class men and women—entire families—began to fall into a world they did not understand.

At the same time that the transient world was being inundated by new inhabitants, its landscape, its economy, was shrinking radically. Jobs became harder to find. Modernization had something to do with it; machines took the place of men and women. And where they did not, the influx of workers from Mexico and points farther south created a class of semipermanent workers who took the place of casual transient labor. More important, perhaps, was the fact that the forgotten parts of many cities began to attract attention as downtown areas were redeveloped, reclaimed. The skid row sections of smaller cities were turned into "olde towns." The old and modest hotels that once catered to transients were upgraded or torn down or became warehouses for welfare families— an arrangement far more profitable to the owners. The price of housing increased; evictions increased. The mentally ill, who once could afford to house themselves in cheap rooms, the alcoholics, who once would drink themselves to sleep at night in their cheap hotels—all were now out on the street, exposed to the weather and to danger, and also in plain and public view: "problems" to be dealt with.

Nor was it only cheap shelter that disappeared. It was also the "open" spaces that had once been available to those without other shelter. As property rose in value, the nooks and crannies in which the homeless had been able to hide became more visible. Doorways, alleys, abandoned buildings, vacant lots—these "holes" in the cityscape, these gaps in public consciousness, became *real estate*. The homeless, who had been there all along, were overtaken by economic progress, and they became intruders.

You cannot help thinking, as you watch this process, of what happened in parts of Europe in the eighteenth and nineteenth centuries: the effects of the enclosure laws, which eliminated the "commons" in the countryside and drove the rural poor, now homeless, into the cities. The centuries-old tradition of common access and usage was swept away by the beginnings of industrialism; land became privatized, a commodity. At the same time something equally important occurred in the cultural psyche. The world itself, space itself, was subtly altered. It was no longer merely to be lived in; it was now to be owned. What was enclosed was not only the land but, in a complex way, the flesh itself; it was cut off from, denied access to, its rightful place in the physical world.

When thinking of the homeless, one thinks too of the American past, of the settlement of the "new" world which occurred at precisely the same time that the commons disappeared. The dream of freedom and equality that brought men and women here had something to do with space, as if the wilderness itself conferred upon them a new beginning, the Eden that had been lost. Once God had sent Christ to redeem men; now He provided a new world. Men discovered, or believed, that this world, and perhaps time itself, had no edge, no limit. Space was a sign of God's magnanimity, a kind of grace.

Somehow it is all of this that is folded into the sad shapes of the homeless. In their mute presence one can sense, however faintly, the dreams of a world gone aglimmering, and the presence of our failed hopes. A kind of claim is made silently. An ethic is proffered, a philosophy—or, if you will, a cosmology—one older than our own ideas of privilege and property. It is as if flesh were seeking, this one last time, the home in the world it has been denied.

Daily the city eddies around the homeless. The crowds flowing past leave a few feet, a gap. We do not touch the homeless world. Perhaps we cannot touch it. It remains separate even as the city surrounds it, entirely beyond us even in our midst.

The homeless, simply because they are homeless, are strangers, alien—and therefore a threat. Their presence, in itself, comes to constitute a kind of violence; it deprives us of our sense of safety. Let me use myself as an example. I know, and respect, many of those now homeless on the streets of Santa Barbara. Twenty years ago some of them would have been my companions and friends. And yet, these days, if I walk through the park near my home and see strangers bedding down for the night, my first reaction is, if not one of fear, a sense of annoyance and intrusion, of worry and alarm. I think of my teenage daughter, who often walks through the park, and then of my house a hundred yards away, and I am tempted—only tempted, but tempted still—to call the "proper" authorities to have the strangers moved on: out of sight, out of mind.

Notice: I do not bring them food. I do not offer them shelter or a shower in the morning. I do not even stop to talk. Instead, I think: my daughter, my house, my privacy. What moves me is not the threat of danger—nothing as animal as that. Instead there pops up inside of me, neatly in a row, a set of anxieties, ones you might arrange in a dollhouse living room and label: Family of Bourgeois Fears. The point is, our response to the homeless is fed by a complex set of cultural attitudes, habits of thought, and fantasies and fears so familiar to us, so common, that they have become a second nature and might as well be instinctive, for all the control we have over them. It is by no means easy to untangle this snarl of responses, but one can at least point to some of its elements. Mixed into it is much that colors the unconscious life of the nation in general: the residue of Protestant attitudes that make of each individual fate a deserved and God-given destiny, and the belief in a radical individuality teaching that all must look out for themselves and that only the weak or failed depend on others.

But there is more to it all than that, and our horror and fear of the homeless argue that something else must also be at work. For starters there is a *resentment*, for in the eyes of many Americans, unaware of the nature of homelessness, the homeless "enjoy" a freedom from responsibility denied to the rest of us, who must work very hard for whatever we have. They are in a sense—at least in how we see them—the "bad" children that we, the better citizens, did not dare to become. They don't wash or do their lessons or chores or come inside for supper or bed. They live out in front of us the forbidden behavior we learned to suppress in ourselves, and in some way it is necessary for them to suffer, if only to legitimize the strained but proper lives we ourselves lead.

Perhaps in a subtle way religion and myth also enter in here. The theme of homelessness, after all, lies at the core of many of our cultural myths. Adam and Eve, Lucifer's fall from Heaven, the wandering Jew—in all of these homelessness is the punishment for disobedience and sin. At some low-humming, primitive level of consciousness there is a connection we make between the homeless and *evil*, if only because their condition suggests in terms of myth that they must have somehow sinned or angered the gods we worship.

Finally, the homeless, in their visible fall from grace, are also like twentieth-century versions of *momenti mori*, the skulls medieval scholars kept on their desks to remind them of death. Those scholars, of course, sought such reminders while we flee them, but flee as we will, there the homeless are, reminding us of what we want to forget: not only about what awaits us if we falter and fail, but also about the nature of the society we participate in but do not have the energy or will to change. Turn away as we do, or roll up the windows of the car and turn the tapes up loud, still certain horrors, certain truths, seep under the doors and past the barriers we erect against disorder and danger and a world we cannot control.

The homeless, then, in their shadowy and assertive presence, embody all that bourgeois culture has for centuries tried to eradicate and destroy. If you look to the history of Europe you find that homelessness first appears (or is first acknowledged) at the very same moment that bourgeois culture begins to appear. The same processes produced them both: the breakup of feudalism, the rise of commerce and cities, the combined triumphs of capitalism, industrialism, and individualism. The historian Fernand Braudel, in *The Wheels of Commerce*, describes, for instance, the armies of impoverished men and women who began to haunt Europe as far back as the eleventh century. And the makeup of these masses? Essentially the same then as it is now: the unfortunates, the throwaways, the misfits, the deviants.

> In the eighteenth century, all sorts and conditions were to be found in this human dross ... widows, orphans, cripples ... journeymen who had broken their contracts, out-of-work labourers, homeless priests with no living, old men, fire victims ... war victims, deserters, discharged soldiers, would-be vendors of useless articles, vagrant preachers with or without licenses, "pregnant servant-girls and unmarried mothers driven from home," children sent out "to find bread or maraud."

Then, as now, distinctions were made between the "homeless" and the supposedly "deserving" poor, those who knew their place and willingly sustained, with their labors, the emergent bourgeois world.

> The good paupers were accepted, lined up and registered on the official list; they had a right to public charity and were sometimes allowed to solicit it outside churches in prosperous districts, when the congregation came out, or in market places. . . .
> When it comes to beggars and vagrants, it is a very different story, and different pictures meet the eye: crowds, mobs, processions, sometimes mass emigrations, "along the country highways or the streets of the Towns and Villages," by beggars "whom hunger and nakedness has driven from home. . . ." The towns dreaded these alarming visitors and drove them out as soon as they appeared on the horizon.

And just as the distinctions made about these masses were the same then as they are now, so too was the way society saw them. They seemed to bourgeois eyes (as they still do) the one segment of society that remained resistant to progress, unassimilable and incorrigible, inimical to all order.

It is in the nineteenth century, in the Victorian era, that you can find the beginnings of our modern strategies for dealing with the homeless: the notion that they should be controlled and perhaps eliminated through "help." With the Victorians we begin to see the entangling of self-protection with social obligation, the strategy of masking self-interest and the urge to control as moral duty. Michel Foucault has spelled this out in his books on madness and punishment: the zeal with which the overseers of early bourgeois culture tried to purge, improve, and purify all of urban civilization—whether through schools and prisons, or, quite literally, with public baths and massive new water and sewage systems. Order, ordure—this is, in essence, the tension at the heart of bourgioes culture, and it was the singular genius of the Victorians to make it the main component of their medical, aesthetic, *and* moral systems. It was not a sense of justice or even empathy which called for charity or new attitudes toward the poor; it was *hygiene.* The very same attitudes appear in nineteenth-century America. Charles Loring Brace, in an essay on homeless and vagrant children written in 1876, described the treatment of delinquents in this way: "Many of their vices drop from them like the old and verminous clothing they left behind. . . .The entire change of circumstances seems to cleanse them of bad habits." Here you have it all: *vices, verminous clothing, cleansing them of bad habits*—the triple association of poverty with vice with dirt, an equation in which each term comes to stand for all of them.

These attitudes are still with us; that is the point. In our own century the person who has written most revealingly about such things is George Orwell, who tried to analyze his own middle-class attitudes toward the poor. In 1933, in *Down and Out in Paris and London,* he wrote about tramps:

> In childhood we are taught that tramps are blackguards . . . a repulsive, rather dangerous creature, who would rather die than work or wash, and wants nothing but to beg, drink or rob hen-houses. The tramp monster is no truer to life than the sinister Chinaman of the magazines, but he is very hard to get rid of. The very word "tramp" evokes his image.

All of this is still true in America, though now it is not the word "tramp" but the word "homeless" that evokes the images we fear. It is the homeless who smell. Here, for instance, is part of a paper a student of mine wrote about her first visit to the Rescue Mission here in town.

The sermon began. The room was stuffy and smelly. The mixture of body odors and cooking was nauseating. I remember thinking: how can these people share this facility? They must be repulsed by each other. They had strange habits and dispositions. They were a group of dirty, dishonored, weird people to me.

When it was over I ran to my car, went home, and took a shower. I felt extremely dirty. Through the day I would get flashes of that disgusting smell.

To put it as bluntly as I can, for many of us the homeless are *shit*. And our policies toward them, our spontaneous sense of disgust and horror, our wish to be rid of them—all of this has hidden in it, close to its heart, our feeling about excrement. Even Marx, that most bourgeois of revolutionaries, described the deviant *lumpen* in *The Eighteenth Brumaire of Louis Bonaparte* as "scum, offal, refuse of all classes." These days, in puritanical Marxist nations, they are called "parasites"—a word, perhaps not incidentally, one also associates with human waste.

What I am getting at here is the *nature* of the desire to help the homeless—what is hidden behind it and why it so often does harm. Every government program, almost every private project, is geared as much to the needs of those giving help as it is to the needs of the homeless. Go to any government agency, or for that matter to most private charities, and you will find yourself enmeshed, at once, in a bureaucracy so tangled and oppressive, or confronted with so much moral arrogance and contempt, that you will be driven back out into the streets for relief.

Santa Barbara, where I live, is as good an example as any. There are three main shelters in the city—all of them private. Between them they provide fewer than a hundred beds a night for the homeless. Two of the three shelters are religious in nature: the Rescue Mission and the Salvation Army. In the mission, as in most places in the country, there are elaborate and stringent rules. Beds go first to those who have not been there for two months, and you can stay for only two nights in any one two-month period. No shelter is given to those who are not sober. Even if you go to the mission only for a meal, you are required to listen to sermons and participate in prayer, and you are regularly proselytized—sometimes overtly, sometimes subtly. There are obligatory, regimented showers. You go to bed precisely at ten: lights out, no reading, no talking. After the lights go out fifteen men lie wide-eyed and sleepless in a room filled with double-decker bunks. As the night progresses the room grows stuffier and hotter. Men toss, turn, cough, and moan. In the morning you are awakened precisely at five forty-five. Then breakfast. At seven-thirty you are back on the street.

The town's newest shelter was opened almost a year ago by a consortium of local churches. Families and those who are employed have first call on the beds—a policy which excludes the congenitally homeless. Alcohol is not simply forbidden in the shelter; those with a history of alcoholism must sign a "contract" pledging to remain sober and chemical-free. Finally, in a paroxysm of therapeutic bullying, the shelter has added a new wrinkle: if you stay more than two days you are required to fill out and then discuss with a social worker a complex form listing what you perceive as your personal failings, goals, strategies—all of this for men and women who simply want a place to lie down out of the rain!

As for the public shelter sometimes provided by cities or states (often only in response to laws suits), it is often worse. A year or two ago I spent several nights in a New York City shelter, at one of the armories pressed into service in recent years. These vast and open arenas, some of which can house more than a thousand men, are jammed to overflowing in the winter and violent all year around. Men sleep in narrow cots arranged in rows on the armory floor—no pillow, no blankets, one sheet—trying to catch what sleep they can in the pale light kept burning all night long. If at three in the morning you climb up a few rows into the seats surrounding the armory floor and gaze down at the hundreds of men on their cots, they look like an army bivouacked before battle, each one vulnerable and alone, turning in sleep, coughing, sometimes crying out or cursing, as if caught in private nightmares none can solace or know.

I find myself, writing about the people in these shelters, trying consciously to avoid using words like "inmates" or "prisoners." For these shelters *are* like prisons, with metal detectors as you enter, and with watchful armed guards hired by the city from private security firms. No attempt whatsoever is made to make men feel comfortable or at home, and they are herded about and treated with the contemptuous indifference or careless cruelty we have traditionally reserved for those to be punished or those without money or power—there seems to be little difference in our society between the two conditions.

It is these attitudes, in various forms and permutations, that you find repeated endlessly across America. We are moved either to "redeem" the homeless or punish them. Perhaps there is nothing consciously hostile about it. Perhaps it is simply that as the machinery of bureaucracy cranks itself up to deal with these problems, attitudes assert themselves automatically. But whatever the case, the fact remains that almost every one of our strategies for helping the homeless is simply an attempt to rearrange the world cosmetically, in terms of how it looks and smells to *us*. Compassion is little more than the passion for control.

The central question emerging from all this is, what does a society owe to its members in trouble, and how is that debt to be paid? It is a question which must be answered in two parts: first, in relation to the men and women who have been marginalized against their will, and then, in a slightly different way, in relation to those who choose (or accept or even prize) their marginality.

As for those who have been marginalized against their wills, I think the general answer is obvious: a society owes its members whatever it takes for them to regain their places in the social order. And when it comes to specific remedies, one need only read backward the various processes which have created homelessness and then figure out where help is likely to do the most good.

But the real point here is not the specific remedies required—affordable housing, say—but the basis upon which they must be offered, the necessary underlying ethical notion we seem in this nation unable to grasp: that those who are the inevitable casualties of modern industrial capitalism and the free market system are entitled, by right, and by the simple virtue of their participation in that system, to whatever help they need. They are entitled to help in finding and holding their places in the society whose social contract they have, in effect, signed and observed.

Look at that for just a moment: the notion of a contract. The majority of homeless Americans have kept, insofar as they could, to the terms of that contract. In any shelter these days you can find men and women who have worked ten, twenty, forty years, and whose lives have nonetheless come to nothing. And in return? Is it life on the street they have earned? Or the cruel charity we so grudgingly grant them? If a social contract has been broken along the line, it is not the homeless themselves who have broken that contract or must now make it good. It is "society," it is us—all of us—who have failed to keep faith with the homeless; and now we owe it to them to "make them whole," as the investors and lawyers like to say, not as a form of charity but as a function of community, of reciprocity, because for the most part they accepted and played, as best they could, the roles society demanded.

But those marginalized against their wills are only half the problem. There remains, still, the question of whether we owe anything to those who are voluntarily marginal. What about them: the street people, the rebels, and the recalcitrant, those who have torn up their social contracts or returned them unsigned?

I was in Las Vegas last fall, and I went out to the Rescue Mission at the lower end of town, on the edge of the black ghetto, where I first stayed years ago on my way west. It was twilight, still hot; in the vacant lot next door to the mission 200 men were lining up for supper. A warm wind blew along the street lined with small houses and salvage yards, and in the distance I could see the desert's edge and the smudge of low hills in the fading light. There were elderly alcoholics in line, and derelicts, but mainly the men were the same sort I had seen here years ago: youngish, out of work, restless and talkative, the drifters and wanderers for whom the word "wander-lust" was invented.

At supper—long communal tables, thin gruel, stale sweet rolls, ice water—a huge black man in his twenties, fierce and muscular, sat across from me. "I'm from the Coast, man," he said. "Never been away from home before. Ain't sure I like it. Sure don't like *this* place. But I lost my job back home a couple of weeks ago and fig-ured, why wait around for another. I thought I'd come out here, see me some of the world."

After supper a squat Portuguese man in his mid-thirties, hun-kered down against the mission wall, offered me a smoke and told me: "Been sleeping in my car, up the street, for a week. Had my own business back in Omaha. But I was bored, man. Sold every-thing, got a little dough, came out here. Thought I'd work con-struction. Let me tell you, this is one tough town."

In a world better than ours, I suppose, men (or women) like this might not exist. Conservatives seem to have no trouble imagining a society so well disciplined and moral that deviance of this kind would disappear. And leftists envision a world so just, so generous, that deviance would vanish along with inequity. But I suspect that there will always be something at work in some men and women to make them restless with the systems others devise for them, and to move them outward toward the edges of the world, where life is always riskier, less organized, and easier going.

It is not that men like these are afraid to work. It is simply that they can't or won't work steadily—not year in, year out, at the same job, for the same boss, in the same place. They're too restless for that, or too adventurous, or simply "trained" badly, too much at odds with the world. They seem, as a group, never to have understood or accepted what it takes to survive in America. Their older counterparts—solitary pensioners, derelict old men—are around them here at the mission, and they are what these younger men, thirty years from now, will have become. But that doesn't bother the younger men. They seem oblivious to their own destinies, or maybe it simply doesn't matter to them, or maybe they take it so much as a matter of course that they no longer worry about it.

It is that, I think, that makes the condition of these men so poignant: one's sense of something in human nature betrayed or made superfluous. They are like a vanishing species of animal whose water holes have dried up or been ringed with barbed wire. One has a terrible sense of waste, not because they did not become, as they might have, supermarket managers or real estate salesmen. It is rather that their restlessness, their nearly mute refusal of the world as it is, and their tethered attempts to escape whatever lay in store for them has led only here: to this ramshackle building on the desert's edge.

Do we owe anything to these men and women who reject our company and what we offer and yet nonetheless seem to demand something from us? We owe them, I think, at least a place to exist, a way to exist. That may not be a moral obligation, in the sense that obligation to the involuntarily marginal is clearly a moral one, but it is an obligation nevertheless, one that might be called an existential obligation.

Of course, it may be that I think we owe these men something merely because I once enjoyed the company of others like them, or because I want their world to be there always, as a place to hide or rest. But there is more to it than that. I think we as a society need men like these. A society needs its margins as much as it needs art and literature. It needs holes and gaps, breathing spaces, let us say, into which men and women can escape and live, when necessary, in ways otherwise denied them. Margins guarantee to society a flexibility, an elasticity, and allow it to accommodate itself to the natures and needs of its members. When margins vanish, society becomes too rigid, too oppressive by far, and therefore inimical to life.

It is for such reasons that, in cultures like our own, marginal men and women take on a special significance. They are all we have left to remind us of the narrowness of the received truths we take for granted. "Beyond the pale," they somehow redefine the pale, or remind us, at least, that *something* is still out there, beyond the pale. They preserve, perhaps unconsciously, a dream that would otherwise cease to exist, the dream of both having a place in the world, and of being *left alone*.

Quixotic? Infantile? Perhaps. But remember Pavlov and his reflexes coded in the flesh: animal, and therefore as if given by God. What we are talking about here is freedom, and with it, perhaps, an echo of the dream men brought, long ago, to wilderness America. I use the word "freedom" gingerly in relation to lives like these: skewed, crippled, emptied of everything we associate with a full, or realized, freedom. But perhaps this is the condition into which freedom has fallen among us. Art has been "appreciated" out of existence; literature has become an extension of the university, replete with tenure and pensions; and as for politics, the ideologies which ring us round seem too silly or shrill by far to speak for life. What is left, then, is this mute and intransigent independence, this "waste" of life which refuses even interpretation, and which cannot be assimilated into any ideology, and which therefore can be put to no one's use. In its crippled innocence and the perfection of its superfluity it amounts, almost, to a rebellion against history, and that is no small thing.

Let me put it as simply as I can: what we see on the streets of our cities are two dramas, both of which cut to the troubled heart of the culture and demand from us a response we may not be able to make. There is the drama of those struggling to survive by

regaining their place in the social order. And there is the drama of
those struggling to survive outside of it.

The resolution of both struggles depends on a third drama occurring at the heart of the culture: the tension and contention
between the magnanimity we owe to life and the darker tendings
of the human psyche: our fear of strangeness, our hatred of deviance, our love of order and control. How we mediate by default
or design between those contrary forces will determine not only
the destinies of the homeless but also something crucial about the
nation, and perhaps—let me say it—about our own souls.

THE PREJUDICE AGAINST MEN

FOR THE PAST several years advocates for the homeless have sought public support and sympathy by drawing attention to the large number of homeless families on our streets. That is an understandable tactic. Americans usually respond to social issues on the basis of sympathy for "innocent" victims—those whose blamelessness touches our hearts and whom we deem unable to care for themselves. Families, and especially children, obviously fill the bill.

But the fact remains, despite the claims of advocates, that the problem of chronic homelessness is essentially a problem of single adult men. Far more single adults than families, and far more men than women, end up homeless on our streets. Until we understand how and why this happens nothing we do about homelessness will make much of an impact.

Most figures pertaining to the homeless come from limited studies or educated guesses that tend, when examined, to dissolve in one's hand. The most convincing figures I know can be found in James Wright's book, *Address Unknown: The Homeless in America.* According to Wright's data, out of every 1,000 homeless people in America, 120 or so will be adults with children, another 100 will be children, and the rest will be single adults. Out of that total, 156 will be single women and 580 will be single men. Now break that down into percentages. Out of all single homeless adults, 78 percent are men; out of all homeless adults, more than 64 percent are

single men; and out of all homeless people—adults or children—
58 percent are single men.

But even those figures do not give the full story. Our federal
welfare system has been designed, primarily, to aid women with
children or whole families. That means that most of the families
and children on the streets have either fallen through the cracks
of the welfare system or have not yet entered it. They will, in the
end, have access to enough aid to get them off the streets and into
some form of shelter, while most men will be left permanently on
their own.

I do not mean to diminish here the suffering of families or children, nor to suggest that welfare provides much more than the
meanest alternative to homelessness. It is a form of indentured
pauperism so grim it shames the nation. But it does in fact eventually get most families off the streets, and that leaves behind, as the
chronically homeless, single adults, of whom four-fifths are men.
Seen this way, homelessness emerges as a problem involving what
happens to men without money, or men in trouble.

Why do so many more men than women end up on the streets?
Let me begin with the simplest answers.

First, life on the streets, as dangerous as it is for men, is even
more dangerous for women, who are far more vulnerable. While
many men in trouble drift almost naturally onto the streets, women
do almost anything to avoid it.

Second, there are far better private and public shelters and services available to women.

Third, women are accustomed to asking for help while men are
not; women therefore make better use of available resources.

Fourth, poor families *in extremis* seem to practice a form of in-
formal triage. Young men are released into the streets more readily,
while young women are kept at home even in the worst circumstances.

Fifth, there are cultural, and perhaps even genetic, factors at work.
There is some evidence that men—especially in adolescence—are

more aggressive and openly rebellious than women and therefore harder to socialize. Or it may simply be that men are allowed to live out the impulses women are taught to suppress, and that they therefore end up more often in marginal roles.

More important, still, may be the question of work. Historically, the kinds of work associated with transient or marginal life have been reserved for men. They brought in crops, worked on ships and docks, built roads and railroads, logged and mined. Such labor granted them a place in the economy while allowing them to remain on society's edges—an option rarely available to women save through prostitution.

And society has always seemed, by design, to produce the men who did such work. Obviously, poverty and joblessness forced men into marginality. But there was more to it than that. Schools produced failures, dropouts, and rebels; family life and its cruelties produced runaways and throwaways; wars rendered men incapable of settled or domestic life; small-town boredom and provinciality led them to look elsewhere for larger worlds.

Now, of course, the work such men did is gone. But like a mad engine that cannot be shut down, society goes right on producing them. Its institutions function as they always did: the schools hum, the families implode or collapse, the wars churn out their victims. But what is there for them to do? The low-paying service sector jobs that have replaced manual labor in the economy go mainly to women or high school kids, not the men who once did the nation's roughest work.

Remember, too, in terms of work, that women, especially when young, have one final option denied to men. They can take on the "labor" of being wives and companions to men or of bearing children, and in return they will often be supported or taken care of by someone else. Yes, I know: such roles can often constitute a form of oppression, especially when assumed out of necessity. But nonetheless the possibility is there. It is permissible (as well as often necessary) for women to become financially, if precariously,

dependent on others, while such dependence is more or less forbidden to men.

Finally, there is the federal welfare system. I do not think most
Americans understand how the system works, or how for decades
it has actually sent men into the streets, creating at least some male
homelessness while aiding women and children. Let me explain.
There are two main programs that provide care for Americans in
trouble. One is Social Security Disability Insurance. It goes to men
or women who are unable, because of physical or mental problems, to work or take care of themselves. The other is Aid to
Families with Dependent Children (A.F.D.C.). It is what we ordinarily call "welfare." It was begun early in this century and was
reshaped more or less into its present form during the Depression.
Refined and expanded again in the 1960s, A.F.D.C. has always
been a program meant mainly for women and children and limited
to households headed by women. As long as an adult man remained in the household as mate, companion, or father, no aid was
forthcoming. Changes have recently been made in the system, and
men may remain in the household if they have a work history sat-
isfying certain federal guidelines. But in poor areas and for certain
ethnic groups, where unemployment runs high and few men have
a qualifying work history, these changes have not yet made much
difference and men remain functionally outside the welfare system.

When it comes to single and "able-bodied" or employable
adults, there is no federal aid whatsoever. Individual states and lo-
calities sometimes provide their own aid through "general assistance" and "relief." But this is usually granted only on a temporary
basis or in emergencies. And in those few places where it is available for longer periods of time to large numbers of single adults
—California, for instance, or New York—it is often so grudging, so
ringed round with capricious requirements and red tape, that it is
of little use to those in need.

This combination of approaches not only systematically denies
men aid as family members or single adults, but it also often deprives

men of homes even as it provides for women and children. Given the choice between receiving aid for themselves and their children and living with men, what do you think most women do? The regulations as they stand actually force men to compete with the state for women; as a woman in New Orleans once told me: "Welfare changes even romance. If a man can't make more at a job than I get from welfare, I ain't even gonna look at him. I can't afford it."

Everywhere in America poor men have been forced to become ghost-lovers and ghost-fathers, one step ahead of welfare workers ready to disqualify families for having a man around. In many ghettos throughout the country you find women and children in their deteriorating welfare apartments, and their male companions and fathers in even worse conditions: homeless in gutted apartments and abandoned cars, denied even the minimal help granted the opposite sex.

Is it surprising, in this context, that many African-Americans see welfare as an extension of slavery that destroys families, isolates women, and humiliates men according to white bureaucratic whim? Or is it accidental that in poor communities family structure has collapsed and more and more children are born outside marriage at precisely the same time that disfranchised men are flooding the streets? Welfare is not the only influence at work in all of this, of course. But before judging men and their failures and difficulties, one must understand that their social roles are in no way supported or made easy by the social policies that at least in small ways make female roles sustainable.

Is this merely an accidental glitch in the system, something that has happened unnoticed? Or does it have something to do with a sort of lifeboat ethic, where our scarce resources for helping people are applied according to the ethics of a sinking ship—women and children first, men into the sea?

I do not think so. Something else is at work: deep-seated prejudices and attitudes toward men that are so pervasive, so pandemic, that we have ceased to notice or examine them.

To put it simply: Men are neither supposed nor allowed to be dependent. They are expected to take care of both others *and* themselves. And when they cannot do it, or will not do it, the built-in assumption at the heart of the culture is that they are *less than men* and therefore unworthy of help. An irony asserts itself: simply by being in need of help, men forfeit the right to it.

Think here of how we say "helpless as a woman." This demeans women. But it also does violence to men. It implies that a man cannot be helpless and still be a man, or that helplessness is not a male attribute, or that a woman can be helpless through no fault of her own, but that if a man is helpless it must be his own fault.

Try something here. Imagine walking down a street and passing a group of homeless women. Do we not spontaneously see them as victims and wonder what has befallen them, how destiny has injured them? Do we not see them as unfortunate and deserving of help and therefore *want* to help them?

Now imagine a group of homeless men. Is our reaction the same? Is it as sympathetic? Or is it subtly different? Do we have the very same impulse to help and protect? Or do we not wonder, instead of what befell them, how they have gotten themselves where they are?

And remember, too, our fear. When most of us see homeless or idle men we sense or imagine danger; they make us afraid, as if, being beyond the pale, they are also beyond all social control—and therefore people to be avoided and suppressed rather than helped.

Here too work plays a crucial role. In his memoirs Hamlin Garland describes the transient farm workers who passed through the countryside each year at harvest time. In good years, when there were crops to bring in, they were tolerated: hired, housed, and fed. But when the crops were bad and men weren't needed, then they were forced to stay outside of town or pass on unaided, having become merely threats to peace and order, barbarians at the gates.

The same attitude is with us still. When men work (or when they go to war—work's most brutal form), we grant them a right to exist. But when work is scarce, or when men are of little economic use, then they become in our eyes not only superfluous but a danger. We feel compelled to exile them from our midst, banish them from view, drive them away to shift for themselves in more or less the same way that our Puritan forebears, in their shining city on its hill, treated sinners and rebels.

One wonders just how far back such attitudes go. One thinks of the Bible and the myth of the Garden and the first disobedience, when women were cursed with childbirth and men with the sorrows of labor—destinies still, as if by intention, maintained by our welfare system and private attitudes.

And one thinks too of the Victorian era, when the idealized vision of women and children had its modern beginnings. They were set outside the industrial nexus and freed from heavy labor while being rendered more than ever dependent on and subservient to men. It was a process that obviously diminished women, but it had a parallel effect on men. It defined them as laborers and little else, especially if they came from the lower classes. The yoke of labor lifted from the shoulders of women settled even more heavily on the backs of certain men, confining them to roles as narrow and as oppressive as those to which women were assigned.

We are so used to thinking of ours as a male-dominated society that we tend to lose track of the ways in which some men are as oppressed, or perhaps even more oppressed, than most women. But race and class, as well as gender, play roles in oppression. And while it is true, in general, that men dominate society and women, in practice it is only *certain* men who are dominant; others, usually those from the working class and often darker skinned (at least 50 percent of homeless men are black or Latino), suffer endlessly from forms of isolation and contempt that often match what many women experience.

The irony at work in all of this is that what you often find among homeless men, and what seems at the heart of their troubles, is precisely what our cultural myths deny them: a helplessness they cannot overcome on their own. You find vulnerability, a sense of injury and betrayal, and, in their isolation, a despair equal to what we accept without question in women.

Often this goes unadmitted. Even when in deep trouble men understand, sometimes unconsciously, that they are not to complain or ask for help. I remember several men I knew in the local hobo jungle. Most of them were vets. They had constructed a tiny village of trenches and dugouts and shelters among the trees and brush, and when stove smoke filled the clearing and they stood bare to the waist, knives at their hips, you would swear you were in a jungle army camp. They drank throughout the day, and at dusk there always came a moment when they wandered off individually to sit staring out at the mountains or sea. And you could see on their faces at such moments, if you caught them unawares, a particular and unforgettable look: pensive, troubled, somehow innocent—the look of lost children or abandoned men.

I have seen the same look multiplied hundreds of times on winter nights in huge shelters in great cities, where a thousand men at a time will sometimes gather, each encapsulated in solitude on a bare cot, coughing and turning or sometimes crying all night, lost in nightmares as terrible as a child's or as life on the street. In the mornings they returned to their masked public personas, to the styles of behavior and appearance that often frightened passersby. But while they slept you could see past all that, and you found yourself thinking: these are still, even grown, somebody's children, and many of them are no better at dealing with life, on their own and alone, than they would have been as children.

I remember, too, a young man in my town who was always in trouble for beating up older drunken men. No one understood his brutality until he explained it one day to a woman he trusted: "When I was a kid my daddy ran off and my mother's drunken brothers disciplined me. Whenever I made a mistake they punished me by slicing my legs with a straight razor." And he pulled up his pant legs to reveal on each shin a ladder of scars marking each childhood error or flaw.

This can stand for countless stories I've heard. The feeling you get, over and over, is that most men on the street have been orphaned in some way, deprived somewhere along the line of the kinds of connection, support, and sustenance that enable people to find and keep places in the social order. Of course economics plays a part in this—I do not mean to suggest it does not. But more often than not something else is also at work, something that cuts close to the bone of social, psychological, and economic issues: the dissolution of family structures and the vitiation of community; subtle and overt forms of discrimination and racism; and institutions—schools, for instance—that harm or marginalize almost as many people as they help.

For decades now, sociologists have called our attention to rents in our private social fabric as well as our public "safety nets," and to the victims they produce: abused kids, battered women, isolated adults, alcoholics, addicts. Why, I wonder, is it so hard to see homeless men in this context? Why is it so hard to understand that the machinery of our institutions can injure men as permanently as it does women? We know, for instance, that both male and female children are permanently injured by familial abuse and violence and the "normal" cruelties of family life. Why, then, do we find it hard to see that grown men, as well as women, can be crippled by childhood, or that they often end up on the edges of society, unable to play their expected roles in a world that long ago betrayed them?

And do not forget here the greatest violence done to men, the tyrannous demand made upon them when young by older and more powerful males: that they kill and die in war. We take this demand for granted in our society and for some reason fail to see it as a form of oppression. But why? Long before the war in Vietnam had crowded our streets with vets, as far back as the Civil War, the male victims of organized state violence wandered across America unable to find or make places in the social world. The fact is that many men never fully recover from the damage done by war, having seen too much of death to ever again do much with life.

Nor is war the only form in which death and disaster have altered the lives of troubled men. They appear repeatedly in the stories men tell. Listening to these tales one thinks of Oedipus and Lear, of tragedy in its classical sense, of the furies and fates that the Greeks believed stalk all human lives and that are still at work among us, no matter how much we may deny them.

Gene, a homeless man I know, was conceived when his mother slept with his father's best friend. Neither of his parents wanted him, so he was raised reluctantly by his mother's parents, who saw him only as the living evidence of their daughter's disgrace. As an adult he married and divorced twice, had two children he rarely saw later in life, and spent two years in jail for beating nearly to death a friend he found in bed with his second wife. When I first met him he was living in a cave he had dug by hand out of a hillside, and he spent the money he earned doing odd jobs on dope or his friends. But then he met a homeless woman on the streets and they moved together to a cheap hotel. He got her pregnant; they planned to marry; but then they argued and she ran off and either had an abortion or spontaneously miscarried—it was never clear which. When Gene heard about it he took to his bed for days and would not sleep, eat, or speak. When I later asked him why, he said: "I couldn't stand it. I wanted to die. I was the baby she killed. It was happening to me all over again, that bad stuff back when I was a kid."

Not everything you hear on the street is so dramatic. There are a thousand quiet and gradual ways American lives can fall apart or come to nothing. Often it is simply ordinary life that proves too much for men. Some have merely failed at or fled their assigned roles: worker, husband, father. Others lacked whatever it takes to please a boss or a woman or else decided it wasn't worth the trouble to learn how to do it. Not all of them are "good" men. Some have brutalized women or left families in the lurch or fled lives in which the responsibility and stress were more than they could handle. "Couldn't hack it," they'll say with a shrug, or "I had to get out." And others have been so cruel to women or proved so unreliable or sometimes so unsuccessful that women have fled them, leaving notes on the table or stuck to the refrigerator, such as the one a man in Seattle once repeated to me: "Gone. Took the kids. So long."

Are such men irresponsible? Perhaps. But in working with homeless men over the years, I've learned that many of them are genuinely unable to handle the stress others can tolerate. Many manage, for instance, to steer clear of alcohol or drugs for a certain period of time but then return to them automatically as soon as they are subject again to the kinds of stress they once fled. It is as if their defenses and even their skins are so much thinner than those of the rest of us that they give way as soon as trouble or too much responsibility appears.

The fact is that most such men seem to have tried as best they can to make a go of things, and many are willing to try again. But if others have given up and said, inside, *the hell with it* or *fuck it,* is that really astonishing? The curious society we've compounded in America out of equal parts of freedom and isolation and individualism and demands for obedience and submission is a strange and wearing mix, and no one can be startled at the number of victims or recalcitrants it produces.

Finally, I must add one more thing. Whatever particular griefs men may have experienced on their way to homelessness, there is one final and crippling sorrow all of them share: a sense of betrayal at society's refusal to recognize their needs. Most of us—men and women—grow up expecting that when things go terribly wrong someone, from somewhere, will step forward to help us. That this does not happen, and that all watch from the shore as each of us, in isolation, struggles to swim and then begins to sink, is perhaps the most terrible discovery that anyone in any society can make. When troubled men make that discovery, as all homeless men do sooner or later, then hope vanishes completely; despair rings them round; they have become what they need not have become: the homeless men we see everywhere around us.

What can be done about this? What will set it right? One can talk, of course, about confronting the root causes of marginalization: the failure of families, schools, and communities; the stupidities of war, racism, and discrimination; social and economic injustice; the disappearance of generosity and reciprocity among us. But what good will that do? America is what it is; culture has a tenacity of its own; and though it is easy to call for major kinds of renewal, nothing of the sort is likely to occur.

That leaves us with ameliorative and practical measures, and it will do no harm to mention them, though they too are not likely to be tried: a further reformation of the welfare system; the federalization of assistance to single adults; increases in the amount and duration of unemployment insurance; further raises in the minimum wage; expanded benefits for vets; detox centers and vocational education for those who want them; the construction of the kinds of low-cost hotels and boarding houses where men in trouble once lived.

And remember that back in the Depression when the welfare system was established, it was paralleled by programs providing work for men: the Civilian Conservation Corps and the Works

Progress Administration. The idea seems to have been welfare for women, work for men. We still have the welfare for women, but where is the work for those men, or women, who want it? Why no one is currently lobbying for contemporary forms of those old programs remains a mystery. Given the deterioration of the American infrastructure—roads, bridges, public buildings—such programs would make sense from any point of view.

But beyond all this, and behind and beneath it, there remains the problem with which we began: the prejudices at work in society that prevent even the attempt to provide solutions. Suggestions such as those I have made will remain merely utopian notions without an examination and renovation of our attitudes toward men. During the past several decades we have slowly, laboriously, begun to confront our prejudices and oppressive practices in relation to women. Unless we now undertake the same kind of project in relation to men in general and homeless men in particular, nothing whatsoever is going to change. That's as sure as death and taxes and the endless, hidden sorrows of men.

VIRGINIA'S STORY

MICHAEL HARRINGTON once wrote that one ought not to talk about "poverty" but about *poverties*. He meant there are so many ways of being poor that no single description or analysis can apply to them all. The same thing is true of homelessness. There are in actuality a variety of *homelessnesses*, each one very different from the others in terms of causes, particulars, and solutions.

What I mean to do here is examine a particular kind of homelessness, one that has gotten less attention than it deserves: a sporadic and recurrent homelessness so much a part of the cycle of poverty in which some people find themselves that it becomes a predictable and "normal" part of their lives.

Ordinarily we think of homelessness as either the result of a long downward slide (as with alcoholics, for example) or as the result of a cataclysmic event—catastrophic illness, mental collapse, the sudden loss of a job or a home. In both cases homelessness seems like a sudden and forced exile, almost a falling off the earth, something that takes people beyond our ordinary social or economic orders and into another alien reality.

But there is another kind of homelessness, one that many poor people learn to take almost for granted. It's a part of our social and economic orders, part of the poverty which takes people, in a seemingly endless round, in and out of homelessness: from low paying jobs to unemployment to shelters to the street to welfare to low paying jobs and eventually, once again, to unemployment and the street.

I want to examine that form of homelessness by writing about a young African-American woman named Virginia I met several years ago in New Orleans. She was then twenty-one, with two young children, and she had just gotten out of a shelter after being homeless for a year. In the time that I've known her she's been homeless three times, and when she hasn't been homeless she's been so close to its edge that it took only the slightest mishap or misstep to render her homeless again.

There is another reason, too, I want to write about Virginia. For several years now homeless advocates have concentrated on the absence of affordable housing or low wages as the main causes of homelessness. But there is far more to most kinds of homelessness than that. If you carefully examine them, you find at work psychological, social, and cultural factors as well as economic ones. And it is only in that larger context that you can understand what homelessness involves, or how and why people become homeless.

Is Virginia's case typical? I don't know. The statistics we have about homelessness don't usually tell us precisely how long or how often particular people are homeless. But I do know this: Virginia is an African-American, and close to 50 percent of the homeless population (more, in large cities) is now African-American. And Virginia is a young single mother without skills, prospects, or a mate, and a preponderant portion of the families now on our streets or on welfare are headed by women in similar circumstances.

I first met Virginia when I went to New Orleans to talk about homelessness at a conference of city administrators. I asked a local homeless advocate to suggest a couple of people who could come to the conference and talk about their own lives. One of them turned out to be Virginia, who was then in a short-term church-run program for homeless mothers in which she'd been given an apartment for three months and help in looking for a job.

I know enough about black-white relations in the South to un-derstand the guardedness and masking that goes on, so my sense of Virginia is largely limited by what she let me see, but I liked her from the start. She was tall and slim with a soft face and high cheekbones and her hair cut boyishly short. There was both gen-tleness and directness in her manner, and a kind of shy diffidence, and she seemed, as do many young black women in the South when faced with whites, to draw her voice—and her whole being too—inward with her breath as she spoke, so that you felt yourself leaning forward, straining to hear, even when you heard her words clearly.

The audience at the conference liked her too. She described her life without self-pity or complaint. Facts followed facts; she didn't editorialize; and as she went on speaking, describing what it was like to live in shelters or walk the streets all day with children, the people listening were quite moved—far more moved, I suspect, by her sorrowful self-possession than they would have been by some-thing more openly desperate or dramatic.

When I went back home to California, Virginia and I kept in touch. Whenever she was in financial difficulty she'd call and I'd wire what money I could. I'd been well-paid for my lecture and Virginia had gotten much less and it seemed only right to send her what she needed until I'd exhausted my fee. Week after week, month after month, I followed, long-distance, the twists and turns of her fortunes. Whenever I went back to New Orleans, I would see her and we'd talk, and then, last summer, when I returned there again to write at length about women who were homeless or on welfare, I had a chance to see, close up, Virginia's struggle to get by.

It doesn't take long, looking at the economic details of that struggle, to understand why Virginia slipped so often into home-lessness. Her welfare payments were $190 per month—that's what the state of Louisiana gives to a woman with two children. With one child, you get $169. With three, you get about $235. For every other child your check increases by about $50, but the total is clearly never enough to lift you out of the most abject kind of poverty.

Measure Virginia's payment against her expenses. When the church program ended she stayed on in her apartment at a cost of $150 a month. Her utilities came to $100. A telephone was a necessity, both for looking for work and sustaining a social world. That was another $30 or so, at a minimum. Food stamps provided her food, but even so the basic expenses I've mentioned came to $280 a month, and she was $90 *behind* before spending a penny on clothing, toys, or transportation.

Virginia looked for work but all she could find were part-time, split-shift jobs at fast-food outlets for minimum wage. Employers in New Orleans, like employers everywhere, prefer part-time and split-shift workers because that keeps the cost of benefits low and means you don't have to pay overtime wages. Say Virginia worked 20 hours a week for $3.35 an hour. That's $60 a week in take-home pay. But she had to pay someone to watch her children, and when you deduct that from her pay and throw in the cost of transportation—$10 a week—you can see that the kind of work she could find didn't much help her at all.

And then there are the welfare regulations. The federal government requires that any money you make be reported to the welfare office so that an equal amount can be deducted from your next monthly check. That means that for every dollar you make, regardless of expenses, you *lose* a dollar, so you're left, always, in the same sorry predicament. And if you don't report your earnings—as sometimes Virginia did not—then you are, according to the law, guilty of fraud.

What happened to Virginia was predictable and inevitable. She fell further and further behind on her bills. First the telephone was disconnected; then her utilities were cut off. Finally, she stopped paying the rent altogether and was evicted. Homeless again, she went back to the emergency shelter she'd been in before she entered the church program. For several months she looked without success for work. And then finally, reluctantly, she chose the only option open to her and did what almost everyone on welfare in New Orleans ends up doing: she put her name down on the waiting list for an apartment in the city's "projects" and took the first one that became available.

Let me describe the projects. There are about a dozen of them scattered throughout New Orleans: huge federally-funded housing developments built in the thirties and forties and now administered by the city. Official estimates put the number of people in the projects at 55,000, almost all of them black, most of them on welfare. But homeless advocates and grass roots leaders estimate that when you add in illegal residents and doubled-up families you get a total closer to 75,000 or even 90,000—and that, if correct, would be close to 25 percent of the city's 330,000 black inhabitants.

I've seen old picture postcards of the projects as they were when first built after the war for the returning vets: neat lawns and tidy two- and three-story brick buildings surrounded by trees, streetlamps, and wrought-iron benches. These days they are dusty and rundown wastelands largely ignored by the city government which administers them. In some projects a third of the apartments are gutted and abandoned; everywhere there are drugs and guns; violence is commonplace and at night you often hear gunfire. When Virginia lived in the projects she kept her windows boarded up so the gangs wouldn't bother her, and she never let the children play outside. "Minute I'd let them out," she said, "I'd hear shootin' and they come runnin' inside. I always told them to git down low and don't be scared."

Life in the projects is the meanest possible kind of life. The only reason for moving in is economic, and once you're there it isn't easy to get out. Look again at the figures and you see why. Rents in the projects are geared to income, and Virginia's apartment, utilities

included, cost her $60 a month. Figure, again, $30 for a phone.
Assume that food stamps provide food. That leaves $25 a week for
all other expenses. That isn't much, but it is more than you'd have
living outside the projects. And if you teach yourself to need little
and expect nothing, you can last forever in the projects, impoverished and in constant danger, but at least not homeless.

But Virginia didn't last. She missed a couple of welfare appoint-
ments and her checks stopped coming. She didn't pay the rent and
again she was evicted. Homeless once more, she moved in with a
friend, an older woman whose one-bedroom apartment was paid
for by a lover. Virginia and the boys slept on a fold-out couch in
the living room and got all of their meals, in return for which
Virginia gave her now-restored welfare checks to her friend. It
was, she told me later, like being a prisoner. But even that didn't
last. The lover grew tired of Virginia's presence and so her friend
asked her to leave.

It is easy to see how Virginia was checked at every turn by economic factors beyond her control, the ones we've grown used to
pointing out when talking about the homeless: rents she couldn't
afford, jobs she couldn't find, and welfare payments so low, so close
to the bone of her needs, that any false step, any single miscalcula-
tion, could plunge her back into homelessness.

And yet, for all that, there is another and equally important side
to Virginia's story, one that reveals not only something about
Virginia herself, or about what else is involved in homelessness,
but also something about America: the nature of the age and society we inhabit, the crosscurrents of social and cultural life which
sometimes catch people up and sweep through their lives and set
them down so far from any hope for order, so distant from a sense
of power or belonging, that homelessness becomes all but inevitable. The easiest way to explain what I mean is to describe

Virginia's early life: her childhood and adolescent experience, and then the particularities of the social and cultural world she inhabits as an adult.

She grew up in New Orleans when the city—to hear Virginia and many others tell it—was far more prosperous, neighborly, and orderly than it is now. The black neighborhoods were thriving, whites had not yet fled the city for the suburbs, and both inexpensive housing and decent jobs were much easier to come by than they presently are.

Virginia had four sisters, two brothers, a mother who took good care of them, and a father who drank a bit too much but worked steadily on the docks as a foreman and had managed to buy a small house. But when Virginia was seven years old her world fell apart. Her mother died. Her father's drinking increased. Her two older sisters and a brother left the house. At eleven, she was left more or less alone in the house with a younger brother and sister. "My daddy was gone all the time," she says. "We was in the house by ourselfs many a night. We never knew where he was cause he didn't want us knowin' his business."

Then Virginia's father was shot and wounded in a bar by a jealous woman. He lost his job and vanished, perpetually drunk, on the streets of the city. The house was sold at auction and Virginia and the other two children moved in with an older sister who had joined the Army. She sent Virginia to a Catholic day school and Virginia's oldest brother became her surrogate father. And then the brother was shot five times and killed in a barroom brawl over a woman.

Virginia nonetheless managed to graduate from high school, but in her senior year she fell in love with a boy and got pregnant. She had the baby after finishing school and stayed on with her sister. Then she met another man and got pregnant again. Neither of the men could take care of her; neither wanted to marry her. Both went off, but Virginia shows no anger when she talks about them: "I don't bear them no grudge in my mind."

Of the first one, she says: "He tried. He wanted to be a man. But he couldn't find no job or nothin'. He got discouraged and got hisself in trouble. I think he was misled to wrongness."

Of the second, she says: "He never had no chance. He grew up in the projects not carin' about anything. That was his lifestyle. Now he got another baby by a woman younger than me."

When I ask about birth control, she says: "See, when you're just startin' out you don't know what you do now. I was only nineteen, and I was a good girl, and my sister, she kept all that stuff quiet."

When Virginia had her second child her sister told her she couldn't take care of her anymore. Virginia went to a Salvation Army shelter and then, after several months, into the church program she was in when I met her.

There's little in Virginia's story that is unusual—not at least in terms of the stories I heard in New Orleans from other women. All of their stories contained many of the same elements: early pregnancies; men drifting in and out; no preparation for work or the world; little family support; and, perhaps most importantly, personal tragedies and traumas that destroyed an orderly world or deprived women of what they needed to survive.

I recall a thirty-five-year-old woman in the projects named Lobelia who had eight children by six different men. She was tough and outwardly cheerful and had been hooked twice on drugs but was clean when I met her and trying hard to replace crack with Jesus. She had a 20-inch scar on her thigh from a recent fight with a neighbor over a man, and she wouldn't, she told me, let any male visitor into the house unless he brought whiskey, food, or money. "I ain't no whore," she said.

I didn't quite know what to make of her until she told me one day that her father had died when she was thirteen. "I went so wild with grief," she said, "there wasn't no controlling me. My mama had the doctor declare me crazy and they put me away for a year."

When she was released she started having sex and then children and soon her mother would have nothing to do with her, and so she went from one relative to another until there were none left to help her, and then, homeless and on welfare, she went into the projects.

Mixed in with economic troubles are these other difficulties: sorrows of the heart and grievances of the soul which isolate men and women and make it impossible for them to order their lives or make sense of the world. Is this a surprise? Jack London, long ago, in *People of the Abyss,* perhaps the best book ever written about the poor, speculated that in a competitive and individualized economic system those who failed soonest were those without the energy and will, as well as the means, to survive. What I'm saying here is delicately different: that those who have the hardest time surviving are neither the weakest nor the worst but often those with the least sense of human connectedness, the most broken relations, the strongest senses of betrayal: the wounded, the abused, the abandoned, the excluded, and all those who cannot on their own discover how to fit into the world or even the reason for trying. I remember once asking Virginia what she most wanted in the world. I expected her to say something about money or a house or a job or a man. Instead she said, in a voice so soft I had to bend to hear: "I want my Momma to be livin.' "

Almost all of the women I spoke to in New Orleans had two or sometimes three sets of children by different men, nearly all of them born outside of marriage. Most women had their first children in their middle or late teens, often with men they say they loved. For both religious and cultural reasons, birth control isn't much talked about or used; abortion hasn't much appeal; and since most of the young men involved are without money, jobs, skills, or prospects, going on welfare is, for most of the women, the only feasible choice.

Here too, one must remember, welfare regulations play a role. For decades family aid has gone only to those households where women and children lived without men. Where men are present—even husbands and natural fathers—no aid is given. Precisely how much effect this has had on family life in poor communities has not, in so far as I know, been documented. But the regulations tend to nullify or destroy whatever romantic or moral impulses men and women may have had to stay together.

Once on welfare and in the projects, women are almost like hostages: bored, tied down by children, isolated from the larger world, and with little hope of changing their lives. They become stationary targets for disenfranchised men for whom sex is an anodyne and a consolation and a way of proving one's worth or simply, in a very direct fashion, that one *exists*. Out of boredom and the human need for company, attention, and pleasure, more children are born. And one must remember, too, that children in the black South, and especially among the poor, seem to have an absolute value unrelated to economic questions. Many black women come from large families—five children, often more. Family is central to their view of the world; children *create* that world, create the order and meaning in it.

I remember a conversation I had with Tanya, a young woman in her late twenties who was a second-generation project dweller. She had three children by two different men friends. One of them, a daughter, was still a nursing infant. Now she was pregnant again. The father was a man she hardly knew and didn't like, and she had slept with him while drunk and without precautions, believing— as do many women in the South—that she couldn't conceive as long as she kept suckling the child. "It wasn't quite rape," she said. "I just lay there, not ready, not caring. But I didn't bother to say no."

Still, she could not bring herself to have an abortion. She'd gone twice to a birth control clinic intending to get one, but she couldn't go through with it. And then her own doctor let her listen to the fetal heartbeat with a stethoscope. After that, she said, "I couldn't do nothing. It was like my own heart I heard." And then she sat there, musing, and asked me, "Would someone like you like me if I had an abortion? Do you think God would like me?"

A few days later I talked with Jeannine, whose father was a school teacher. She had wanted to be a journalist. But in her first year at college she fell in love and got pregnant and now she has four children by two different fathers. She had recently had an abortion. "You know," she said, "I hate my life. I hate myself for wasting it. I once tried to give the kids away for adoption. But the very worst time in my life was when I had an abortion. I didn't want the baby. I knew I shouldn't have it. But afterwards, when I came back, that's when I tried to kill myself."

Religion? Tradition? The fear of God? The inherited, oppressive, and patriarchal notion of women merely as mothers, as breeders? I don't know. Perhaps. Certainly, at times, talking to these women, I had a sense that they were trapped in roles and traditions they've inherited rather than chosen. And yet these families, which echo the large families from which these women come, provide at least some sense of connection to the past, to a culture, some sense of purpose and location in troubled lives which might otherwise be too empty and crimped to bear.

I remember a conversation I had with Tanya's two older children—a boy of ten, a girl of eight. They told me that between them they had two real daddies and considered Tanya's present boyfriend to be a third. They felt that all of their daddies' other children by other women were their brothers and sisters—eight in all, they said, toting it up on their fingers, trying, several times, to get all the names in the right sequence. And some of the mothers of their daddies' other children had become their surrogate aunts, and the children of those women in turn, by still other men, were, they thought, like cousins—all part of a haphazard web extending outward and endlessly expanded by the formation of new sexual liaisons and the making of new babies.

Within this network relationships were not always determined by biology. Tanya's son, for instance, felt closer to his sister's natural father than he did to his own dad. And the sister, in turn, spent much of her time at the house of her brother's daddy's new girl-friend, who, she explained, she had started to love.

Hard to follow? Too unfamiliar? It's true that when I asked Tanya's children if they wouldn't have preferred their real fathers present all the time they nodded yes in unison. But nonetheless these families, odd as they may be, sometimes *work*. They are not simply the evidence of the collapse of what we think of as "nor-mal" family life, they are also a necessary variation of it: a system of connections, established through sex and procreation, that act as a buffer against loneliness and create not only a meaning for life but also a social world, a human world. Seen from one angle they obvi-ously reveal the difficulties people have in creating order around themselves; seen from another they are a way of *making* order, a way of making lives.

And there are two other crucial elements at work in Virginia's life that must be mentioned here: the racism that surrounds her and the whole question of culture, the choices presented to her in terms of who she is and how she can survive. I link the two to-gether because it isn't easy to separate them in the South. There are, for instance, certain aspects of behavior or sets of values to which African-Americans in the South, and especially in the proj-ects, seem to cling: language, music, large and extended families, and the idea of children as a good in themselves. But since those in the projects are ringed round by a still-racist society, prevented in most ways from becoming free and equal in the larger society, there is no way of telling precisely which aspects of their own culture they would keep or leave behind if they were free to choose. Given that, one can only give a rough indication of how both are at work in lives like Virginia's: a culture that partially sustains her and a pervasive racism that forces her into a closed and unhappy world.

Talk to Virginia about this and she stays pretty mum. These are not things you discuss with white people. But I know how wary Virginia is when she and I walk downtown or sit together in a restaurant. She wants it to be perfectly clear to people there's nothing romantic or freely sexual between us; but she's also worried that people will think she's a whore and that there is merely business involved. Black and white don't usually mix in New Orleans, and certainly not two by two. No matter what the law of the land says, every black person in New Orleans, or in the entire South for that matter, or maybe in all America, knows there remain two separate worlds and a set of invisible passbook rules nowhere written down but everywhere in effect.

How much does all of this enter into Virginia's troubles? I cannot say. But surely it is not surprising if she often acts ineffectively or without aggressiveness in a world which is still, as she understands it, off limits to her. She is expected somehow, all on her own, to succeed in a world from which she was systematically excluded as a child, and in which, in her mind, she has no place.

What about rage? About this subject, too, Virginia remains self-protectively silent, though it would hardly be surprising if, behind her prudent demeanor, she felt a cumulative fury with white welfare workers, white shelter providers, white employers, white apartment managers and, yes, with me—a white man supposedly an expert, (at a properly safe distance) on a world she experiences every day.

There is, too, the whole question of culture. Debates about African-American culture rage everywhere around us, and black men and women are faced with agonizing choices pertaining to the larger culture and their own traditions: how much to embrace, how much to cast away, how to mediate between their needs for a culture and the sense that it must be discarded if they are to succeed. There's a growing sense in some African-American intellectual and academic circles that the trade-offs required of those who want to find places in mainstream America may well be a bad bargain, and that the gains to be had are matched by what is lost in terms of identity, community, and a sense of the past.

For most black Americans a terrible tension exists that is not unlike the familiar agony of Native Americans. For the pull of the past *is* there, especially in the South, where some of the sustaining traditions of black culture remain at least partially intact. There's a whole world in the projects which outsiders cannot enter, but you can sense it from a distance. It's there in the speech: a patois so private, so dense, that it is like listening to a foreign language. It's there, too, in the music, in the systems of kinship, in the perception of time and space, in attitudes towards pleasure, work, leisure, and community. And it's there, still, in the astonishing capacity for generosity and sweetness, in the residual passion for relationship rather than competition, in a system of values that somehow raises life itself to a crowning position unchallenged by success or accumulation. Obviously, the culture I'm describing is in disarray. Most of those who maintain it do so in part because they have little choice. But if they hold tight to it, unwilling to let it go, that's natural enough. There's something so joyless and pained about the society we expect people to enter that one can easily understand why—in cultural if not economic terms—some men and women are reluctant to enter it, or to trade away what little they have for the little we offer in return.

Much of this applies to Virginia. It's in her background and it exists side by side with the more obvious issues of rents and wages. Erik Erikson, writing about Martin Luther, once argued that certain great men were culturally significant because they were forced to resolve in themselves deep-seated and schismatic cultural crises. The same can be said of more ordinary people—Virginia, for instance, though in her life, as in others, it is failure rather than success that we see, as if some people suffer in themselves cultural crises they cannot, on their own, resolve or heal.

But Virginia, of course, has not failed yet. Her story so far has neither an unhappy nor a happy ending. I go back now to where she was when I first saw her last summer, on the living room couch at her friend's apartment, about to leave and with nowhere to go.

Had I not been there she might have been homeless again. But she had one welfare check in hand and asked me for a loan of $200. With the total, she said, she'd be able to move into an apartment. I tried to tell here there was no point in it, that even if she got a place she couldn't keep up the rent payments and would be out on the street in two months. "I don't care," she said. "I ain't goin' back to the shelter. And I got a feelin' this time that somethin' good is gonna happen."

One Sunday with newspaper in hand we went hunting for apartments. Virginia wanted to get as far away from the projects as possible, so we drove out to an area known as East New Orleans on the city's edge. Only a few years ago developers moved into what was rural territory and began building housing developments and apartment complexes for an anticipated invasion of babyboomers that never materialized. Now the rents are low and the apartments are filled with people usually down on their luck, and there are still open spaces and stands of trees and, at twilight, a whole host of country smells, though it is only twenty minutes by bus—"a straight shot," says Virginia—to downtown New Orleans.

We had only to look at two places before Virginia found what she wanted: a rather dingy one-bedroom apartment in a colonial-style complex with a brimming but dirty pool, a laundry room, and both black and white tenants. The ad in the paper had said something about moving in for $199, but Virginia talked to the manager alone and when she emerged she had handed over $400—$235 for the first month's rent and the rest, he had explained to her mysteriously, for "one-time unrefundable charges."

The apartment was on the first floor, out on the edge of the complex where the blacks were put. It had a glass door in the living room that slid open to a swampy common that once was a lawn. The whole place smelled of mildew and mold and you could see its presence on the wall for a couple of speckled feet above the damp shag carpet. But Virginia loved it. It was the nicest place she'd lived in, she said, "since my daddy's house." The manager who had overcharged her took a liking to her—it was the South, after all—and dragged out of storage an old box spring and two torn high-backed velvet chairs and a lopsided table that non-paying tenants had left behind. Said Virginia happily: "It's mine, my own, my first real home."

And then, to my surprise, suddenly something good *did* happen. Virginia had a friend who worked as a maid at a downtown hotel, and for more than a year she had called the hotel every few weeks to see if there was a job for her. Three days after she moved into the apartment she called again and they told her yes, if she'd come in the next day to be interviewed, they would put her to work.

Within a week she had a steady job and had found someone to watch her children. It was a good job as such jobs go. The hotel was locally owned and the owners treated their employees in a familial way. The pay was close to $5 an hour and there were scheduled raises and a health plan and a credit union and even below-cost hot lunches in the employee cafeteria. It was clear, Virginia told me, that if you did your work and showed up on time, you could stay there a lifetime. "You're gonna have to show me," she said, "how to open a bank account and write checks and *save*. I never done it before."

But there was one small hitch. The hours and pay weren't steady. In the winter when the hotel was full Virginia might work seven hours a day, six days a week—forty-two hours in all. But in the summer when the flow of tourists slowed, she might work only three or four days a week, and only five or six hours a day.

Now, for the last time, look at the figures. During the busy season Virginia can take home perhaps $700 a month. Measured against her expenses that doesn't work out badly: $235 for rent, $100 for utilities, $30 for the phone, $30 for transportation to work, $25 for hot lunches—it comes to $430 or so a month. Because of her earnings she won't get food stamps, but that still leaves her about $65 a week for food, clothing, toys, etc. Maybe if she's disciplined and lucky she will, as she said, be able to save.

But what happens when things slow down? Figure four days one week, three the next, say fifteen days a month, maybe six hours a day. That's about $400 a month in take-home pay, not quite enough to cover all her expenses, though they'll be slightly lower. She'll get some food stamps if she reapplies for them every time her income dips. But what about other expenses? Under such circumstances it isn't hard to imagine what will happen, just as it's happened before. She'll fall behind; the phone will be cut off; the lights will go; there'll be a monthly struggle to come up with the rent, and when she fails to do it, the eviction notices will start, and sooner or later she'll be homeless again.

That hasn't happened yet. Virginia still calls, though less often than she once did, and less in need of money than of the sense that somebody, somewhere cares what happens to her. But she's having trouble making do. The tourist season is over and she's working less—four days in two of the last three weeks, she told me. She has a bit of money saved up and the manager of her complex tries to give her odd jobs around the place, but what she really needs in order to survive is what nobody poor in America gets: a loan to tide her over, or welfare money to supplement her salary, or some kind of grant so that she can learn to do something else.

What comes to my mind when she calls is an image I first had years ago, during the period when she was in the projects. She'd called me up back then in despair, at the end of her rope. She didn't want money. She'd asked for something else. "Kin we come live with you," she said. "Kin we come live with you?"

I said no, I was sorry, and I sent her some more money, and the image which came to me then and is with me still was from *Moby Dick*, when, at the end of the book, the *Pequod* sinks beneath the waves, and the crew, made up of members of every imaginable oppressed and immigrant race, is sacrificed to mad Ahab's will and rage. I kept imagining Virginia among them, calling out from the sea as her head goes under: "Kin we come live with you?"

Maybe that's overly dramatic. After all, Virginia is still afloat. And maybe, just maybe, since homelessness is such a "natural" part of her life, it isn't in her mind quite like going under forever, but is, instead, simply a way of getting from one stage of poverty to another.

But I'm not certain of any of this. Virginia keeps her sorrows hidden, and I've never seen the full depth of the desperation she feels. How long can she keep it up? How long before exhaustion or hopelessness wear her down; or before she begins to solace herself with alcohol or drugs or sex; or before, with a sigh, she slips back into the stasis and safety of welfare and the projects? And what about Virginia's children? What's the cost to them of all of this? What happens to them if she becomes homeless again or decides to seek permanent refuge in the projects?

So the image of sinking persists: Virginia, along with millions of others, caught in the swirling currents of different kinds of poverty and homelessness, each of them on their own, but joined together in the downward spiral of their fates. The modern equivalent of Ahab's madness is all around us, spelled out for us in the ghettoes and projects of America. Economics? Of course. Wages and rents? Obviously. But the crisis goes so much deeper, and the wounds are so much more varied, it would take another Melville to reveal them all.

FREEDOM & ITS DISCONTENTS

Author's note: *What follows here is from a work in progress. I've spent the last year or two in the attempt to think through, almost from scratch, certain notions I've long held about culture, order, freedom and, in particular, morality and ethics. What concerns me is the present state of the freedom we've fought for, and what we've made of it, or how we've fallen far short of the grand moral ideals or hopes with which we began. What follows is meant to sum up or explain many of the themes in the earlier work which appears here; but it is also an attempt to push those themes forward, to see where they lead if followed to their end and to put them together in a way that raises certain insights and notions in the earlier work to the level of principles.*

I

I WANT to write about secularism here, about the secular traditions of thought to which we are heirs in America, and especially about the contemporary condition of secularism: the present state of the high ideals and moral and social visions which have fueled secularism from the Enlightenment onward but now seem, if seen clearly, rather suspect and played out, a residue of the past rather than a vision for the future.

I write as a secularist, as a man brought up believing in the secular tradition, and especially in the notion that social visions, systems of meaning, and codes of individual behavior can be constructed on entirely secular terms, without reference to anything beyond the human mind and heart—not God, not God's wishes or laws, and certainly not the wishes or laws of those who presume to speak in God's name.

I should make clear why I talk about secularism rather than humanism. Humanism can be summed up as the notion—I will use Orwell's simple phrase here—that "Man is the measure of all things and that our job is to make life worth living on this earth, which is the only earth we have." But what I mean by secularism is something slightly more specific and has to do with morality, with ethics: the belief, the assumption, the assertion that the sources, ends, and means of human meaning and moral value can be derived from and sustained by a purely human frame of reference.

And by secularism I mean, in addition, the tradition most of us in America who are intellectuals or academics have inherited: a way of reading history, society, and human nature; a profound respect for reason; and a deep skepticism of all the religious traditions which presume to define good and evil in terms of the will of God. And I mean, too, the systems of value at work among us, our belief in public and civil institutions as adequate bases for morality, and beyond all that, the dominant notions of human nature, rights, and freedoms we take so much for granted that we see every deviation from them, especially those made in the name of faith or God, as reactionary and retrograde, a part of the past we must overcome.

I will argue here that something has gone radically wrong with secularism, and that what's gone wrong may not, in fact, be inherent in secularism itself but is instead rooted in *what we have made of it,* in what we have brought to it as Americans: a set of attitudes and needs and a kind of moral naiveté which reveals more about our nature as Americans than it does about secularism itself.

I've intentionally taken my title from Freud's *Civilization And Its Discontents.* Two of its main points seem to bear directly on modern secularism, and I want, briefly, to examine them here. The first has to do with the nature of civilization itself: the demands it puts upon the individual psyche and its cost to individuals in terms of happiness or satisfaction. Freud sees the tension between the order of civilization and individual instinct as fundamental, inescapable. Order depends, he argues, on the sublimation of instinct and desire, on the ability of civilization to repress, control, and redirect all of the energies in the individual striving for satisfaction or free expression. The price we pay for the safety and order offered us by civilization is the happiness we might otherwise have gained from instinctual satisfaction, and we are therefore more or less doomed, within all civilizations, to lives of manageable unhappiness. No matter how passionately we dream of true freedom, full instinctual gratification, or the complete expression of our powers, the hidden dynamics of civilization make these impossible—imaginable, of course, but never attainable.

This view lies at the very heart of Freud's vision. It was, in part, a response to the violence and irrationality he saw at work everywhere around him in the early part of the twentieth century: his attempt to come to terms with what it is that leads men endlessly away from rationality and towards destructiveness. And it lies, too, close to the heart of Freud's belief in the *heroism* of reason—the courage he believed must be marshaled among us to lead rational lives within a system of order that prevents all but ameliorative and partial forms of satisfaction, joy, or freedom.

This view leads, too, directly to the second of Freud's notions I want to discuss here: his notion of religion as an illusion, a retreat from truth, a self-deluded attempt to escape our inevitable human destinies. The order and meaning religion offers—its consolations, its promise of absolution and redemption, its assurance of grace and heaven and an ultimate and triumphant joy—all of that, according to Freud, is merely an expression of superstition, of yearning, of a series of orchestrated illusions meant to protect us from the truth of civilized life or the demands of reason. Thus for Freud the great work of modern life is the heroic struggle to leave such myths behind, to come to honest terms with the conditions of our lives, to learn to live with the reality of our natures, powers, and pains, and thereby, in the end, release ourselves from the illusions and hapless yearnings which prevent us from seeing the world clearly or inhabiting it well.

Freud's view of religion can stand in general for the standard secular view of religion, a view which runs all the way back to the Enlightenment and has marked almost all secular thought since then. The great dream at the heart of secularism has always been that religion would slowly wither away, giving way, as it did so, to reason and a generosity of spirit or a morality rooted not in a fear of God or the hope of heaven, but in a sense of community and a belief in the common good. The fear and fanaticism engendered by faith would gradually be replaced by a maturity of vision, an understanding of self, and an ethical complexity that would leave behind, as part of the infantile past, the illusions, fantasies, and superstitions which had marked the childhood of man. The religious divisions and hatred separating us one from another would disappear, and the senses of gratitude, awe and indebtedness traditionally felt for God would be transferred to the human world and relocated in a universalized community. Values would no longer be enforced or maintained through oppression or fear, but instead would rise naturally and directly from human reason, instinct, and sympathy. Men and women would give freely to one another what had once been demanded by God.

I think I've put that fairly. These are the attitudes which have dominated secular thought in America from its beginnings, and they have certainly defined and produced the perception of religion which marks even now most of America's intellectual and cultural life. Of course these days many among us talk about "senses of the sacred" and the need for myth; the "new age" has reintroduced to common realms of discourse all kinds of beliefs and illusions that are beyond the grasp of science or reason. But little of this has changed the ways secularists think about traditional or organized religion, and none of it has anything whatsoever to do with our secular ideas about how value and meaning are to be formed and maintained. In this regard, whatever their other differences, most secularists remain squarely aligned with Enlightenment belief: the childishness of religion must give way to a more worldly wisdom, one derived from both experience and reason.

This brings us back, again, to Freud's notions about civilization, his belief that a true wisdom or a mature rationality will also, by its very nature, involve a tragic or stoic recognition of the costs of civilization, an awareness of the shadow cast always upon us by *Thanatos* or death, by the ineradicable human capacity for destruction and self-destruction.

Immediately an irony asserts itself, for this aspect of Freud's thought—his critique of religion, so central to his beliefs—is precisely the part denied by American secularists. Oh yes, of course: secularism is largely Freudian in its attitudes; but the Freudianism it has embraced is a mediated Freudianism, a revisionist Freudianism, one modified by men like Wilhelm Reich and Erich Fromm and Norman O. Brown and Herbert Marcuse, all of whom argued, in one way or another, that civilization and freedom and the lifting of repression and the denial of the past would involve few risks, would simply allow us to leave pain behind and find, in reason and experience, the joy denied us by religion. To see life as dark, or as essentially tragic, is, by its very nature, un-American, and so we have quite readily, as American secularists, greedily latched on to everything that allows us to deny the darker vision offered us by Freud. Our *true* natures, the ones denied by the limits of culture and to be reclaimed through reason, have always appeared to us only good, only innocent—a condition conferred upon us by nature but denied us by our institutions.

Absurd? Not as absurd, I admit, as I've made it sound. But absurd nonetheless. There's always been such a deep strain of positivism at the heart of American secularism, so much of a residue or taint of Protestant reformism, and perhaps so much pure American optimism, or romanticism, or utopianism, that Freud's resigned notions about the cost of culture and safety have simply been totally alien to most of us. Happiness, we believe, if pursued, is attainable; all forms of human relations are perfectible; all that it requires is a rearrangement of institutions, or a throwing off of old repressions, or perhaps a revolution (but always a gentle one) to bring about the future we've envisioned and a human nature free of sin.

All of this, I suppose, should come as no surprise. The forms of secularism which dominate our thought in America are a strange hodgepodge of contradictory ideas, many of which exist so far beneath the surface that we're hardly aware of them. Look briefly at the elements which meet and combine in our secularism and you can find remnants of Renaissance individualism and hope, Enlightenment skepticism and rationality, bourgeois Victorian notions of reformism and the desire to intervene in others' lives, the evolutionary liberalism of nineteenth-century England, traces of New England transcendentalism, a hint of the French Revolution, a lot of Locke and Mill, a good bit of Rousseau, a bit less of Kant, surprising amounts of Nietzsche, something of Hegel's idea about history, spirit, and progress, a lot of Marx's utopianism and consciousness of class, a great deal of pragmatism and positivism, and some—but not nearly as much as you'd think—of the combination of Deistic skepticism and hope which defined the thought of America's founders and the constitution they wrote. And there's also at work in it a good bit of science, or perhaps "scientism" would be a better word: the hopeful science of the 19th century, when men transferred from religion to science, and from science to the social and moral realms, the idea of the inevitability of evolution or progress: the steady development of mankind toward moral wisdom and social order.

Beyond this, or actually entangled with it, one finds a number of originally religious ideas rooted in English and American Protestantism. Among these are, most importantly, a belief in the perfectibility of human nature and society and the complementary notion that we can somehow hope to establish in one form or another something close to heaven on earth. Indeed, seen clearly, certain ideas fundamental to much of modern secularism—especially those associated with progress, improvement, and coercive "uplift" or rehabilitation—have their most obvious and deepest roots in religious ways of seeing the world. Analyze any of our contemporary American debates and the positions of secular, liberal, or left-wing Americans and you can find, surprisingly, but clearly preserved, many of the assumptions and attitudes held by the Puritans toward community, deviance, sinners, and rectitude—though these, of course, have been transformed, and now we speak about health rather than sin, and are ready to put such ideas to use in the name of secularism rather than faith.

To this mix, already complex, one must add our particular psychology as Americans. We are, as a people and as individuals, more fully given than most others in the world to a belief in our own virtue and innocence. We have a brief history as a society; a knowledge of our own corruption has not yet seeped into our bones; we seem to believe that we left the worst diseases of authority and the soul somewhere behind us in Europe, and that wilderness America from the start somehow offered us a renewed innocence or grace that others, elsewhere in the world, do not have. We're dreamers, and in our dreams we have managed—and manage even now—to keep alive the notion that we alone, among all others, will be able to combine freedom and order, power and innocence, and that we'll thereby have the best of all possible worlds: full plates and clean hands, good sex and good consciences, the chance—ah, were it so!—to effortlessly satisfy the demands of both desire and duty with the very same set of actions.

In other words, much of the endeavor to which we are committed as secularists has far less to do with reason and skepticism than with *conviction* and *faith*—both aspects of religion. In this sense our critics and opponents are right: secularism is a religion and a form of faith, and that may be why we hold to our views with such desperate tenacity and with so much blind devotion, for we are possessed of and by a certainty which only faith can generate.

In this light it is no accident that we saw at the Democratic convention, and then at the inauguration, Bill Clinton with his backwoods Baptist smarmy good-boy earnestness surrounded by zealous secular academics and experts of all sorts dead set on righting society's wrongs with an endless series of interventions and programs—an extended 12-step program for the nation backed by the state's coercive powers. Our secular claims to innocence, our postures of virtue and authority, our beliefs in the power of "moral" government (as opposed to a *just* one) to set things right, to correct errant behavior, to improve private moral life—all this is the modern form of what, in older days, was brought to rough and frontier towns by the "civilizing classes": a social vision marked by a fastidiousness of virtue so sure of itself that self-doubt never entered in, nor any doubt of its own right to force upon recalcitrant others the order so ardently desired.

And here another irony presents itself. For while we are quite ready, as secularists, to share in Freud's view of religion, and to treat its zealotries with contempt and disdain, almost everything Freud had to say about religion *is now true of secularism itself.* This presumed force for tolerance, this belief supposedly grounded in reason, this tradition of skepticism, has now become something else altogether, has grown into its near opposite, and it now partakes of precisely the same arrogance, the same irrationality and passion for certainty, the same pretense to unquestioned virtue against which its powers were once arrayed. In short, just as religion was once largely a mask for the infantile yearnings and fears of men, so too, secularism now becomes a mask for the same things. In our desperation, in the way we cling to belief, and in our self-righteousness, our contempt or disdain for others who do not believe what we believe, secularism has, indeed, taken on all the trappings of a faith—and a narrow one at that. One thinks of the final scene in Orwell's *Animal Farm*, when the once rebellious pigs have become so like the farmers they've overthrown that the other animals, watching through a window, can no longer tell the difference between them.

I do not mean here to demean the extraordinary ideas which may still lie half-forgotten and largely unexpressed at the heart of secular belief. The role secularism has played in the last couple of hundred years has usually been an honorable one, powered by deep and praiseworthy human passions and hopes: for liberty, equality, and fraternity; for men and women to become true makers of value; for a freedom and ethical maturity that we dreamed would appear when the last vestiges of dependence on authority and the submission to the powers of the past had been eliminated.

But along the way something quite curious happened. We bred out of secularism the deep seriousness that once informed it; the senses of tragedy, complexity, and ambiguity which once marked it as a legitimate response to the mindlessness of others have disappeared. And we've picked up along the way the bags and baggage of those mindless others: a passion for totalizing thought; a conviction that we know better than others what is good for them; an increasing reliance on coercion, a readiness to force upon people through law what reason cannot teach them; and a sense of superiority or virtue which makes us contemptuous of others and allows us to sacrifice their freedoms to our ends.

The attitudes I am describing cut across almost the entire range of contemporary secularism, whatever other ideological differences we may have among us. They're present, obviously, in the Marxist notions of the new man, or in the speech and behavior codes now enacted on campuses, or in the fury with which abortion rights defenders denounce as charlatans or knaves all those who persist in thinking of the fetus as a person and alive. All of the positions I've named may indeed be defensible on one ground or another, but what's important here is *how* they're held: with a monstrous certainty that assumes first the tone of self-righteousness and then the form of coercion or tyranny, and which reduces all those in opposition to unworthy representatives or inhabitants of a corrupt past that must be entirely changed or destroyed before the world can move on.

The astonishing thing about all this is that such certainty, such freedom from self-doubt, should persist at the heart of secularism even after the past century, after two world wars and countless examples of the ways in which predominantly secular forms of ideology have failed to produce the results that were anticipated or promised. After all of that, we seem still comfortably convinced that all of those evils can safely be ascribed to circumstances or peculiarities of history or cultural quirks or forms of excess that are merely incidental to secularism and of which we ourselves could never be guilty. We never seem to falter—even in the face of evidence and history's testimony—in our belief that it would take little for us as secularists, had we the power, to repair what is wrong, or adjust or remake it so that such horrors disappear forever, their place taken by a community of gentle and reasonable human beings magically set free of the very impulses Freud saw as intrinsic to all civilized life.

What we've learned, of course, or what we *should* have learned but have refused to learn, ought to trouble us deeply, ought to send us rushing back to examine the easy assumptions we've made about the world, the convenient and endlessly tractable models of human nature we've constructed, usually out of pretty thin air. What we know now, or ought to know, is that men are just as ready to kill in God's absence as they kill in his name, and we ought to know, too, that the furies and fanaticism associated with religion are not merely born there but have their roots deeper down in human nature, and that they can as easily be expressed in the guise of reason as in the name of faith.

Is this, in itself, not enough to have caused us to question any ideology, including our own, that promises a permanent and radical change in human nature or which claims permanent hegemony over evil? From the French Revolution on, secular ideologues have seen their glorious dreams give way, in their own hands, to furious forms of cruelty or violence they never intended. And we've seen the same thing in our own time in Russia, China, Cuba, Nicaragua, and even, yes, in lesser forms, here at home in America, and yet we go on speaking as if none of this had ever happened, or, if it did, as if it has nothing to do with *our* secularism, our ideologies.

Like all true believers, we brush away anything that might call into question our dreams or contradict what we want to believe. If it is communism in Russia or the behavior of the Khmer Rouge in Cambodia or totalitarianism in China, we content ourselves with muttering that they've gotten things wrong because of something foreign or "Oriental" in their natures and that the fault lies not in secularism or its ideologies but in the particular people who subscribe to them. Here in America, whether it is the condition of the schools we are talking about or divorce rates or children born out of wedlock or violence or the moral condition of our communities, we steer all thought away from the possibility that something in our system of beliefs may be faulty or responsible and content ourselves with blaming the conservatives or Jessie Helms and the fundamentalists—as if they alone stood in the way of the heaven on earth we envision. Endlessly, we explain away all problems in terms of what others have done or not done, and we never bother to ask ourselves whether there might not be something flawed in our vision or more complicated about the world than we realize.

I remember what it was like decades ago to argue with young Catholics about the Trinity or the divinity of Jesus. Precisely at the point where these became matters of faith, those who believed in them became most obstinate and angry. They could not afford to subject such questions to the same skepticism or examination they reserved for other matters, because then the whole edifice of belief by which they located themselves in the world would come tumbling down. The criticism one brought to bear on their faith must have seemed to them as if it were directed personally at them, at their egos, at the whole world they inhabited, because they could make no distinction between self and belief.

Is it any different now with secularists? What fury one finds, what outrage, when one calls into question any of the shibboleths and superstitions by which we habitually define ourselves. Abortion? Questions of gender? Public schooling? The possibility that some believers or religions may be closer than we are to certain essential truths? On these and any one of dozens of issues one runs smack into a level of fury that equals in intensity anything I've ever seen in religion, and the likeliest explanation is simply that we, like all believers, can no longer afford to subject our views to rigorous examination, if only because they, and with them our egos, our hopes, might dissolve before our eyes.

The curious thing here is that even religious men and women can be beset by doubt, by crises of faith, by deep elisions of belief in which certainty vanishes and they fear for their souls. But secularists? It is hard to find much evidence these days of anything similar in our zealous public stances, and how often does one hear it in private from one's colleagues or friends? Our capacity for denial and evasion, for the circumvention of fact and truth, has led us clearly away from the rationality, the skepticism, the courage required by doubt, which were once thought to be the hallmarks of genuine secularism.

All this, perhaps, has something to do with despair. After all, we don't, as secularists, have a God above or a heaven ahead, don't have much in the way of other-worldly hopes to assuage our pain in this world. As our culture grows increasingly divided and disorderly neither we nor anyone else appears able to control it, to set it right. Life in America doesn't seem to provide many of us with deep satisfaction or a feeding source of identity, and therefore we cling ever more desperately to our ideologies, our familiar dreams for the world. These offer us our only senses of location and hope, and who can be surprised if we hold to them like drowning men to debris or like children to departing parents?

Nowhere can you see the failure of the secular endeavor, or the bad faith and intellectual dishonesty we've brought to it, more clearly than in the realms of ethics and morality, in our vain attempts to create systems of value to replace those once offered and held in place by religion. It is here, in relation to value, that you can see our dreams writ large and our successes writ small, for this is where we have failed most completely: in our attempt to construct, maintain, and transmit a binding moral system that might effectively illuminate individual lives and order a free society.

From the Enlightenment on, this particular project, this specific notion of moral re-creation or re-envisioning, has been at the very heart of secular thought. It has been the implied and overt center of the argument made against religion and in the name of secularism: that we can create, in the absence of religious systems of value, something of equal moral power to take their place. Much of our critique of religion as both regressive and repressive, as well as our claim to a reasoned and free secular future, depends squarely on the viability and power of our promise of a new moral order.

Well, how has the struggle, the adventure of living ethically without God, turned out? Look around. Is what we see around us what we imagined as a just and moral order, or one which might justify our critique of religion? Oh, I know, not everything we see around us can be blamed on secularists. I understand how strenuously we deny all responsibility for what surrounds us, by arguing that the changes we'd like to make have barely been begun, or that we've been stymied by others who stand in our way, who have prevented us from bringing about the world we envisioned. We

look at the disorder and ethical confusion around us and ascribe it
to conservatives, or the greed of the 1980s, or late-stage capitalism,
or a breakdown in community, in all of which we, of course—
clean-handed and innocent as usual—have played no part.

But that won't wash. For several decades now the levers of institutional and popular culture have been in our hands. We've
controlled the arts, the sciences, the universities, the public schools,
much of the federal and local bureaucracies, and most of the popular culture. We've overthrown countless restrictions and cultural
limits, have vastly extended the realm of individual freedom, have
largely determined taste and behavior and the rise and fall of
particular values. Of course there has been a backlash too—the
culture clashes and the "culture wars" now visible all around us.
But for the most part we've won, and if our victory has been
neither final nor complete, and if freedom remains limited and
contested, the secularization of the culture has in fact been pretty
successful. Though what has emerged has made few of us happy,
we cannot pretend any longer that what we see around us in terms
of values can be blamed on those who have opposed us. Much of
what we see and decry is clearly rooted in secularism, is the out-
come of the freedom for which we've fought, and if it isn't close
to what we dreamed, then that may have far more to do with our
own moral failures and errors than it does with the resistance from
others we have encountered along the way.

It is true, of course, that our present moral condition has many
sources and roots, and that many of them have little to do with secularism. America is a huge and relatively new society consisting of
many competing ethical and moral traditions, all of which are continuously beset by astonishingly rapid rates of change, and by a
popular culture as powerful in its influences as established institutions. We have never really had here the kinds of deep rooted
and time-worn traditions of behavior and value which in other

societies form the basis of an established moral and social order. For close to 200 years a set of fundamentally narrow Puritan and Protestant values dominated most of our public institutions, but these were imposed from above on our rivalrous ethnic traditions and our frontier values, which had a powerful and recalcitrant life of their own. From the beginning we've been a wilderness nation, a nation defined as much by its margins as by its center, and the freedoms we prize have always been expressed in the absence of, or at the expense of, an established social order. Go back to our great national texts—Twain's *Huckleberry Finn,* Hawthorne's *Scarlet Letter,* Melville's *Moby Dick* and *Billy Budd*—and you will find there in one symbolic form or another the crises now at work in our contemporary lives.

And then, too—it would be negligent not to point this out—there's the fact that freedom remains among us so unevenly distributed, so incomplete and partial for so many groups of marginalized people, so unmatched by distributive justice or a genuinely participatory politics, that one cannot be surprised if large numbers of Americans seem to be unconstrained by norms of moral conduct. The freedom we have can perhaps be explained in Marxist terms as the florescence of late-stage capitalism in which freedom has been confused with consumerism, and in which we vainly attempt to act out in our privacies, or as "life-style" choices, the desire for liberty which is thwarted in terms of politics or community.

And yet having said all that, one must still recognize that secularism has indeed played a significant role in what we see around us: first in its concerted attack on older religious values, and secondly, in the inability of secularists to create, side by side with freedom, or out of freedom, a compelling new frame of moral reference to replace the old one.

Clearly, the rebellion made in America in the name of personal, cultural, aesthetic, moral, and political freedom was in the main a rebellion led by secularists and against religion. The reason for that is obvious: the existing restrictions on freedom were rooted in Protestant and often Puritan religious doctrine. Despite all our talk about the separation of church and state, their powers throughout American history have been intertwined, inseparable. The laws of the land were often, and in some cases even now remain, the direct translation into public policy and life of punitive and repressive religious doctrines and attitudes.

Inevitably the contest between the new (freedom) and the old (order) became a contest between those rebelling against the supposed word of God and those obedient to it. In such a context it was only natural for the attention of secularists, and those seeking freedom from the old order, to be drawn mainly to the breaking of limits, the destruction of mores and values, rather than to questions of value or morality. It was natural that certain ideas—those, say, of duty, or guilt, or personal responsibility—were often perceived by secularists to be weapons of tyranny, instruments of repression, for indeed they are used that way, not only by churches but by authorities of every sort, including governments, schools, and families. "Morality" was seen as (and often was) the enemy of freedom, an obstacle to freedom.

And it is here, precisely, we come to the second area of secular responsibility. For freedom is after all (even the partial freedom we've established) only a preliminary clearing of the ground from which a more mature, or more complete and *moral,* freedom can arise. In terms of moral life, a *genuine* moral life (which must begin in freedom), the breaking of taboos in the name of freedom, the clearing of the ground, is only a start. Freedom in itself guarantees nothing; it is merely the beginning of a task; it is itself a question: *how shall we live?* And I am not certain, even now, that we have begun, in earnest, to answer that question.

The odd thing, of course, and the thing that makes our task even more difficult than it would otherwise be, is the ambiguity, the incompleteness, of our victory. Around us, still, many people struggle to return to the moral past, to curtail freedom, to reinstate or reinvigorate the forms of repression against which we struggled.

And yet the old world, for better or worse, is gone; America, for all its tensions, for all of the old Puritanism still at work, is nonetheless—in terms of culture, or individual choice, or the chance to live out one's will or imagination, or simply *make a self*—an astonishingly free place: not yet free, and, yet, astonishing. What we've done, you see, is to break the old order and its repressive power. But because its residue remains, because others, with other values, still cry out against us, we remain distracted by our unfinished task: to recreate, within freedom, a new moral life.

But that doesn't mean the second stage of our labor can be legitimately avoided, or that we can excuse ourselves for having failed at it. And it is here that our critics may be right, here that they may correctly fault us for making claims we cannot substantiate, for offering arguments based only on dreams. All along we've implied that we had schemes, remedies, insights, and moral alternatives that would be adequate to both freedom and a society as complex as our own. We would be able, we argued, through one means or another, to fix into place and keep there, on a broad scale and for the entire society, new systems of meaning and value upon which individuals could base their moral lives and in which entire communities, whole nations in fact, could find a moral order.

But have we in fact done that? Have we offered up anything of value, anything that touches the soul and gathers together human powers in a way that makes for moral wisdom or a moral life? Again, look around. Does what we see lift the heart? Is there anything here to indicate that we know how to do what we promised or that we know at all what we are doing?

We know, of course, how religious systems create and maintain universes of moral values: by grounding morality in a sense of divine and immutable law and making use not only of guilt, fear, and hope of reward, but also the human capacity for wonder, awe, and gratitude. Architectonic worlds are envisioned which cradle each human life and locate each individual gesture, work, and act in a universe of meaning. Moral values are rooted in an entire cosmology, and human behavior is understood to derive its significance from an eternal drama in which all men and women are participants. The magnified and simplified conflicts between good and evil or God and the Devil become points of reference, compass points in a geography of meaning that exists simultaneously in the individual soul and at the furthest edges of space. We can ignore them, violate them, push against them, or dispute their ultimate meaning, but nonetheless there they are, like stars: something to steer by. Their presence, their existence outside of us, though presenting us with a demand, also confers upon us a kind of release, a respite, for they exist regardless of what we do or how we fail them.

Remember, it is not only Western or Judeo-Christian societies which are organized in this way. Tribal societies and indigenous peoples do something similar, relating moral norms to myths of origin and the acts of the gods, thereby anchoring, in the mystery of a *beyond*, even the most commonplace human acts. True, communities and families (often extended families) do the day-to-day work of moral grounding in countless ways. The rituals of daily life encode and enforce certain norms; repetition and resistance to change kept them in place. But always, everywhere, such systems are anchored in *belief*, in explanatory religious myths which defy reason but are nonetheless accepted beyond all questioning and related to even the smallest thing—the fall of a sparrow, say—in a context that includes life and death, origins and endings, the war between good and evil, and, as a precipitate, the moral lives of men and women.

Have I made it sound too pretty, too perfect? I need not detail here the harm such systems can do, the ways they not only locate people in a particular world of meaning but *trap* them there, stifling imagination and intelligence, denying them the full use of their powers. I need not explain the violence such systems do, the bloodbaths and schisms that arise from them, the injury they do to dissenters and nonbelievers or to truth itself. But we know too that such systems "work"; they do what they are meant to do in terms of culture; they keep alive at its heart a vision of order and meaning, a sense of significance of moral acts, moral lives.

And what about us? What do we have to offer as secularists in the place of such religiously rooted systems? What *have* we put in its place? Can we, in fact, put *anything* in its place? And here the answer must be, I fear, that we don't know. We simply don't know. Oh, for the moment, as always, we pretend we know. We do it with smoke and mirrors and sleight of hand and a bravado and rhetoric that mask our confusions. When we argue about anything, take any position, about school vouchers, say, or against the censorship in schools of certain texts, or against prayers said at graduation, what we're arguing is that these are not only antithetical to freedom (which they are) but that they are also unnecessary because we—the secularists, the secular state, the secular schools—can successfully substitute for these antiquated means of maintaining a coherent society or a moral order a new set of visions, a new order.

But there's the rub. At every imaginable level, in both public debate and the privacy of our own lives, this is a work that has hardly begun. There has been no systematic effort whatsoever to discover for ourselves, or for others, a universal set of principals, a frame of moral reference, that can adequately illuminate individual lives and serve as a compelling ground for a collective or communal sense of morality. What we do have, of course, are what we've always had: hunches, hopes and dreams, assumptions that we manage to keep intact by steadfastly refusing to examine them with the same skepticism we reserve for the beliefs of others. The end result of all of this is that we are usually in the position of criticizing others with great certainty and glee while, in fact, behind our zeal, we have little of real value to provide as alternatives.

I do not mean that secularists cannot be, as individuals, moral men and women. Nor do I mean that we cannot, on a small scale, and in particular situations, teach others to be moral men and women. There are plenty of ways—too many to enumerate here—that secular individuals learn to be generous, just, honest, and dutiful human beings. We learn it from parents, we learn it from rare and great teachers, we learn it from books, and sometimes experience itself takes us by the throat and teaches us directly about human suffering or justice—this happened, for instance, in the southern freedom marches and often to people in the Peace Corps. And then, too, more often than not, we make do by locating bits and pieces of moral wisdom here and there, usually (and ironically) in the religious traditions against whose repressive limits we've rebelled.

But what we do not do, what we cannot do, is discover or create ways to leave religion behind as the organizing basis for moral life. We can't locate with any common agreement or compelling public rhetoric a different ground for morality, a different but distinct frame of moral reference. That, after all, is what we have implied all along we would be able to do, would do. But we haven't done it, and we don't really know whether we can do it, whether it is possible to do.

Thus, for the moment we have neither a clear-cut set of moral principles nor compelling frames of moral reference with which to replace what we've left behind. Even the idea of natural law, which, for awhile, took God's place as the bedrock foundation of moral thought, has been jettisoned. What we're left with is hazy and confused and hammered together out of bits and pieces of the past, and we leave all moral choice to individual preference, conscience, or judgment, and though this sounds fine on paper or in theory, it continuously breaks down for want of a mode of discourse, a dimensional moral language in which to think or speak, or a communicable way of understanding the notions of duty or responsibility or what Kant called categorical imperatives. We are no good at framing these things, no good at teaching them or even learning them, largely because we lack a tradition, *a commons* of discourse, or a commonly accepted hierarchy of aims or "goods" by which people might learn to construct moral lives for themselves.

To have, as we do now, a secular ethic in which duty is conflated with desire, and in which morality is almost entirely identical to will, inclination, and ideological preconception, is to have no ethic at all. It is merely the rationalization of convenience or appetite. We have grown quite practiced at laying claims to freedom, or in finding a basis upon which to constrain the behavior of others, but we can't seem to locate either categories or imperatives by which to measure, change, or judge *our own* behavior. Kant's dictum that we can usually recognize duty by the way it conflicts with desire may seem harsh on its face, but there is truth to it. One of the few ways we know we have hit upon a universal principle of behavior is that it requires *us* to change, demands that we act or refrain from acting in ways that are at odds with preference. But in that sense alone, in the sense of a rigor of moral thought applied to the self, how many of us can be said to have done the hard work that our present condition requires of us?

Part of the problem is that we've neither common and acknowledged traditions nor texts to guide us in the search for principles. They've somehow been forgotten or discarded along the way. Once, it is true, we had a supposed "canon": a set of texts held in common and which, if studied (or so it was held) might lead us not only towards an understanding of a shared past, but also in the direction of wisdom; they would teach us not *what* to think about morality or truth, but *how* to think, or what one ought to think *about* in order to come to moral wisdom. But all agreement about what constitutes a canon has now disappeared, and even before that it had ceased to function in any serious way. One can still go back, if one chooses, to Socrates and Plato and Aristotle, or to Mill and Locke and Hume, or to Kierkegaard and Hegel and Kant, and painfully construct for oneself a set of principles to guide behavior. But how many of us in fact do this? How many of us, as secularists, once school has been left behind, bother to struggle our way through these texts in order to find how to use freedom, or what to do within it?

And then there's the Constitution—we must not forget that. But the Constitution is a *political* document, not a moral one, though certainly a moral sensibility guided it, infused it. But it nonetheless tells us far more about the behavior and limits of the state than it does about individual moral choice. It creates a space for freedom, it guarantees us freedom, it confers upon us certain rights; but in terms of what to do within that space, or how and when to exercise our rights, it falls appropriately silent and leaves the creation of a moral life, or the discovery and exercise of particular values, to the people, to *us*.

Thus we come again back to square one, back to the task which remains unfinished, which has barely been begun. We may indeed have some idea about what to do as citizens, as political beings, but it leaves us still, as moral creatures, as ethical agents, in a darkness and confusion created by the destruction of the old moral order and our refusal or our inability to create a new one. This refusal, this inability, this confusion hidden behind our ideologies and our dogmas and our pretenses to moral certainty, renders the very heart of secularism vacant and vacuous, empty of wisdom. There's a void there that reveals a bad faith of terrifying proportions, an emptiness that renders all of our other arguments and positions, our criticisms of others, especially in relation to their ways of preserving value, suspect and false.

Back in the old days, in the innocent hey-day of American secularism, when Dewey-eyed we saw the moral future clearly unfolding itself before us, we may innocently have thought that freedom was the hardest part of the task and that the creation of value would follow without much effort. We imagined it would happen, well, *naturally*. Repression would lift, religion would lose its power, and somehow decency and generosity and a natural appetite for goodness would rise to the surface of human affairs where the mechanisms of secular society—community, family, school, individual conscience—would keep them in place. We might have had our disagreements about particulars. Marxists thought a revolution was necessary; socialists thought a peaceful redistribution of power and wealth was both required and possible; liberals imagined it would take only the triumph of reason, the defeat of prejudice, and decent people running the state. But all of us were equally sanguine and sure about the direction of history; new systems of value, we were certain, would simply accompany and follow the political changes we envisioned.

Even now I'm not sure how we could have been so foolishly certain of ideas so sloppily held. Perhaps our illusions had something to do with our belief in the unassailability of our own virtue. Or maybe it was simply the result of supreme moral arrogance: the notion that any power we might acquire would lead only to goodness. Or maybe, more probably, it was a combination of things: innocence, naiveté, wishfulness, self-delusion, and, yes, even stupidity. A host of figures—think here again of Reich and Fromm and Marcuse, among countless others—had convinced us, because we wanted to believe them, that evil was a function of repression, that freedom and pleasure would lead inevitably to generosity and moral "health," and that merely by liberating energy, by transforming culture, we could redeem our full powers, our true natures, and watch them fill, like water rising, the cultural spaces we had cleared.

But that was back then. And can anyone now, in the light of the present day, seriously and honestly hold such views? Those familiar platitudes, those hidden assumptions, ought long ago to have given way to something far more serious and reflective and skeptical about easy fixes or ideological dreams. For nobody then talked about *work*, about the hard labor of creating values, the immense effort involved—especially in relation to a society as divided,

young, huge, and wild as our own—in maintaining and trans-
mitting values. From Rousseau's hazy notions of a "civil religion"
down to our own day, to Dewey's progressive schools or James's
moral equivalent to war or the ideas of Ivan Illich and Paul Goodman about de-schooling, we've always side-stepped these questions, have always adorned our calls for change and freedom with
rhetorical flourishes and utopian schemes and forms of pretty fu-
turism that may indeed touch the soul or lift the heart, but melt
away like dew when set against the harsh realities of the world
around us: the immensity of the disorder which confronts us, the
moral devolution at work, and the divisions which separate us ide-
ologically. Everyone among us, always, has or alludes to a magic
program, a final solution, a sure-fire, can't miss, just-let-us-try-it
blueprint for change that promises at one fell swoop to renovate
the whole shebang, totally transforming the entire society from
top to bottom. But nobody seems to have anticipated or known
what to do about reality: AIDS and fist-fucking or gangsta-rap and
the powers of MTV or drug-deal shoot-outs or a third of all children born out of wedlock or the confusion of desire with duty or
the madness of a sexuality that manages, god help us, to combine
license with Puritanism and produce the worst of both: incessant
sex and continual unhappiness.

The closest we've come to replacing the morality of religion
with a secular alternative is in our contemporary psychology. It
is here, in our popular forms of therapy, our fashionable notions
of "cure," self-improvement, empowerments, etc., that we can see
most at work our fuddled attitudes toward responsibility, reciprocity, indebtedness, duty, guilt, and countless other problems of
value and behavior. In this regard psychology has become a scandal
and a joke, a form of ritualized ignorance in which almost every
human act is shed of genuine moral content. The church and its
doctrines and priests may have been devoted as much to power
and control as they were to the health of the soul, but the ignorance and illusions they foisted on their followers were nothing

compared to the conspiratorial ignorance now maintained in the therapist's office—those silly catechisms of pain and self-justification which have led to familiar bromides like "self-esteem," "dysfunctional family," "addiction," and all of the other supposed explanations for angst and disorder which lift from our shoulders the weight of moral incumbency and labor.

I remember years ago working with vets who had returned from Vietnam distressed not only by what they had suffered but also by what they had done: the destruction of villages, the murder of innocents. They would have nothing to do with religion, since most of them had been encouraged by their priests and ministers to go to war in order to defeat the godless communists. But one could if one looked at least find in religion a set of concepts and rituals designed for the healing of their moral distress: atonement, expiation, absolution—all parts of a moral language or discourse that at least accredited, whatever its other purposes, the depth of the anguish men feel when they've done something wrong. But our psychology? Secular psychology? There was nothing in it of use to the vets, nothing appropriate to their remorse, their need to comprehend what they'd done or to find a way to put the past to moral use. In matters involving morality or guilt our psychology is entirely silent, or else it finesses such issues by defining them as something entirely imposed upon us from the outside, a fiction that must be unlearned if we are to achieve the happiness or pleasure we dream about. The best our psychologists can do is "delayed stress syndrome," a descriptive category devoid of all ethical or tragic content, making of the vets' moral crisis little more than a malfunction of the adrenal system or a problem in neurological misfiring.

What's happened in psychology has also happened in countless other realms of contemporary discourse: a kind of flattening, an emptying-out, a shift from moral frames of reference rooted in religious belief and traditional modes of repression to secular systems from which repression has largely been banished but from which all depth of moral understanding, and all sense of an individual moral universe, a "surround" of moral meaning, seems to have disappeared. What has vanished among us is not so much the idea of right and wrong, but the deep moral context in which we once considered right and wrong, the moral universe in which men and women searched for answers and for "the good" and struggled to come to terms with what they had done or what they ought to do. No doubt what caused the vets so much pain after Vietnam (as it causes many of us pain) was not only that they had done something to regret, but that they had no way to deal with it, no frame of moral reference in which to think about or resolve the terrible questions it raised for them.

I remember, too, a few years ago in California, how someone discovered behind an abandoned abortion mill hundreds of discarded fetuses in dumpsters. As best I can recall, a Christian group approached state officials and asked to say some kind of prayer when the fetuses were buried. But this proved too much for certain secularists. They went to court and argued against the rights of the Christians to say their prayer and petitioned the judge to declare the fetuses "waste human tissue." When they won, the fetuses were buried without a prayer, though for all I know the Christians, at some distance, may have murmured a few words to speed them heavenward.

Waste human tissue! This is what we've come to, as secularists. This is what we fight for in court. I honestly doubt that souls exist and rise, and I've never believed a God exists who listens to our prayers. But so what? I can understand the human horror or grief one might feel at the desecration in a dumpster of life-to-be or what-might-have-been-life. Is a reverence for that life-to-be or sorrow at its degradation so out of the question that we must forbid its expression in prayer? Here, juxtaposed with one another, we have the illusions of religion and the "mature realism" of secularism. And which one seems more frightening, more dangerous, closer to death than life: the religious fiction that the soul of a fetus floats up to God, or the secular notion that nothing more is involved here than a discarded appendix or hemorrhoid?

This is the dead-end of positivism and the will's triumph: this reduction of all mystery and potentiality to a moral wasteland that permits us to make of reality whatever is required to satisfy our needs. The issue here is not abortion or women's rights; it is, instead, what we do to reality and language and even to ourselves in the name of those rights: our hope of avoiding all guilt by avoiding ambiguity, our dream of preserving our own innocence by ignoring whatever calls it into question.

Think here of the early and great secular voices that filled us, when we were young, with a sense of truth as deep as any offered by religion, ones that seemed to promise us not only freedom but a richer and more profound way of seeing, of being in the world. Think of the voices that stirred us, made us aware of the great human tasks awaiting us—the voices of Victor Hugo and Jack London and Charles Dickens and Emma Goldman and Walt Whitman and the later Freud or the early Marx and all those others who drew us towards them not only with ideas but with the resonance of their voices, the depth of their sensibilities, convincing us that, yes, we could, even in God's absence, find in ourselves a capacity for wisdom and human generosity and courage equal to the complexity of the world.

And with that in mind look again at what surrounds us: the moral dogmatism, the mad desire for certainty, the shrill ideologies which present themselves in the guise of secularism. And look, too, at what we ourselves have become: living examples of what can go wrong in secularism or the foolishness and vacuity into which it can devolve.

Every Christian zealot who shivers at night in fear because the state requires him to send his child to our schools is right to do so—not because of what we're going to teach his child about ethical or spiritual life, but because we've so *little* to teach. Oh, we may manage with perseverance and luck, and the help of popular culture, to tear the child away from Christian values and the terrors of hell and the sweet simplicity of Creationism—we're not, after all, so bad at doing that. And no doubt we'll dwell a bit on right and wrong. Don't cheat. Don't fight. Share. Wear condoms. Don't laugh at different others—or not unless they hear God's voice. These are such nice notions. Who can argue with them? But behind or beneath all this, where the great structures of value used to be, the overarching depth of a universe where each act had a meaning, or where, at least, a muscularity of thought, or the true adventurousness of reason, or an indwelling in mystery, might lead us toward the truth—well, it's there that the Christians are right to quiver and blanche, because in those vast inner and outer regions where conscience used to dwell, we presently proceed blindly, without direction or thought.

II

What is called for now is the conscientious re-envisioning of the whole secular endeavor: an effort to rethink, as if from the ground up, the basic tenets of our beliefs. Such an activity must be communal, shared, creating a realm of discourse among us in which we must struggle to exercise the same skepticism, the same rigor of reasoning and thought, that we now bring to bear on the ideas of others. It must include not only a re-thinking of our familiar and habitual public positions, but also a truthful accounting of how secularism works, where it has taken us in our own lives, the ways it has or has not helped us to locate ourselves in the realm of meaning and value.

We've had beginnings and hints of new ways of thinking and feeling: John Rawl's work, for example, or Robert Nozick's, or that of Richard Rorty. But even here something essential has been missing, for while all of these men have attempted to find a basis for a universal secular morality, they haven't cut deep enough, gone far enough, towards the real problems at the heart of secularism; they have given us answers but haven't required from each of us the self-analysis, the *individual* re-thinking of fundamental questions which our time now requires. What we need are not so much new theories, new analyses, or new programs for change, but a willingness to go back to the very assumptions of secularism, the most fundamental ideas or attitudes, the very things we've taken most for granted, in order to find out how these really work, or *if* they work—not only in the world at large but in our privacies, our solitudes, the night world where we hunt, at three in the morning, still awake, for something to hold on to, something to give a meaning to our lives.

I know how hard it is to do this. We're so fearful of losing the cultural ground we've gained, so frightened by the possibility of religion's resurgence, so distracted by the foolishness and knavery of others, that we have little inclination or energy left for the collective task of self-examination. But what choice have we? It should be clear by now that the secular systems of meaning we've created do not in fact constitute a sufficient response to the world around us, or a sufficient foundation for an ethical future. And what's up for grabs now, what hangs in the balance, are the ways we will in the future define *every* aspect of our shared condition: freedom, order, virtue, good and evil, moral responsibility, reciprocity, and obligation. What we think, say, and do now will create the social and moral realities others inhabit, and to shirk our task now, or to rest easy with what secularism has become, betrays the future in whose name we claim to speak.

It's almost as if, in order to move forward, we have to go back to the very beginning of secularism, back past Marx and Freud, back past the reformers and the evolutionists, back past the era of revolution and the early glory of secular ideology, back past all our favorite positions and ideas in order to ask ourselves again, in new ways, the questions which secularism has claimed to answer since its beginning.

And how to do that? We can't actually go back in time, can't unreel history. But what we can do is to think or reflect our way back; we can set aside our habits of thought, our desperate certainties, our frayed and questionable ideologies, in order to once again think through our beliefs, think our way towards and then beyond them, think our way towards a secularism more appropriate to our time and condition, more appropriate to the future now upon us.

We come, then, roundabout, but inevitably, to the idea of thought, or reflection, or the inward work that needs to be done in each of us, by each of us, before we can claim again an outward mission or a purpose for a secularism worthy of respect. What I want to do here, at least briefly, is to think about thought, to examine what kind of thought may now be necessary, and what this thinking, this reflecting, may demand of us. The main problem, of course, is that we have largely stopped thinking, have merely made use, without thought, of old assumptions, old ideas, which we recite again and again *as if* we were thinking, as if they came from thought. And this failure to think, this acceptance without thought of all we take for granted, is responsible for much of secularism's failure, the fact that it no longer touches, as it once did, the hearts and minds of others.

As secularists, we have only our own minds, our reason, our shared capacity for thought, to fall back on in times of crisis, or to offer us, *in extremis,* a way out or forward. But almost everywhere now, at precisely the point in time when thought has become most necessary, it has also become most rare—almost as if because we are so desperate, because our situation is so precarious, we are afraid to think, afraid of the abyss which will open below us, afraid of the uncertainty, the terrors, which await.

Oh yes, of course we argue about things, endlessly devise positions, hatch new schemes, martial defenses for those already in place. We analyze, dissect, explain, criticize, and predict. But listen carefully to all this and you almost never come upon real thought, never the willingness to call our own received truths into question, or to set them aside for the moment in the name of deeper or greater truths which may appear once we ready ourselves by acknowledging the need for them.

What interests me here, in particular, is a specific kind of thought, *reflective* thought, *reflection*—by which I mean the conscious attempt to think one's way past the habits of thought one has already learned or the received ideas so much taken for granted they amount to a faith. The capacity for reflection, the willingness to reflect, must lie, I believe, at the heart of all secular life, and its absence, our present failure to engage in it or practice it, empties much of what we say of the significance it might have, and it renders our words and positions hollow and false.

It is odd, I know, in a situation as chaotic and busy as is our own, where schisms and disagreements divide us, and where all seems tension and discord, to argue the virtures of *thought,* or to call, in the midst of so much noise and action, for reflection, for *a pause,* for the renewal of an inwardness that may seem the opposite of public action, public life. But that, in fact, is what seems to me necessary. Action without thought, or a public world that lacks, at its center, an inward depth, or a privacy of reason and reflection, can only lead to disaster, no matter who is in charge of it or making its laws.

What I want to do here, then, is to look briefly at reflection, to try to describe what it is, what it means, and in a very general way, where it leads. What follows are, in fact, reflections on reflection, attempts to examine how a new secularism, or a new secular ethic, might be thought through. Nothing I present here is meant to be definitive; how could it be? Everything I write is meant only

to be suggestive, provocative, exhortative: a place to begin, a goad
to others who, reading it, may be tempted into a similar beginning. Toward that end I've left these reflections in the fragmentary,
episodic form in which reflection almost always occurs: as a series
of flashes, insights, or meditations which rings a subject round and
illuminates it from the sides, in a series of views or angles as opposed to a whole or completed vision of truth. Stonehenge is an
image which comes to mind: a center defined only by what surrounds it.

III

Secularism is predicated on the notion that men and women can
and will seek out, in their privacies and inward lives, a moral frame
of reference that transcends the cant and rhetoric that surrounds
them. If we can't do that, if we won't do that, then all claims made
for secularism and the belief systems rising from it become fraudu-
lent. Thus, reflection is what secularism itself demands: it is the
claim made at its beginnings and it lies, still, at its heart. We must
be willing to become, by the rules we have chosen to live by, genuinely reasoning and deeply reflective creatures; if we do not or
cannot do that, then, clearly we can make no genuine claim to
moral seriousness. And if we can make no such claim to seriousness, then how can we put forth, seriously, or expect others to
accept, the variety of assertions we make about countless other issues in terms of secularism or reason?

What would it mean to be a deeply reflective man or woman and
to follow out the meaning of experience and ideas and arrive at
profound and compelling conclusions? What does it mean to embark seriously on this quest, putting aside prejudices, delusions, and
the need for certainty and trying, as best one can, to see clearly,
to understand fully? Thinking for oneself, or seeking truth, does

not mean merely thinking over and against the oppressiveness of authority or received wisdom. It also means thinking over and against the fashion and cant of the times, against even the popular forms of our own revolt. It means going beyond the shallowness of thought of both one's antagonists and one's comrades, and it means recognizing not only the ways in which others obscure the truth and delude us, but the ways in which we are tempted to obscure the truth and delude ourselves.

There is a passage I came upon just the other day in Kenneth Clark's book, *The Nude,* that I think is oddly appropriate here. He is writing about Botticelli's "Birth of Venus," describing the haunting expression on her face, and he points out that it is the same one that Botticelli uses in his portraits of the Madonna: "... That the head of our Christian Goddess, with all her tender apprehension and scrupulous inner life, can be set on a naked body without a shadow of discord is the supreme triumph of Celestial Venus."

For those of us who are secular, and for whom Venus seems far more worthy of worship than the Madonna, the task remains fundamentally the same as the one that faced Botticelli: to graft to secular life certain aspects of traditional spiritual life, most notably the inwardness, the consciousness of interiority, that once marked—at least in theory, or at religion's heart—the proper relation of the soul to God. Religion often creates a profound inwardness in the subjective lives of men and women. There is a way in which secularism can do the same thing; even pleasure, deeply pursued and felt, can create the honey-combed thoughtfulness or reflectivity without which the self is emptied out. That we do not do this much in America, that for all our talk about self, our inner experience often remains flat, thin, or non-existent, is a measure not of the limits of secularism, but of what we have made of it. This flattening out, this corruption of inward space, this loss, if you will, of what Clark called "scrupulousness," has perhaps less to do with God's absence than with the particular cultural habits of thought we've inherited. And just as we have struggled to learn how to use our bodies, how to try to reach, through and in them, the pleasures and capacity for love unused within us, so too we must now learn again to use the reflective mind in ways we have forgotten or ignored. This is part of the secular *discipline*, something each of us, individually, must seek to do on our own, learning two things at once: the full, integral depth of inner life, and also how to speak or act this into the shared communal world.

Ah, yes, of course: we have universities, journals, departments, conferences, symposiums, and so on. But my God! How much of this reveals genuine thought or the presence of the humility, the irony, the *knowing-of-nothing*, with which all real thought, as Socrates knew, must begin? Who among us, after all, is willing to call into question—as we must—the very categories, disciplines, or languages in which we have been taught to think? Who will go back—as one can, if one tries—to the emptiness, the silence that is there before and beyond thought and offers itself to us when we have given up the ghost and admitted ignorance? That is the ground of all thinking, as close to innocence as we can get: the whispered *I don't know* in response to the questions of friends, students, colleagues, or the self. But think back, now, to universities, departments, colloquia: how many times have you heard in response to a question the answer *I don't know* or even *let us think and see?* Oh no: whatever confusions may lie behind our expertise, whatever errors we have made, whatever forms of doubt or even madness may plague us in our private lives, ah, despite that, we always in public have an answer, are always expert and adept, and meaning or wisdom unroll themselves from our mouths and lie themselves down at our feet so easily that all truth is lost.

I don't know . . . That, in the midst of our confusions, our failures, the vast confounding of our hopes and beliefs and dreams by history, is where we must begin. It is where identity begins. It is

where—oh yes, Socrates was right about this—*knowing* begins. If
we know nothing else, let us know that. Or perhaps it is safe to say:
all "knowing" teaches us what we have left to know. Without this,
for secularists, there can be no real thought. No God has spoken to
us; nothing was written for us in fire on the walls of the world. If
we are to eventually know anything, if the world is to come close,
if truth is to reveal itself, this will occur only in those spaces
cleared out by the acknowledgment of our ignorance and to which
we are led by a humility we have yet to find.

It is only when instrumental or purposive or argumentative
thought stops, only when the mind is cleared of what must be
thought or is already thought, that a kind of knowing begins in
the silence or emptiness thought leaves behind. The source of this
knowing remains unclear; all thinkers who acknowledge it explain
it in their own particular ways. But it is true—psychologically
true, subjectively true, true as experience—that often a negation, a
nullification, is required before an affirmation offers itself. Then,
and only then, something speaks through and to us. Perhaps it is
merely a deeper part of the mind speaking to us; or perhaps the
world whispers to us; or perhaps we do in fact remember, as Plato
thought, what past lives have taught us, hearing a music so faint
that only in perfect silence, with an emptiness of mind, can we
hear it. Still, beyond all these interpretations, an experience remains: the experience of something, from somewhere, offering
itself with a fullness that astonishes us. It is a landscape where one
discovers something essential, the hints of a clarity, a kind of illu-
mination, that calls into question all notions of beauty or truth
held before. Michaelangelo's last few pietàs come to mind, especially the 'Randanini Pietà,' where essence seems to become all
and beauty has been cleared away so that truth can enter, filling
the space that beauty's absence leaves behind.

Reflection sinks deeper than reason, dips into memory and states of being, tries to call up from flesh remembered pleasures and sensations, tries in some profound way to order experience, not by defining or explaining it, but by feeling out its form, by raising to consciousness the implicit and emergent meanings that reveal themselves only in reflection. Though an order may well be uncovered or revealed, there is no purposeful seeking of order; that is allowed to occur or not, as it will. Think here of scuba diving, of the novel world beneath the surface, of the state of watchfulness or awareness and the deep looking that occurs. Reflection is something like that, a sinking inward and down into a dimensionality created inside by experience and memory and previous learning, but through which the mind now ranges trying not to expropriate things, but in a different way, involving less of will and more of receptivity, to allow things to present themselves with an innocence previous systems of order and meaning denied to them.

Reflection is in that sense a search for meaning rather than order, a *going beyond* into territories which are understood to be the appropriate ones merely because they are unfamiliar and nothing there, seen for the first time, makes sense. With reason, our topics and purposes are given; thought is purposive and constrained, we think towards something, we almost always have an end in mind: a particular thing we want to order, see, discover, reveal, or clarify. With reflection, purpose takes a back seat, becomes less significant, we have less of an end in view, the logical and rhetorical rules are set aside; what thinking becomes then is full of surprise, novelty, and sometimes danger; we know we are on the right track when we are startled, or when something we find or think suddenly calls into question, much to our surprise, the ways we have done things before or lived our lives.

Reflective thought is also, in a sense, precisely that: *reflective*. It seeks itself. It reviews itself with the same skepticism, the same doubt, we bring to the thought of others. It raises to itself—objectively, carefully, painstakingly—all of the objections that others might raise to it, and it attempts to answer those criticisms not with an eye towards convincing, but towards fidelity to the truth. It involves, also, a suspiciousness of self, an awareness that our own particular enthusiasms and prejudices may reveal far less about the truth of the world than they do about ourselves and our needs. Marx was right about this: consciousness is always conditioned; and Freud was also right: there are unconscious motives and intentions at work in all of us. Reflection is an attempt to deal with both factors, both sources of mystification and delusion. True, because these factors lie beyond consciousness, no one can be entirely successful at erasing them. But surely we must do the best we can. One thinks here of the well-known exchange between Camus and Sartre. Camus, responding to Sartre's criticism of his own work, says that nothing—no ideology, no radicalization of thought—can save either Sartre or himself from being bourgeois. And Sartre responds simply by saying, yes, but we can be the best bourgeois we can. He means that we cannot entirely recondition our thought, cannot out-think our material and given position vis-à-vis society; but we are responsible for thinking past the initial habits and safety of our familiar thought, can, indeed, think our way beyond it, if we try.

Out there (let us imagine thought an *out there*), a clarity gradually emerges as one leaves behind the familiar noise of public life, the cacophony of voices, the incessant barrage of problems, solutions, programs, policies, facts, and opinions. "Out there" one *can* remember, or listen inwardly to all that offers itself, or hear the hum of the stars. Think, here, of those isolation tanks in which one can entomb oneself, suddenly aware of breath, of the beating of the heart, and perhaps—one imagines it—the whisper of blood in its veins. This too occurs in thought: in the solitude, the silence, the emptying-out and the leaving behind that occurs as each who thinks puts aside familiar ideas and modes just as one strips naked to enter the sea. And then one begins; or, rather, *it* begins: that gentle delicate pressure on the skin of light, of unseen things barely felt, not yet understood or ordered, gently tapping, tugging here and there: invisible still, and so softly, so gently, one would never have known, save in solitude or silence, they were there. This is the first moment of thought, the moment of pausing, of setting out, of letting in: the moment of trepidation and hanging back and fear of the unknown. Now, poised, about to begin, the gravidity of reflection is clearest, is made *almost* holy by the intensity of anticipation and the great undertow of fear—as if a wind blew back from beyond somehow making us stay where we are, or at least reluctant to proceed. Right then! Let us go, each, down the long corridor or lane to the door that awaits in the side of the world. And then in. *And then in:* think ahead with the body, with its eyes and hands; think ahead through its fears, its hungers, the strangeness it feels exceeded only by the strangeness it *wants* to feel.

Go back, for instance, to Plato or Aristotle, and you find there the attempt to use reason transcendentally, to lift oneself beyond the commonplace social order of the day and to find a way of seeing more clearly, of judging more rightly, of coming to terms with some larger and deeper notion of goodness or justice. Such an inwardness need not in any way depend upon a belief in a purposive God or divine intervention in human affairs; the secularist can, in fact, leave almost all such questions open, can suspend both belief and disbelief, can search, in silence and solitude, for something

beyond ideology, for principles and truths upon which an ideology—the action of ideas in and on the world—can be both based
and, more importantly, judged.

Do this and pretty quickly certain elements usually related to
religion (but not necessarily *religious*) begin to come back into
view: not God and his angels, no heavenly host or horned devils,
but access to certain senses of connectedness and relation, certain
stirrings of astonishment, wonder and, yes, sometimes, love. Though
we have chosen to live without religion and as if God does not
exist or intervene, surely we cannot and need not live without the
emotions I have named, because when we try to do that too much
dries up within us, too many of our powers go unused. These
senses, these feelings, create in us the beginning of meaning, the
root of belonging; they locate us in the world as it is, and they create for us—if we are lucky, attentive and thoughtful—a good part
of the ground out of which ethics and morality arise.

Nietzsche writes at one point, addressing himself to both poets
and philosophers (in the supplement to *Human, All Too Human*):
"The most grievous thing the thinker can say to the artist is:
'What, could you not watch with me one hour?'" Watch with
me! This is a cry for the suspension of certainty, for momentarily
putting one's beliefs in abeyance, for the willingness to watch and
wait and understand without finalizing knowledge, without falling
prey to the temptation for totalization. Watch with me. This, indeed, is what secularists must say to one another and to all those
around them who remain mad for certainty, order, and systems.
Think here of Kafka's notion of the world rolling itself at the feet
of those who remain silent in reflection. Watch in this fashion and
two things happen: first, something appears in or from the world,
making itself known, that would otherwise remain hidden. And,
too, something happens in the self, in the inwardness of being: a

space is formed into which the world can enter, an interiority in which self becomes other than it would otherwise have been, begins to expand, to grow, into what believers call soul.

Of course, not all reflective outcomes are equal and there is as much danger or risk awaiting us in the adventure of reflection as there is in any other foray into the unknown. Certain men— Nietzsche is one, Heidegger another—seem in the vast reaches of thought to lose their ways, or to wander so far away from what is human, or grounded in life, that the abstractions at which they arrive seem to lend themselves as easily to cruelty as to wisdom. There is something in reflection, then, to be wary of: the currents of thought which can carry us into regions further and further from the heart. One thinks here of the ancient Jewish rules for studying Kabbalah: the admonition that this must be undertaken only in the company of others, for to venture into those regions entirely alone is to risk madness, or the loss of the soul.

Read through Neitszche and you can see this happening, can see madness as it approaches, as the sweet dream of leaving the madness of systems behind slowly develops into another kind of madness: the loss of all felt relation to living others. It is as if, at times, reflection can take you so far from anything fleshed or familiar, and into such distant regions where all is clear but somehow cold, that ideas become *all;* living others cease to be ends, as they were for Kant, and become sacrificed once again to a beauty or wholeness of thought.

Whether such dangers also offer themselves to religious mystics or contemplatives is something I do not know. Perhaps in the spaces separating the yearnings of men from the vision of God are similar coldnesses of vision and icy clarities of thought where living others become trivial. It is possible, I suppose, for the soul to outstrip the heart and leave it so entirely behind that the soul and its yearnings become almost perverse, or perhaps in some way evil.

In those higher regions to which mind or spirit aspire, the leaving behind of flesh, of the particularities of existence, of irony and the laughter attendant to it, may become in itself a kind of "fall" subverting all clarity of vision or apprehensions of the truth one seeks. Just as mind and spirit may be necessary to the full experience of the body, so, too, body, flesh, the groundedness of being, may be necessary to the adventures of spirit or reflection. Leave body too far behind, forget the joys and frailties of flesh, ignore the suffering of others, and reflection is emptied of the wisdom, the generosity, the *care-fulness,* that would otherwise attend it. Heidegger calls reflection a "thinking-toward-Being," but, in fact, the best thought, though it leaves certainty and systems behind, does not leave "Being" behind; it remains rooted in Being, rooted in flesh. Indeed, it can be said to "move" Being from one condition to another without leaving it behind at all—*if* the heart remains open, and a part of thought.

More than one person has said to me, in the midst of discussions of value or thought: 'But if I no longer can believe what I already believe, what can I believe?' And I have no answer to that—I must admit it. What can one say? Merely, live on a while? Or, watch with me? But can men and women stand this? Can they hold themselves and their yearning in abeyance, suspending not only belief, but also hope, to see what emerges from their anguish? I don't know. At this point far more questions than answers crowd themselves into the mind. Oh, yes: one is tempted to offer premature answers, or to assuage, far too soon, the anxieties which rise up to fill the space emptied of certainty. In the dark, of course, we are all inclined to whistle. But what would happen if we sat silent instead? If we let anxiety wash over us, and the fears of ego, and the waves of disorientation which follow the letting go of conviction? Would it be as bad as we think? Imagine: we are alone in a room; all is quiet; we let the mind go, and we find ourselves once again in an innocence where Freud has fallen silent, and Marx, and Darwin. We know nothing for certain: how we got here, where we are going, or where the light switch is to save us from darkness. But for the moment there is the window, with the sky beyond. Here is the table, a plate, a cup half-filled with coffee. Here is the chair we sit on, and the floor it stands on, and here are our bodies: the thigh, the hand, the elbow. Here too is the mind, and contained within us, in this flesh, the flowing of life and the yearning of the heart . . .

No, there is no certainty; and yet, outside of us, the world remains. Inside of us . . . well, here *we* are, looking out. It is here we must begin, in this emptiness, devoid of belief: no uniforms, no flag, no doctrine, no king, no god. There is only this facticity of being alive and aware in a world. Oh yes, there is history behind us and the future ahead and, around us, the disorder, the cruelty, the present madness of men. So what? Is this, really, more than we can bear? Must we have, to survive this, the systems of meaning, the maps, we fear to be without? I know how much we want them; we are so used to having something in our hands: a diagram, a *text* to guide us, to make us think it will be all right . . . But we don't know that. It may *not* be all right. And yet here we are still: in a room, solid, fragile, in the *flesh,* thinking our way forward or into being. Can we stand it? Can we live through it? Why not? What makes us quake with fear or cling, as we do, to what we once believed and no longer believe but *must* believe—or so we think—to survive. When ideology vanishes *we* do not, nor do those suffering others in whose company we find ourselves, nor does the task— always there—of learning how to live among them. Outside, *outside,* there remains a world. Is that not sufficient? Is it too little? There remains, out there, children, work, love, the variety of satisfactions filling one moment and gone the next but somehow preserved in both the mind and flesh. There are voices which call to us and creatures who offer themselves and hands not always cruel but sometimes tender, receptive, forgiving. Is *this* not enough? Is twilight not enough, with the darkening of the sky and the sense we have—sometimes, sometimes—of being creatures alive on the earth and aware, beneath the immensity of the sky, of the glory of our littleness? Give up belief, abjure certainty, and nothing is lost: the world flows in, like water, to fill the territories we have cleared; sit still and you can feel, even in uncertainty, the blood as it runs in the veins, desire as it asserts itself, the heart as it beats, and the mind as it strives for meaning, strives to find it and to make it.

⟡

"I believe in a world in itself, a world governed by laws I try to apprehend in a wildly speculative fashion." That's Einstein, writing about a physical universe so much more apprehensible and sure than the psychological or moral realms. Why can't we think the same way? Why can't we believe in a reality toward which we think, and yet which is always, in so far as we can be sure, beyond thought? After Einstein, physicists have settled for a reality that is little more, as Merleau-Ponty points out, than a "tissue of probabilities." The positivism and idealism which were there at its beginnings have long since faded away. Yet we, in our theories of mind, a la Freud, or in our theories of politics, a la Marx, continue to argue, think, and act as if what we imagined must ineluctably be true, or that we cannot, for all our good will, be wrong. But Freud, too, is wildly speculative. Marx is wildly speculative. All of us bring to the workings of history a set of certainties which may well be wrong, and yet something within us will not permit us to concede this, just as the believer cannot concede that his notion of God's desires are simply the human meeting of wish and need and tell us little about the mystery beyond.

⟡

I do not mean to suggest that most of us can live without ideology or systems of meaning. We can't. But when such systems become habitual and are set beyond questioning, and when we cling to them out of despair rather than a love of truth, and when, in order to maintain them, we have to put truth aside and blind ourselves to experience and cease to think—then, yes, we must struggle again, if only for a while, to find a vision founded on fidelity to truth rather than despair or our need for hope. Of course—who does not know it?—all around us there is a world so much at odds with our wishes or wills it sometimes stops the heart with fear. Who would not, in such a setting, cling for all they are worth to what is familiar or promises consolation? Surely, even as the plane plunges towards the ground and the passengers cry out in fear, it is soothing to hear a voice whisper, absurd as it may be, that it will be all right. But surely, too, some of us can live without that, can go beyond that in the hope of finding something new. What we are talking about here is a capacity for hiatus, for the know-nothing-ness which overwhelms us when experience calls certainty into question or when what we learn conflicts with what we hope.

It is from this capacity for hiatus, for a pause in certainty, that both wisdom and generosity arise, for it is only here, where certainty ceases, that others, *the other,* can appear to us as they are, in the fullness of their own subjectivity, and as equals. The vacuum created, then, by the suspension of belief, fills with others; what has been lost in terms of certainty is replaced by the presence of the world.

All of this is asking a lot, I know. For who will we be if not superior? And how will we survive, if not through our particular and present hopes? We can't know that, in advance. No doubt the particular process I am suggesting will be a rough one and difficult to bear. Men and women were not made by nature to live without certainty or order or with the indefiniteness that such a journey requires. We know that. We know that whether we are talking about ideology or God or a moral system or simply a division of the world into the saved and the damned or *we* and *they,* what most people seem to constitutionally require is not only an ordered world but one in which they are closer to the center, the truth, than others. Egos and psyches do not fare well when myths and frames of reference must be called into question or left behind. Exile is not a comfortable condition—even in terms of ideas.

And yet this, precisely, is what the present condition demands of us as secularists. This is where an acknowledgment of the present moment or our present situation leads us. No amount of intellectual gymnastics or the blaming of others or the repetition of claims will change that. To avoid at this point in time the task assigned to us is in effect to consign secularism to the trash bin of history, since it can neither proceed nor succeed as it is.

Suppose certainty was gone; suppose, in terms of ideology, we admitted the tentativeness and incompleteness of all political "truth" or schemes for the future; suppose, indeed, we understood that all of our systems of understanding and plans for improvement were flawed, and soon to be surpassed or replaced by different kinds of understanding, different plans for the future—what then? And having already set aside the absolutes and revelations and doctrines, what is left? Is everything, then, merely "relative" or arbitrary? I don't think so. I don't think, in the struggle to approximate truth or goodness, we need level or equate all notions, all frames of reference, or all moral systems. The saint and the ax-murderer do not automatically become equal; nor do dreams of freedom and dreams of domination become simply interchangeable systems of understanding or order between which we are equally free to choose. No, even when certainty is gone, there remains the task of searching for the good, of discovering how we ought to live, for trying to see as much of the truth, or to acquire as much wisdom as we can, even when we know we can never see the truth entire and must never mistake what we think we know for a final, or the only, wisdom.

I keep coming back in my mind to a word Heidegger often used: *extremis.*

What does it mean to reflect in extremis? It means we have come to an edge, to a passage, to a desert or wasteland we must cross together if we are to find any sort of moral order, any set of binding values that we might take seriously. Nietzsche, writing a hundred years ago, talked about a "passing over," a transition to be made between "the last man" (men who saw no future for themselves) and the "superman" (those who had learned those arts of heart and soul the "last men" lacked). No amount of explaining what Nietzsche meant by the "superman" will ever free it from the overtones it has taken on in the light of what fascism made of it. Nietzsche foresaw none of that and would have forsworn most of it, and yet much that he wrote paved the way for it, *cleared* a way. Nonetheless, the condition he recognized as soon to appear is certainly upon us now. Throw out as we may the concepts of a "last" or "super" man and still the need for a *passing over* presents itself: a passing over from our shrill and desperate dependency on certainty to the courage to live in and with the freedom we insist upon.

There are those among us, on all sides, who cry out with one scheme or another for re-creating a premature and artificial order, mainly by depriving someone else of freedom or coercing others into circumscribed behavior. Those on the Right do this; those on the Left do this; all those in between, close to the center, do it. But this is not a passing over, and in any case it cannot work, mainly because this is America: new, huge, rapidly changing, with permeable borders and many conflicting systems of value, all of which make it highly unlikely that any one group or ideology will ever be able to win or force the obedience or allegiance of most members of the society. For this reason each position, each vision, each set of values, will remain a *minority* position, and it is hard to imagine any single voice or vision rallying and holding for long a majority of Americans. Freedom moves too fast, too formlessly, for that.

Thus, if we stand little chance of making order, then disorder, as well as freedom, is what we must learn to live with: disorder and the tension between conflicting values, and the sense still with us of America as a wilderness (though in our time it is a wilderness in terms of values, or of culture, rather than nature). We must struggle now, not only *for* freedom, but *with* freedom, to find a way to be both free *and* good, a way to combine our partial liberty with at least a beginning of wisdom. This too is what it means to speak of passing over: a capacity to enter the moral wilderness and seek out principles of moral order that leave freedom intact, or ways in which different expressions of freedom can be combined or made congruent so as to create a complex moral and social order— something that will eventually come to feel like a culture or a home. Thus, the passing over we speak of must include for us, as secularists, a capacity to leave one failed order behind and survive the confusions in the midst of which another must be made. And it means, too, a simultaneous passing over within the self: a slow, disciplined, intentional growth into the kinds of maturity, the senses of patience and generosity, which may in the end emerge from the disorder which, for now, marks our world and our lives.

A passing over, then, is an exilic passage in search of a home or a way to feel at home in our human condition. Even that limited endeavor, that constrained and careful advance, that passage from despair, not to joy but simply to a way of keeping on, will require from us something of a super-human effort, though it will not make us supermen. We stand on the edge—that is what extremis means. We can go no further, not as we are—that too is what ex-tremis means. And one step further, only one step, will take us entirely into the inevitability of a wasteland that awaits, the dangerous time (already upon us, not fully realized) of furies, rages, and men turned against men: beasts fighting for what little bits of meaning they can find.

Extremis means the cliff, the precipice, and the long fall beckoning downward, and, barely seen in the distance, a shining of rooftops, of clustered houses, where we can imagine—in the narrow streets, under shuttered windows—feeling at home. Extremis means the distance, the dangers, between where we are now and where we want to be: the rocky landscapes we must cross, the dry riverbeds, the beasts and the men who wait poised to leap as we pass, wearing faces full of fear and rage, like our own.

All reflection now occurs in extremis: in extreme times, at the extreme edge—a dangerous edge—of human destiny. Up to and perhaps through Nietzsche's time it may well have been possible to maintain the comfortable illusion that reason and violence (or murder, or evil) were antithetical to one another, and that reason, or thought, offered a clear alternative to the frenzies, the fanaticisms, exercised in the name of religion. But now we have seen, as reason entered history, as philosophy wed itself to politics, as first Hegel and then Nietzsche and then Marx began to assert the role of reason in history, how reason itself can eventually lead to violence or murder; how it, too, like faith, lends itself to error and to excess.

Around us now, conservatives and true believers lead the assault on reason, arguing that these have not proved themselves out, have not led towards, or brought about, what was promised. And because of that many people now call forth, once again, the notions of faith, of God, of absolute systems of morality and punishment. They have a point: reason may indeed lead to slaughter. But faith also leads to slaughter. And this, then, is also what defines our condition of extremis: the knowledge that both faith *and* reason lead to slaughter, that both religion and secularism, beginning with hope and promising perfection, lead us back to our eternal capacity for murder.

Was there ever a time men were not in extremis? Perhaps not. Perhaps it is merely our explanations of extremis that vary, and we are simply called on from time to time to re-describe the *particular* extremis in which we find ourselves: our time, our place, our selves. What marks our contemporary extremis, the extremity of our condition, is the vast shrinkage of the moral realm, our refusal to acknowledge or create a moral center for our actions, our lives. In our century we have been drawn ever forward by freedom and technological possibility toward the implementation of will, the satisfaction of desire, the realization of imagination—without serious thought (save for a few plaintive voices raised here and there) for the ethical center around which all human activity, no matter how glorious or daring, must be organized.

As things stand now, the cleared spaces we leave behind as we live one freedom or another into the world have become a wasteland. It is as if the battles we wage for freedom leave the moral ground on which they occur leveled, strewn with rubble, where only exiles, maimed survivors, and savages can live: shadows drifting from ruin to ruin, little more, in moral terms, than beasts.

It is there, in that wasteland, in the ruins of failed values, of discarded norms, of wrecked cathedrals and collapsed academies, that we now confront one another; it is there we stare into cracked mirrors and see with horror our own faces: no longer human. Now, having almost lost language, reduced by habit to little more than grunts and cries, we are compelled by our condition to turn to one another, to begin to reason together, to reflect, to speak honestly—that is, as human beings. It hardly matters if this wasteland, so new-seeming to us, is as old as human time, as old as consciousness. It hardly matters if our memory of what has fallen or gone is faulty, and that there never really existed on this ground—no matter how grand our recollection, how deep our yearning—much more than these ruins. This moment, this possibility of a beginning, of a re-thinking of moral life, may be, in fact, eternal—or at least as old as man. The beast-face we see in the mirror—fragmented, cracked—may be, indeed, the face of man, the face man has worn, inside, until now, and *also* now. It may well be—I rather think it is—that the beginning which offers itself to us on this ground was and is always there for us, and that the only difference between one age and another, one set of historical circumstances and another, is that sometimes cherished illusions wear thin and our ideologies, exhausted, allow us to see clearly the *necessity* of a beginning, allow us to hear the beginning that can be said to call to us from inside, from the wasted parts of self, our unused human powers.

Philosophers, especially modern philosophers, are always hearing this call, which says *begin*. This much they have in common: an acuity of hearing which allows each of them, in solitude, to hear, from the edge of consciousness, the plea to at last begin. And yet, at that point, they diverge. Their thought shoots off in as many directions as matter did after its first explosion, out toward every degree of the huge and curving horizon, and so too, now, each man or woman knows at some level we must begin. But how? And in what direction? With what end in mind? For it is here, in extremis, in the land most wasted, where the devastation is greatest, that many, and not only a few, hear inside themselves the call *begin*. But it is also precisely in extremis, where *begin* is most fully heard, that a genuine beginning becomes most difficult, and that the possibility of fragmentation, of conflict and disorder, are greatest. Each, hearing in themselves, from beyond themselves, the cry *begin,* moves almost instantaneously in a direction of their own making, out toward the particular compass point from which—they will swear it—they heard the cry first come. And now the voices rise; the arguments begin. Like travelers lost in an unfamiliar land, to whom all points on the horizon seem equally inviting, we furiously argue with one another, knowing that our lives depend on the right choice—and yet having no common agreement whatsoever of which choice is right. Each of us hears the same cry as the others, but no one can in fact begin, because each is convinced that we must begin *together,* must move as one, and that only he or she knows where and how to move, and that a beginning depends on the control or coersion of others. A stasis asserts itself, or a mad whirl without forward motion, in which each traveler, furious now, and desperate, knows he or she must begin, but cannot begin. Thus all find themselves together, imprisoned in extremis.

In such a condition, in this condition, we must begin. But how? There is no answer save this: you must begin. But how? Begin. But how?

Begin.

If I could, here is what I would produce on the page which follows: an entirely blank page, and from margin to margin, perhaps an inch from the top, an inch-wide band of mirror, so the reader, peering down, would see his or her own eyes. That's all: the blank page and your own reflection. Now, in the silence, in the blankness of the page, each must say to himself, begin, and each must begin to ask himself, how? This too is where reflection begins—the community of reflection that depends for its vitality on the willingness of each, in their own solitude, to ask themselves: how? This is where moral reflection begins because at this point in time we know that thought (even our own) can lead to murder, and that our own particular dreams of order, meaning, and safety are always these days brought into being at the expense of others, at the expense of their freedom, their dreams of meaning. And so, we must begin to ask ourselves how, while at the same time accepting into our reflections, as never before, the image of the other, the value of the other as equal to our own: the other, then, in all his difference, even his apparent malevolence, as a part of the kingdom of ends worthy of moral consideration.

Let me, then, revise my page. A band of mirror, and the page blank, save for the phrase, clearly printed and central: *the other*. For now, *now*, we must begin to think ourselves forward from this impasse reflectively and morally, by which one means with a radical and limiting concern for the other in all his or her (frightening) differences.

What a task! And yet this *is* our task, here in the antechamber of thought, at the beginning: to think our way through to modes of discourse and a simultaneity of differences that preserves at its heart a sense of moral order and obligation that can guide our own behavior while at the same time allowing others their freedom.

Oh, I know, I know. We think the issue is the behavior of others: their excess, the threat they pose to us. No doubt this is and should be of concern; we are all, and always, in danger. But the alleviation of that danger is *social* thought, *political* thought. It is not *moral* thought. Moral thought involves how *we* should begin, how *we* should reflect, how *we* should behave. And here, I think, we can safely say something clear: all thought, to be moral, must not only occur in freedom, but must be about the limits and obligations of self. Moral thought must involve our own search for the good, for a moral order in which we ourselves can live. It cannot be otherwise. We may think "about" morality, of course: how to get others to act as we want them to, to be good. But for thought to become moral in itself, the purpose of our thought must be the transformation of self. It is *we* who must want to find and act according to "the good."

This does not mean we abnegate a concern with the behavior of others. Every rational man or woman concerned with social order, culture, or value will obviously be concerned about and troubled by what others may do. But a *moral* discourse can begin only when each is willing to consider—deeply, reflectively, voluntarily—*their own behavior*, and to set side by side with their own legitimate desire for freedom (such a desire is always legitimate) a profound concern for what in such freedom should or should not be done. This does not mean—let me make this especially clear— merely figuring out how to defend or justify what one already desires or does. Such thought is by no means moral reflection, though obviously it is what all of us almost always do. I mean something very different: the attempt by each of us—in solitude and then communally—to discover universal principles ("imperatives," Kant called them) of moral order by which we judge and determine our own behavior.

Of course we have moved well past Kant's time. Our perceptions of psychology are different than his and more complex; we have developed a whole new rhetoric of desire, new attitudes toward our own natures, and new understandings of the powers at work on, and against, and even *hidden within*, reason and judgment. Therefore our formulations, our categorical imperatives, might differ from Kant's. And yet the process, the manner of moral reasoning must remain the same: (1) the search for principles of order and action; (2) the acceptance of the other as a binding consideration (an end rather than a means); and (3) a readiness to live by—even if others do not—the principles or imperatives we objectively, and with good will, discover.

If we do this, if enough of us do this, if enough of us accept the inwardness of this searching and rigor of mind, then, perhaps, even in our differences, when we turn at last to speak to one another, we will have something of value to say, and we will also be able to hear.

Morality. Reflection on morality. This is our task and our burden. It is the only way, in the silence which precedes or permits thought, we can respond to the cries rising from history which now crowd every solitude and fill our silent moments with horror. Thought, then, beginning here, where we are, must involve itself with this: our condition in history. And this, perforce, involves us immediately with something else, the problem of thought itself: where it can lead. And because we can only measure or judge where it has led by looking at the world, we cannot help but look at all suffering others, those who are victims of reason as well as those who are victims of its absence. This cannot help raising for us, as secularists, as rationalists, the specter of our own culpability, or the culpability of reason itself. And it raises for us too the most serious imaginable questions pertaining to morality or prospective systems of ethics, for we must now concern ourselves with ways to safeguard others against ourselves, or with ways to bind ourselves so tightly to a notion of goodness, or to the idea of others as ends in themselves, that violence will become, if not unthinkable, then at least something other than reason's inevitable end.

For reflective thought to lead in the direction of morality several elements must be present. The first of these has to do with will, intentionality: we must indeed, with what Kant called good will, search for principles that can, if universalized, form the foundation of an orderly society. But other elements are equally important, for without them the search for universal principles can lead us toward tyranny. These other necessary elements are two in number. First, we must begin with the notion that freedom is a good in itself and necessary to any moral order. It is the only ground from which a genuine moral order can arise, since without freedom men and women cannot be said to choose, and where they are not free to choose they cannot be moral—not in any real sense.

And the second element is equally significant: that we understand that whatever system we devise, whatever "whole" we can imagine, cannot include any others *against their wills*. That is, a democratic order, a genuinely free order, can only arise when all members have helped in its creation, when all feel (as they have a right to) the order they inhabit has its roots in their own natures, their own deeply felt desires, values, and needs.

The impulse to encapsulate others in our systems of thought, to see them only through the lens of our systems of thought, to define them and judge them only via our systems of thought, is perhaps the worst of all our present secular tendencies. Indeed, almost all of our secular systems of thought are set up so that a denial of the system, or an insistence on remaining outside of it, is instantly seen as evidence of a recalcitrance that can only be corrected by the system in question. Thus, just as the believer sees the nonbeliever as a sinner who must be cured by God, the Freudian sees the nonbeliever as a neurotic who must be cured by therapy, and the Marxist sees the nonbeliever as a victim of false consciousness or repressive tolerance who can only be cured by coercive re-education. Each of us exists for the other only as a counter, a character, to be put to use in, or made a part of, one system or another.

It was for this reason that Kant defined living others not only as *ends* but as *purposes*: that is, free willful creatures who must be allowed to remain outside or beyond the limits of our invented systems. We can try to reason with them, can try to inspire or lead them, perhaps to teach them. But we are only allowed (by our respect for freedom, and by morality, which must be *based* on freedom) to do any of this on and from a ground of freedom which belongs commonly to all and is a greater value, a higher good, than the particular system we hold dear.

I know this is difficult to imagine or swallow. For we see around us everywhere behaviors, actions, modes of being, and kinds of speech which we want to legislate or educate out of existence. I am not talking here about the ax-murderer, or the children in gangs firing at random into crowds or houses; clearly, in this territory, it is not difficult to find a moral and universal basis for condemning, limiting, preventing, or punishing such action. I am thinking, instead, about men and women who, for instance, may want to prevent their children from learning evolution, or who want to teach their children that the Jews killed Christ and must therefore be converted, or who would like to bring to bear on the rest of us a set of limits based on one set or another (think here of the Black Muslims) of suppositions which disturb us.

Such behavior is no doubt frightening. As secularists, we would be much happier and probably better off if it didn't exist. But remember: to people such as those I'm describing much of *our* behavior, as secularists, is immensely disturbing and even frightening, and yet we understand that our freedom requires that they live with their fright; they cannot enclose us within their own dreams of order, or the orders they receive from Christ, because we have a right to exist outside their system; we stand on freedom's ground. But if we do have such rights, so do they. Their illusions, their fantasies also arise from and exist on a ground of freedom, and the terrible tightrope we must walk, the terrible burden which is ours, the one forced upon us by our understanding of freedom, is that we must simultaneously protect our freedoms from others and refrain from denying them theirs.

This is not merely a cute intellectual paradox. It is the practical situation which confronts us every day. All of us—this certainly includes secularists—are tempted to establish order and bring the future into being by denying to threatening others the freedoms we fear they will "abuse." Freedom is in fact a ground of contradictions in which each man's truth and exercise of freedom appears to someone else as madness and an abuse of freedom. But few of us are strong enough to live without systems of thought or see beyond them long enough to see the other clearly, and therefore we endlessly encapsulate others in our mad systems of protection and consolation. Who does not do this? No one among us is either naked or free; each of us is clothed, imprisoned, first by our *own* systems of thought, and then by the systems of thought through which others see us, and in which they hold us captive.

＊

All thought, all reflective thought, that begins in silence and with listening, begins therefore with life and ultimately leads us back toward life—but only if we remain aware of, attentive to, the moral implication of thought, only if we envision at the end of thought, not a perfected world or life in the abstract, but a world of specific and suffering and imperfect others. And this gives rise to another irony: the fact that thought, which wants to issue forth in a great arc, wants to begin with life and then soar reflectively, and then descend at the end into a perfected world—this soaring thought, thought as it wants to be, must in fact, because it exists in history and among men, inscribe a lesser arc, beginning with life, then soaring, and returning finally not to perfection, but to what in the present remains only possible: the flawed world of flawed others we all must inhabit.

This is the tension, the burden, of thought: that it must return always to the possible, the present, the world, *humanity*—not humanity as it might be or must be, but to humanity *as it is:* in the absolute presentness of its contemporary existence.

And herein lies the task, the yoke, the pain, of thinking: the fact that those who think themselves away from things as they are must eventually return to things as they are, must remain perpetually doubled in vision, shadowed by irony, aware, simultaneously, of what vision can offer us and what the world requires.

Kant took us to the edge of a precipice; he understood, as if for once and for all, the bifurcation in thought which necessarily confronts all those who replace religion with reason. He understood the situation in which we must think morally, or what happens when duty and desire are treated as if they could be one thing. In this he presaged Freud, who was a Kantian in the deepest sense, understanding full well the immense chasm between what we imagine or will and what we are. Wherever men have gone beyond this understanding, or tried to heal the wound in themselves which corresponds to the chasm between is and ought, things have gone radically and tragically wrong. Our knowledge of this adds to our burden, our sorrows. But it should also add to our wisdom, and remind us about the terror that waits for both self and others when we think ourselves into the territory of imagination where God's will once challenged man but which remains, now, empty: a territory in which, when duty vanishes, all things become not only thinkable but doable, and where we mistakenly try to bring into being a perfectibility that can only be imagined, not lived.

It is only natural to speculate, theorize, analyze, and thereby map the human future. It is in our nature. And it is in our nature, too, to grab at certainty, to reach for big truths that explain and fix all in place. But the desire to be certain, as natural as it may be, does not mean that we *can* be sure—not to the extent that we can dismiss all those who believe other than we do as fools, knaves, lackeys, or diseased. Each human theory, idea, or prejudice must always be preceded—invisibly, unstated—by the words "I believe" or "I think" or even (think of Pascal) "I bet." I do not mean to suggest that all is solipsistic or arbitrary. It is not. But all our theorizing or even our certainty is only a "moving toward" the world—an approximation, an approach. Think, here, very simply, of a cat or the bark of a tree. We reach out; we touch; in that touch we are beyond ourselves. But the cat or the tree also remains largely beyond our touch. It is somehow there, in the world, independent of our knowledge of it: closer to us than before we reached out, yet further, still, than we might like. So it is with thought and the world. With Freud we reach and touch; with Marx, we do the same. And yet the complexities at work in the thoughts and lives of men remain, still, beyond that touching and reaching, and they may in their workings soon confound us again.

No matter how different from our own the ideas of others may be, no matter how such ideas may imply values or an order we dislike, no matter, even, how we may oppose them in political or moral ways, we nonetheless should not, and may not, act as if the mere difference in our ideas makes us superior, or wiser, or better. Others' notions may appear to us as "wildly speculative" but they are no more speculative than our own. "I am no more able," Einstein also said, "to invoke any logical argument to defend my convictions, unless it be my little finger, the sole and feeble witness to an opinion buried deep under my skin." He was talking about the physical universe, but the same thing may well hold true of morality and psychology. We are acting out of conviction and guesswork rather than absolute knowledge, and those who do not understand that *something*—some part of reality, or perhaps most of it—lies beyond what they believe are doomed thereby to be defeated both by history and life. If history and life teach us anything, it is that the certainties of every age are called into question by the certainties of the next and that beyond every set of certainties lies a world of complexity and mystery we have barely entered and must learn again to enter and make our home.

IV

Taken seriously, thought through, secularism may well be the most difficult inner discipline of all—that, I think, is what we must now understand. It requires us to proceed steadfastly, and yet without recourse to the traditional forms of hope or consolation that have in the past allayed human suffering or pain. We have cast aside the familiar maps and texts men use in exploring the heart or the soul or ways to escape their travail. When ego falters, when pride wanes, when ideology wears thin, when despair or the presence of death force their ways past our shredded defenses and are simply there, silent beside us in the midnight dark, then, either the most courageous or stupid of men, we have few sources of sustenance, few illusions or myths to comfort us. To choose as we have, to risk all on God's absence, to cling as we do to the emptiness we inhabit, is a form of risk that has few rewards, a mad wager which, even if won, gains us nothing and takes all our chips.

The believer, of course, can fall back, in the face of failure or sorrow or loss, on the kindness of God or a bosomy universe soon to enclose him, to take him back in. There's the sense, too, if you're lucky enough to feel it, as fundamentalist believers sometimes do, of being held in God's palm, of being lifted up, or having, always, in the midst of distress, an anticipated access to another and a truer home. And secularists? In moments of despair or the presence of death, it is true we have living others, and sometimes the shreds of ideology or a stoical wisdom that murmurs *courage*, but beyond that what we have can be found only in reflection, only in solitude, only among the faint whispers which in silence fill us with something more than ourselves and for which we are too proud, too stubborn or wise, to use the name *God.* . . .

In this, the emptiness which fills us with a longing for what we have chosen to accept as *absent*, we often come ironically close to the passionate mystics and religious contemplatives whose longing and love for God was so great it denied them his proximity or the easy consolations available to less adventurous believers. I don't mean to say—I will be crystal clear here—that in our disbelief or non-belief or belief in *nothingness* we have hidden a religious yearning; I mean only that if we actively embark, as we must, on an inwardness, a discovery of interiority, a going beyond certainty, there is this we share with the mystic: the danger of emptiness and silence, of the gravidity of a yearning which may lead—this is always the risk—to exile rather than a homeland, and to terror rather than joy.

This is not, then, a discipline for everyone. The early certitudes of the Enlightenment, which have lit our way for so much of the secular journey, are no longer supported by history, and we are forced now to live—if we look honestly at the world, or at ourselves—with a knowledge that most sensible people would rather not have.

We know now, or we should know, that good and evil are locked so tightly in embrace, so everlastingly, in both the public world and in our private psyches, that it is impossible to separate them or even at times to tell them apart. Dream as we do of apocalyptic transformations and inexorable human advances or perfected worlds, the world rarely moves in such convenient trajectories. Instead it moves in cycles, in rising and falling spirals, especially in relation to moral wisdom. Technology may advance steadily; nature may gradually yield its secrets up; but where human inwardness is concerned we are confronted by another story altogether. Men are quite capable—history teaches this over and over—of entirely forgetting the hard knowledge they earn at such terrible expense to others and themselves. It is not, after all, the ultimate victory of reason or good that renders our choices significant or calls on us to act; it is rather the fragility of human values, the fact that they have always been in the balance, that demands from us the effort to preserve them.

This is, I think, a hard knowledge, and even secularists themselves cannot live comfortably with it. How or why we came to believe that we could somehow teach tens of millions of people to accept it, or use it to replace religion, is no longer clear to me. What *is* clear is that secularism—in its genuine form, its most demanding form (and can there be another form?)—will stay a minority point of view forever, both in the world at large and here at home in America. There is little doubt, after all, that in the years to come the moral and social disorder in America will steadily increase, the schisms among us will deepen, individual confusion and dissatisfaction will grow, and the few traditions still remaining to us from the past will give way still further to the triple pressures of popular culture, technological change, and our poignant, innocent dreams of a happiness no longer attainable. As that happens, more and more people on every side, in need of solace or meaning, will seek out in dogma, faith, or one ideology or another the senses of self and location the culture no longer provides. Secularism, save in its worst and most hysterical forms, is not likely to flourish in such circumstances.

I know: as secularists it is hard for us to relinquish the image we have of ourselves as a vanguard, a brave and inevitable wave of some glorious future. Those who find their bearings and satisfactions and moral limits in unalterable absolutes divinely inspired still strike us as the remnants of a past already left behind. But it is in fact we, and not they, who may be the exceptions to the human rule, the products of an American experiment in freedom gone awry, the result of a brief and quirky moment in Western history in all likelihood soon to be superseded by new waves of mindlessness and belief we cannot imagine.

Reason, after all, leaves so many hungers unsatisfied, so many desires unappeased, and life itself, in general, remains so hard, that it is only natural for people to seek sustenance in the one place it cannot be denied them: a realm of mystery and succor so distant one can believe about it anything one wants. In matters such as these genuine secularists even now constitute a relatively small cadre of dissidents and eccentrics, at odds with thousands of years of human history and testimony. There is little reason to think things will be much different in the future.

Can one, in the light of all this, postulate a secularism, an alternative secularism, one that simultaneously does justice to the world as it is and that a grown man can take seriously? I think so. I think its preliminary outlines can be found in the secularism of the past, in our own contemporary experience, and perhaps in those distant regions of thought to which reflection leads us.

What would such a secularism entail?

First: a complexity of thought equal to the complexity of the world, something that would, by its very nature, indicate that the human heart and mind, even in God's absence, can locate or create systems of meaning that allow mystery to exist, that make room for irony, and that put the respect for truth ahead of our needs for certainty or order.

Second: a sense of humility. Those who are religious can derive humility from the ways in which the will is limited and human wisdom confounded by a god whose intentions lie beyond our understanding. To feel, as secularists tend to do, that history and meaning lie entirely in human hands, no doubt restores to us a power that is rightfully ours; but this must be counterbalanced by our own sense of limits, a recognition that what we intend or imagine rarely comes into being in the form we desired. The ambiguity of outcomes, and the inevitable mixture of good and evil in all consequences, is something we must learn to remember as a check on our arrogance and the plans we endlessly make for others.

Third, there's honesty: not only the discipline of telling the truth to others, but also of being honest with ourselves, of letting experience and fact call into question our faiths and allegiances. We cannot continue to project, as we do now, our beliefs *onto* the world; they must rise *from* the world, must form themselves in response *to* the world. To see past ideology and out into the world beyond—that, difficult as it may be, is not only where honesty begins; it is also where wisdom is born.

And, there are, too, our own lives. Here (*especially* here) we are beholden to report back honestly (honestly!) about what in secularism works and does not, or about what it means to live as we do, without absolutes, consolation, or hope of heaven, or about the light that sometimes floods in on us or the darkness that overwhelms us. Into the realm of public discourse must now come the private, human voice: whispery, insistent, speaking its way out of and into a darkness that can be lit only by the truth. We may feel ourselves alone here, but we are also *with* one another, and it is that combination of alone-ness and with-ness that confers upon our voices the absoluteness of their significance, their inexhaustible value. It is we who are responsible for the moral and social world others inhabit; the quality of their lives—I mean this literally—depends on our fidelity to truth.

And beyond this? Let me list here, as they occur to me, some of the traits I'd like to see in my own comrades or children. They're not the ones that will necessarily emerge from a mature secularism honed by time or worn smooth by experience into wisdom. They are, instead, the traits with which we must *begin*, the attitudes required if the shy truths of the world are ever to offer themselves to us again, returning from the distances into which our shrillness, our passion for certitude, have driven them.

- An intellectual and moral stance that includes an open acknowledgment of all we don't know, and that demands from us a willing suspension of both belief and disbelief in the face of a world still unfolding its truths to us.
- A recognition of the tentativeness, speculativeness, and incompleteness of all human truths, especially those which are taken to be most final or complete.
- A rejection of all totalizing systems of order or modes of thought which refer only to themselves as a way of categorizing or judging the world and others by a single set of standards.
- A privacy of moral introspection that makes a permanent adventure of reflection and thought; an understanding that such an adventure may take us into territories we have not anticipated and which will call into question, in terrifying ways, what we want to believe.
- A willingness to subject our own beliefs and actions to a more rigorous and skeptical examination than we bring to bear on the behavior of others.
- A realization of the tragic complexity of all human action and of the irony of all outcomes; a realization of the fact that whatever we plan, intend, or imagine will always fall short, when introduced into the world, of what we imagined, intended, or planned.

- A generosity toward all living others and a compassion rooted in the knowledge that all living others are suffering and fallible creatures (as are we), facing death (as do we), and moved (as we are moved) by terror, appetite, and love.
- A love for the freedom of others that equals our love for our own.
- A sense of absolute responsibility of oneself as a maker of value: a deep consciousness of the way each individual human act, choice, or word creates, as did God's, a world others inhabit.
- A consciousness of the sustaining and restorative joys still found in the world as it is (even as it is!): the pleasure, satisfaction, delight, and joy it offers to us, and for which, in the midst of all else, and even in our own pain, we owe both thanks and something in return.

Is this enough? The list could go on and on. I've said nothing here about courage, or about the capacity for solitude, or for living in disorder or chaos, or about a loving hunger for experience, or for seeing with one's own eyes, or about a talent for finding comrades or love, without which we founder in the darkest of times, or about, most importantly, the powers of reciprocity and empathy which sometimes dictate we act for others and against our own reason and interests, even when reason or morality counsel otherwise.

I will dwell a bit longer on this last item because of its importance. A few months ago I was describing to my daughter, in a conversation about ethics, how certain Vietnam vets who I had known had instinctively, without thought, thrown themselves into danger to protect their comrades. "I know," she said, quoting Thomas More, "human nature is a treaty in itself." For there is that, too, you see, that reservoir of powers within us that Freud collectively called Eros, the cluster of drives, hungers, and appetences which exist side by side with aggression and destructiveness and draw us towards one another—as if nature intended it—in dialogue, community, fraternity, and even love.

Must these powers function only as they seem to do now, only in relation to those who think and feel as we do, the mirror images of ourselves? Or can we, somehow, learn to extend these powers outward, away from self and the easy company of the like-minded, toward men and women whose behavior and beliefs radically differ from our own and who make impossible the order we imagine? If we can't then secularism and reason will merely end by isolating us, as they do now, from others and the world.

And in return? What is it, in return for the austerity of this task, this travail without apparent end, that secularism has to offer us? Is there anything to rescue us from this working man's nightmare of all labor and no pay?

It may not be quite so bad a bargain as I have made it sound. There is, to begin with, the joy of living in a world that is allowed to exist in all its complexity and need not be reduced or simplified in order to leave our beliefs intact. There is the sense of oneself as a free woman or man unbound by dogma or authority and able to live or think oneself into a territory relatively unknown to others. There is the possibility of regaining a sense of oneself as a maker of value, and of recovering a pride, even a wonder, in relation to human nature and its works. For if we have invented, as a species, war and tyranny and countless other evils, we have also discovered, created, or at least *named,* liberty, fraternity, equality, and countless other goods, and we have collectively, if imperfectly, labored our way toward them out of the ignorance, innocence, and the muteness of beasts.

There's freedom: the freedom to tell the truth, to question ideology and all that's given or already known, to let the mind or heart move along the great arcs of human seeking without having to trim or restrain them in order to satisfy others. There's a sense of integrity, of keeping faith with conscience and truth and suffering others, of what the Buddhists call "right relation": a feeling not so much of happiness but of *satisfaction*, or the deep conviction that we've managed to live (if we have) on our own terms while still keeping faith with the world.

There's a sense of power, but of a particular kind: a power derived not from authority or control, but from being a creature at home on earth; of not being beholden to others or protected by a web of illusions and lies; of freely forming a private and feeding relation to whatever lies "out there," beyond the fractious disagreements and distracting passions of the age. Or it may well be that "out there" is really inside: the inner voice or force or stillness or murmuring silence that Socrates called "the daimon" and which creates, in the self and yet deeper than self, a sense of connectedness, a relation to something that remains undefined and yet is, indeed, a source of grace.

There is a sense of connectedness, gratitude and—dare I say it?—even *blessedness*, for if we know, as secularists, that what we value in the world has not come from God, then we must also know that it has come to us from the hands, labor, and suffering of other men and women, both the living and the dead. Whatever we make use of, whatever we hold dear—bread, wine, language, music, ideas, the forms of shelter, our ways of making love—has been made or prepared for us, worn smooth, turned fully human, by others; we are sustained by their efforts, cradled by their presence; even in the separateness and isolation we often feel we are actually held, for our entire lives, in a web of reciprocity and obligation that requires of us a silent saying of "grace," a continuous giving of thanks, that must be spoken with our lives.

And finally, if we can only find some way to gather its elements together, to teach it, as we have not yet learned to do, to the young, there's one final gift secularism has to offer: a way of signifying our lives, of understanding, even without reference to God, why each human gesture matters, and why the weight of the moral world rests on each word we utter or is present in every human act. Think here, for a moment, of Darwin, Marx, and Freud, each of whom changed, perhaps forever, the way we think about ourselves. First came Darwin, putting us squarely at the heart of nature, revealing the way that nature and the past actually, physically, collect in each one of us, dwell in each of us, create in and through each of us, what nature and man will become in the future. And then came Marx, who located ordinary men and women, and their labor, their suffering, their hunger for freedom, at the heart of history, made us *makers* of history, revealing the power coiled within us, waiting to be used. And finally there was Freud, locating within us, within our psyches and the dramas we make of our lives, not only nature and history, but also the essence of the eternal struggle between Eros and Thanatos, creation and destruction, love and death.

Is this, and this alone (though we have access to far more), not enough, in itself, to resignify our lives and make us conscious, once again, of the weight, the seriousness of our moral responsibilities? We are, each one us, in everything we do, the face the human past turns to the human future. Can't we learn, in the light of that fact, once more to feel, as we lift a hand, or pause before speaking, or put words on a page, or take another in our arms, the full significance of what we are about to do, or the terrifying responsibility for doing it carefully, conscientiously? If we could do that, could actually feel, inside of us, the weight, the power, of what is gathered there—then we might understand at last, and perhaps even be able to pass on to others, the deep meaning of the secular life, or what it offers to those who attempt it.

"Live," said Camus, "neither with hope nor resignation." Those words are perhaps his credo, and I know of no better words for those of us who are secularists. If we unpack this injunction it means, among other things, to expect nothing and yet be grateful for all, or to find a home in the world while understanding that exile is our lot. This is not a piling up, an accretion of values or attitudes. It is a stripping away, a paring down to our human condition: putting as little as possible between self and the world, between self and truth. One remembers other phrases in Camus's notebook. "Only the body is generous." And elsewhere: "The soul is never right." What do these phrases mean? Of course the soul is never right: distracted, greedy for Paradise, at odds with the world, crying out always for what is impossible or has not yet come. And the body? For Camus it is this, the body and the world, the body in the world, that promises us the only possibility of joy or completion we will have. It is here, in the flesh, in the fleshed presence of others, in the immediacy and terrifying facticity of life itself, that we must learn the arts of generosity and compassion, must struggle, on our own and for the sake of others, to side with Eros against death.

This is where the discipline of the secularist has its beginning: in the tragic sense of the poignant arc of each human life, its appearance out of nothingness and its return to nothingness, the almost dizzying boon of each person or thing as it comes forward to meet us, emerging from a vacancy which, without its presence, would be all. Think, here, of the desert and its silence (so familiar to Camus), the way, in its emptiness, a solitary figure on the horizon, approaching, gathers a meaning to itself entirely defined by, revealed by, the emptiness around it.

It is here, in this emptiness, in the secular consciousness of an emptiness from and in which others appear, that tenderness begins, and all consciousness of value. It is here that gratitude, awe, and love have their roots. It is here that ethics and morality begin, here that one can begin to understand the absolute and innate value of each living thing. "Above the revolutionary absolute," wrote Victor Hugo in 'Ninety-Three, "there is the human absolute." And it is this, the human absolute, the existence of others beyond all our systems, all abstraction, all mental fabrication, all ideology, that demands from us a response, or calls to us, from beyond ourselves, from beyond the limits of our own ways of seeing.

This demand too, coming as it does from beyond us, from the living world, is as powerful and transformative as anything that issues from God. It offers nothing in return, promises no heaven, no grace, no rising together on winds into glory. It allows us no hope and yet forbids resignation. It hands us only the task of being fully human, and, at the same time, the solitude, the loneliness of struggle within which this task must be accomplished.

One would be a fool not to see the pain attendant to such a task or the sorrows inevitably rising from it. It offers us as much anguish as joy, and long stretches of loneliness which define and yet counterbalance our moments of joy. For those who inherit or choose this task, death remains all that awaits us at life's end, and only the closure, the final release it promises to us, can stand in the place of what, for the believer, is merely the beginning of eternal life. We live, as secularists, always on the edge of an abyss, of an ending which those who believe in heaven and God need not confront. We are confined, for our joy, to a space defined for us only by solitude or the presence of others. If we have any consolation in the face of death, if something bids us welcome it, it is not that some eternal part of us goes on, but only that the world we love continues—if, indeed, we have been lucky enough to learn, on our own, *how* to love it.

Surely one can see how this ought to, or at least might, open the heart, resignify our gestures, and confer upon both our freedom and the freedom of others a value so great that it becomes almost, if not wholly, absolute. For those who have God, it is God's presence that gives meaning to life and confers upon others (or at least their souls) the absoluteness of their value. For us, it is God's absence which does, or ought to do, the same thing. For us, the truth does not exist somewhere beyond us, glorious and entire. For us, it has not yet fully appeared, it comes to us piecemeal, in bits and pieces, learned from experience or discovered in reflection or else—and this is crucial—spoken to us by others who share with us the same ground of being and freedom. For us, as secularists, each human voice, each human speaker, must take on much of the value once accorded to God. The truth we seek emerges from and in others, others whose partial truth may differ radically from our own, and thus the truth cannot emerge—not fully, not as the truth of the world—until each living other has had a chance to speak and be heard.

It is only at this point, in relation to truth, the collective gathering of truth, that one can fully understand the humility required of the secularist, as well as the full meaning of what we supposedly hold dear: freedom, fraternity, equality, and justice. Taken together, they comprise the necessary conditions, the essential "human condition," for the speaking and hearing of the truth. Only in the spaces they open and define can we learn to grant to every living other a value equal to all others, and our own. It is here that the incumbency falls upon us to listen, to truly listen, to truly hear and to seek in every human voice—no matter how its truths call our own into question, no matter how strangely it rings on our ears— something that partakes of the same mystery, the same hidden *beyond*, from which our own truths are drawn.

When God's voice falls silent, when the intensity of its low perpetual hum no longer gives the universe or our own destinies their meaning, then what follows may seem at first like silence or like Babel. But it need not be. We must learn, now, in the silence and noise which surround us, to locate amid the shrillness and cries and falsehoods filling the air, the voice of each man and woman who truthfully speaks—as we must speak—out of the full depth of our common longing, terror, sorrow, and joy.